THE PENGUIN POETRY LIBRARY

KIPLING

Rudyard Joseph Kipling was born in Bombay in 1865. His father, John Lockwood Kipling, was the author and illustrator of *Beast and Man in India* and his mother, Alice, was the sister of Lady Burne-Jones. In 1871 Kipling was brought home from India and spent five unhappy years with a foster family in Southsea, an experience he later drew on in 'Baa, Baa, Black Sheep' (1888). The years he spent at the United Services College, a school for officers' children, are depicted in *Stalky and Co.* (1899) and the character of Beetle is something of a self-portrait. It was during his time at the college that he began writing poetry and *Schoolboy Lyrics* was published privately in 1881. In the following year he started work as a journalist in India, and while there, produced a body of work, stories, sketches and poems – notably *Plain Tales from the Hills* (1888) – which made him an instant literary celebrity when he returned to England in 1889. *Barrack-Room Ballads* (1892) contains some of his most popular pieces, including 'Mandalay', 'Gunga Din' and 'Danny Deever'. In this collection Kipling experimented with form and dialect, notably the cockney accent of the soldier poems, but the influence of hymns, music-hall songs, ballads and public poetry can be found throughout his verse.

In 1892 he married an American, Caroline Balestier, and from 1892 to 1896 they lived in Vermont, where Kipling wrote *The Jungle Book*, published in 1894. In 1901 came *Kim* and in 1902 the *Just So Stories*. Tales of every kind – including historical and science fiction – continued to flow from his pen, but *Kim* is generally thought to be his greatest long work, putting him high among the chroniclers of British expansion.

From 1902 Kipling made his home in Sussex, but he continued to travel widely and caught his first glimpse of warfare in South Africa, where he wrote some excellent reportage on the Boer War. However, many of the views he expressed were rejected by anti-imperialists who accused him of jingoism and love of violence. Though rich and successful, he never again enjoyed the literary esteem of his early years. With the onset of the Great War, his work became a great deal more sombre. The stories he subsequently wrote, *A Diversity of Creatures* (1917), *Debits and Credits*

(1926) and *Limits and Renewals* (1932), are now thought by many to contain some of his finest writing. The death of his only son in 1915 also contributed to a new inwardness of vision.

Kipling refused to accept the role of Poet Laureate and other civil honours, but he was the first English writer to be awarded the Nobel Prize, in 1907. He died in 1936 and his autobiographical fragment *Something of Myself* was published the following year.

KIPLING

Selected Poetry

Edited by CRAIG RAINE

PENGUIN BOOKS

PENGUIN BOOKS

Published by the Penguin Group
Penguin Books Ltd, 27 Wrights Lane, London w8 5tz, England
Penguin Books USA Inc., 375 Hudson Street, New York, New York 10014, USA
Penguin Books Australia Ltd, Ringwood, Victoria, Australia
Penguin Books Canada Ltd, 10 Alcorn Avenue, Toronto, Ontario, Canada m4v 3b2
Penguin Books (NZ) Ltd, 182–190 Wairau Road, Auckland 10, New Zealand

Penguin Books Ltd, Registered Offices: Harmondsworth, Middlesex, England

This selection first published in Penguin Books 1992
5 7 9 10 8 6 4

Typeset by DatIX International Limited, Bungay, Suffolk
Set in 10/12 pt Monophoto Ehrhardt
Printed in England by Clays Ltd, St Ives plc

Contents

CONTENTS

CONTENTS

CONTENTS

CONTENTS

CONTENTS

Introduction

At the outset of his long literary career Rudyard Kipling was apparently content to recognize the distinction between verse and poetry, and, if we are to judge from his letter to Caroline Taylor of 9 December 1889, equally content to accept that his own place was below the salt: 'I am not a poet and never shall be – but only a writer who varies fiction with verse.'

Almost a year later, in September 1890, Oscar Wilde recorded a similarly modest assessment of *Plain Tales from the Hills*, turning his phrase like a bayonet. If Kipling's title could boast of its artlessness, the unvarnished simplicity of its artistic means, Wilde was not inclined to disagree: 'one feels as if one were seated under a palm tree reading life by superb flashes of vulgarity'. (Interestingly, Wilde's use of the final *mot injuste* is foreshadowed in *Departmental Ditties*, where Sleary 'Bade farewell to Minnie Boffkin in one last, long, lingering fit', rather than the 'kiss' one might justifiably expect.) This atmosphere of placid congruence – that Kipling's place was with *hoi polloi* – is misleading. What Wilde ruefully perceives as a limitation is precisely what Kipling knew to be his originality – the discovery for literature of the underdog. This is a bent which determines the arc of Kipling's career from early tales of Anglo-Indians to the later poem 'A Charm':

> Take of English earth as much
> As either hand may rightly clutch.
> In the taking of it breathe
> Prayer for all who lie beneath.
> Not the great, nor well-bespoke,
> But the mere uncounted folk
> Of whose life and death is none
> Report or lamentation.

When T. S. Eliot, in the course of an essay of fine advocacy, identifies, as a weakness, Kipling's lack of 'inner compulsion', the absence of a Figure in the Carpet, he overlooks Kipling's uncommon fascination with the common man and the common woman – his helpless under-doggedness.

The atmosphere of congruence between Wilde and Kipling is also misleading because, a year earlier, Kipling had already struck against 'long-haired things/In velvet collar-rolls', preferring to side with the less fashionable military types in India who 'hog their bristles short'. Kipling's acceptance of the distinction between verse and poetry, between high and low art, was not simply benign, but also a wry, bitter, bristling recognition of the way the battle-lines were drawn. That note of resignation, the calm declaration ('I am not a poet and never shall be') could quickly alter to a timbre of puckish aggression, as it does in 'The Conundrum of the Workshops' (1890), where the tower of Babel is an early casualty in the history of criticism:

> They builded a tower to shiver the sky and wrench the stars apart,
> Till the Devil grunted behind the bricks: 'It's striking, but is it
>   Art?'

The poem itself is striking and memorable, but is it poetry? Or is it merely verse? For myself, I find the Old Testament cadence of 'builded' finely judged and the two verbs 'shiver' and 'wrench' beautifully economical in the way they adumbrate, first, the height and the breadth of the tower, and, second, the scale of the driving ambition – the desire to 'wrench the stars apart', a desire whose scope is curtailed by the unBiblical bathos of 'grunted' and 'bricks'. This is a particular instance where, as it were, the pigment of the language can be described by the critic with a modicum of the vividness that Kipling brings to the scar of Matun in 'The Truce of the Bear': 'Flesh like slag in the furnace, knobbed and withered and grey'. In each example, Kipling's language is patently not inert, but, like the harp of True Thomas, birls and brattles in Kipling's hands.

We think of Kipling as a special, borderline case, but he is not. Arnold memorably damned Pope and Dryden as 'classics of our prose' in his essay 'The Study of Poetry', a critical manoeuvre Eliot then used against Whitman in his essay on Pound: 'Whitman was a great prose writer. It [his originality] is spurious in so far as Whitman wrote in a way that asserted that his great prose was a new form of verse.' As one who has fallen short of poetry, then, Kipling is in the best possible company. It is apposite that Pope should be a fellow defendant, since the advertisement to 'An Epistle to Dr Arbuthnot' provided Kipling with the title of his autobiography: 'Being divided between the Necessity to say something of *Myself*, and my own laziness to undertake so awkward a Task . . .'

To substantiate his case against Pope and Dryden, Arnold quoted, maliciously:

> To Hounslow Heath I point, and Banstead Down;
> Thence comes your mutton, and these chicks my own.

Of course, counter examples could be cited against this damning quotation from the 'Second Satire of the Second Book of Horace Paraphrased'. One might list more obviously poetic lines of Pope like 'Die of a Rose in aromatic Pain', but better are lines that merely, yet perfectly, enact the unremittingly alert language we call poetry: the exact comedy of bowls 'Obliquely waddling to the mark in view'; the just comparison of learned commentary to the silkworm and vice versa ('So spins the silkworm small its slender store,/And labours, 'till it clouds itself all o'er'); the finely calculated reversed foot in the middle of the line 'Keen, hollow winds howl thro' the bleak recess'; the incriminating guinea vividly 'gingling' down the tell-tale stairs; the punishment for erring sylphs:

> Or Alom-*Stypticks* with contracting Power
> Shrink his thin Essence like a rivell'd Flower.

What a couplet. Elsewhere in Pope, the words 'power' and 'flower' are contracted to 'flow'r' and 'pow'r', which is what the metre requires here. Yet the words are written out in full, so that they exist, perfectly, precariously, between expansion and the threatened contraction. Notice, too, that Pope chooses not the obvious adjective 'shrivelled', but 'rivell'd', which calls to mind the expected word 'shrivelled', then gives it to us short of one letter – shrunken and contracted to 'rivell'd'. A further punishment for sylphs re-imagines drinking chocolate, and its preparation, with a paradoxical and poetic combination of microscopic intentness and boldly inverted perspective:

> Or as *Ixion* fix'd, the Wretch shall feel
> The giddy Motion of the whirling Mill,
> In Fumes of burning Chocolate shall glow,
> And tremble at the Sea that froaths below!

By now, even the accident of orthography, 'froaths', makes its illusory contribution to the poetry – seeming more frothy by virtue of its extra vowel, silent though it is.

Examples, however, do not answer the general point behind Arnold's particular example. To do that, one must establish what verse actually is. Once establish *that* with certainty and we can see if Kipling holds to the norm and does indeed write verse rather than poetry. By verse, however, I do not mean light verse. Though we seldom trouble to distinguish between them, verse and light verse are easily differentiated. In light verse, the interest, the meaning, resides, paradoxically and primarily, in the intricacies of the form: the content is merely the pretext to activate the elaborate metrical mechanics, just as the steel ball-bearing in a pin-table is only of interest in so far as it gets the pyrotechnics going. Verse, on the other hand, is a transparent medium which is important only as a vehicle for the meaning it carries – and which, therefore, is distinguished from prose only by the use of rhyme. Unsurprisingly, examples of pure verse are hard to find. Garrison Keillor's 'Mrs Sullivan', however, is the perfect instance, *das Ding an sich*: its message is wryly feminist and its medium, when Keillor reads it on radio, is the purest prose anecdote because the enjambement ensures that the unobtrusive rhymes are utterly inaudible.

> 'Function follows form,'
> Said Louis Sullivan one warm
> Evening in Chicago drinking beer.
> His wife said, 'Dear,
> I'm sure that what you meant
> Is that form should represent
> Function. So it's function that should be followed.'
> Sullivan swallowed
> And looked dimly far away
> And said, 'Okay,
> Form follows function, then.'

> He said it again,
> A three-word spark
> Of modern arch-
> Itectural brilliance
> That would dazzle millions.
> 'Think I should write it down?'
> He asked with a frown.
> 'Oh yes,' she said, 'and here's a pencil.'
> He did and soon was influential.

The mystery here – why is this prose anecdote set out as verse? – is solved as soon as one realizes the problem facing Garrison Keillor. His material is too short to be a prose anecdote and it would be ruined by padding or elaboration. However, it is too subtle to be a straightforward joke taking up two lines. So it is awarded the poetic treatment – capital letters and rhymes. In fact, it would make a respectable prose poem, did we not have the mistaken conviction that the prose poem should have a heightened quality of 'froathy' language. In reality, there is no reason why a prose poem should be anything other than a piece of prose which is too short, too short to be even a very short short-story – what the Germans call *eine kleine Prosa*. Eliot understood this perfectly in his prose poem 'Hysteria'. The prose poem, however, is not a remedy one might expect Garrison Keillor to discover. The solution he finds is ingenious enough.

Even if we accept the Keillor as a singularly pure example of verse – and therefore as a standard which Kipling's poetry manifestly surpasses – we are still obliged to confront the issue of versification. Surely, as we try to distinguish between poetry and verse, a further difficulty arises when, unlike the Keillor verse, the lines are differentiated from prose not only by rhyme but also by versification?

> To Hounslow Heath I point, and Banstead Down;
> Thence comes your mutton, and these chicks my own.

Is this merely versified prose? Further, why does versification seem to imply the versifier, an epithet with unmistakably derogatory connotations, while the poet somehow escapes the mechanical universe of metrics into the more plastic and subtle dimension of rhythm? Of course, the two terms are supposedly neutral and interchangeable, because versification (the principles of metrical practice) and rhythm both depend on the repetition of stress.

Nevertheless, our prejudice is that metre is less subtle in its repetition than rhythm, however strained and inaccurate this looks when seen against the long tradition of English poetry. Modernism in poetry did not go metric in this country. In Russia, things were different, despite the best efforts of Mayakovsky. The metres of Russian poetry, from Pushkin to Pasternak, demonstrate enormous subtlety. The Russian poet can deploy metres which, in English, arrive in the ear tainted with comedy, whereas in Russian their associations are majestic.

There *is* an element of pure prejudice in our unthinking, negative response to complex metre. At the same time, the Russian example isn't a clinching counter instance because it is on the English milieu that Kipling is dependent. English culture is no longer receptive to metrical virtuosity. Readers can no longer identify or name even the easier reaches of prosody. In fact, translations from the Russian which attempt to preserve the original metrical complexities only succeed in investing the host language with laughable syncopations. Given this negative predisposition, Kipling's detractors might adapt a phrase of his own and use it against him to evoke the unseemly air of vigorous, even raucous, improvisation in his verse. The phrase comes from 'Naaman's Song': 'In tones like rusty razor-blades to tunes like smitten tin'. While one can acknowledge the drift of the charge easily enough, one could not concede either its accuracy or justice without first citing passages, like the Biblical cadences of 'Gertrude's Prayer', which, finally, make the charge implausible.

Even a professed admirer like T. S. Eliot enters the caveat that Kipling is musically deficient: 'what fundamentally differentiates his "verse" from "poetry" is the subordination of musical interest'. In an earlier and less well-known review in *The Athenaeum* of 9 May 1919, Eliot's view of Kipling was more decidedly negative but the limitations in Kipling's poetry were substantially the same: Kipling, the young Eliot found, had 'ideas' but no 'point of view', no 'world', and the music of his poetry was music only 'as the words of orator or preacher are music', persuading 'not by reason, but by emphatic sound'. The older Eliot has the same reservations, but is less dismissive. Nevertheless, though he hedges the judgement with modifications, the charge, that Kipling's verse is musically deficient, remains on the charge-sheet, damningly. Kipling, we are given to understand, writes terrific tunes but misses out on melody; we like his songs, but where are his lieder?

Obviously, one can point, as Eliot could, to Kipling's free verse in 'Song of the Galley-Slaves' and 'The Runners', but these are exceptions which simply prove the rule. Which is that, for every poem like 'The Runes on Weland's Sword', with its curt, two-stress line, there are hundreds of poems whose metre is as subtle as a barn-dance, as predictable as the fiddler at a ceilidh. One thinks, for instance, of 'The Ballad of the *Bolivar*':

> Leaking like a lobster pot, steering like a dray –
> Out we took the *Bolivar*, out across the Bay!

Yet consider these lines, from earlier in the same poem:

> We put out from Sunderland loaded down with rails;
> We put back to Sunderland 'cause our cargo shifted . . .

The line 'Leaking like a lobster pot, steering like a dray' is actually made up of a trochaic tetrameter catalectic, followed by a trochaic trimeter catalectic. Which only means that the stresses fall as follows:

> Leaking like a lobster pot, steering like a dray –
> / v / v / v / , / v / v /

The tetrameter has four stresses, while the trimeter has three. The pattern here is repeated in the earlier line: 'We put out from Sunderland loaded down with rails'. But the effect is completely different since the pattern hasn't yet established itself in the ear. Thus the absence of a caesura – a pause in the line to divide the tetrameter catalectic from the trimeter catalectic – means that there is a double stress at 'Sunder*land load*ed' which enacts rhythmically what the line depicts, which is a loading down, a weightiness at the centre.

And the following line is another tiny miracle of rhythmic subtlety: 'We put back to Sunderland 'cause our cargo shifted.' Again, deprived of the caesura, the ear cannot decipher and demarcate the two halves of the line, so that the whole line is poised ambiguously between the (as yet unresolved) metre and the natural rhythm of speech. On the one hand, 'We' wouldn't naturally take a stress, whereas 'put' would. On the other hand, the metrical imperatives reverse this natural pattern of stress: 'We' is stressed and 'put' recedes. The line, then, is decidedly shifty about its rhythmic status and the instability is added to by Kipling's use of a full trimeter and the 'extra' syllable (making thirteen in all) – so that the cargo's shift is embodied in the line itself.

These are not crude effects 'like smitten tin', nor are they isolated effects in Kipling. We do not discover them because, like Eliot, we do not expect to discover them. Instead we listen impatiently for the blunter satisfactions of the chorus, eradicating subtleties along the way by assimilating them to the main template. Yet the subtleties are everywhere. To take an example readily to hand, 'smitten tin' contains its own tinny, off-key echo, exactly inexact – not *tin-tin*, but *ten-tin*.

I can't think of a poet in the language who attracts more prejudice than Kipling. Orwell, an avowed admirer, is perfectly prepared to rewrite the poetry so that the dialect is standardized. But dialect is Kipling's greatest contribution to modern literature – prose and poetry – and he is the most accomplished practitioner since Burns. Without his example, Eliot's great avant-garde coup, the cockney pub conversation in 'A Game of Chess', would have been inconceivable. The bonus of dialect is easy to illustrate: which is the most lascivious, the standard English 'lascivious', or McAndrew's Scots version, 'those soft, lasceevious stars'? To the non-dialect speaker, at least, the Scots variant is infinitely more seductive than its less wheedling standard English version. Orwell would probably concur about Kipling's use of Scots – for some reason, the Scots dialect is exempt from the snobbery which attaches to other dialects. The real problem for Orwell is the cockney dialect of Kipling's soldiers, which he finds intrinsically comic – though he attributes his own 'underlying air of patronage' to Kipling. In the short stories, Mulvaney's Irish is a similarly insoluble problem for many readers. It is, the argument runs, a caricature with no foundation in phonetic reality. It is stage Irish. In fact, just as Scots would make a distinction between the urban Glaswegian accent and the more refined delivery of Edinburgh's Morningside, Irish-English likewise contains multitudes – the harsh accent of Protestant Belfast, the soft erosions of Catholic Killiney. In Mulvaney's speech, Kipling offers us only one of many alternatives – the broadest of the dialects, true – but one which, however unrepresentative, has its counterpart in rural reality. The inability to pronounce 'th–', which means that 'thousands' comes out as 't'ousands', while not universal, is easily observable. ('Inability', though, is the wrong word, because it suggests deficiency where in truth there is only difference.) I do not believe that Kipling intended, in Orwell's words, 'to make fun of a working-man's accent'. I think it more likely that Orwell, an old Etonian and a writer who, in *Down and Out in Paris and London*, worries that his accent will instantly discover him as a gentleman, is transferring his own attitudes to Kipling.

After all, Orwell is not a reliable reader of Kipling's poetry: faced with the dove-tailed ironies of 'The Winners', its 'water-tight, fire-proof, angle-iron, sunk-hinge, time-lock, steel-faced Lie', Orwell is taken in: 'Sooner or later you will have occasion to feel that he travels fastest who travels alone, and there is the thought, ready made and, as it were, waiting for you.' Orwell has missed the warning signals sent out by Kipling to dissociate himself from his ostensible ruthless moral: '*Down to Gehenna*, or up to the Throne,/He travels the fastest who travels alone'; 'Win by his aid and the aid disown –/He travels the fastest who travels alone'. Kipling knows that the recommendation of ingratitude as a moral precept is repugnant. Orwell is more concerned with the poem's alleged proverbial memorability. For him, it is a moral mnemonic – good bad poetry whose survival is its justification. It is a tag. As praise, this is decidedly back-handed – and I should like to remove the curse by quoting the end of D. J. Enright's British Council leaflet on T. S. Eliot at the time of his centenary in 1988. 'Many of his lines, felt "as immediately as the odour of a rose", have entered the language in the form of catch-phrases or adages.' Enright goes on to quote, lavishly, without any sense that there is some impropriety in the gift of memorability. Of course, Eliot's intellectual bona fides is impeccable. It will be some time, however, before the taint attached to wide popularity leaves Kipling, as, at last, it has left Dickens – another writer of genius belittled for decades by our cultural custodians.

For them, Kipling's very virtuosity is suspect. The sestina is the artiest of poetic forms, almost Fabergé in its insistence on surface over substance. Successful sestinas, though, invert the given limitations of the form, subduing the obtrusive repetition until it is invisible. Elizabeth Bishop's 'A Miracle for Breakfast' is one perfect example. The other is Kipling's 'Sestina of the Tramp-Royal'. The strict, cramped, formal demands are belied by the unbuttoned dialect and its illusion of relaxation and roominess. The tone rambles and spreads itself and Kipling solves the technical problem of the sestina by making its repetitiveness part of his speaker's character. He does this boldly and immediately in the first stanza, by adding an *extra* repetition at the beginning of the third line:

> Speakin' in general, I 'ave tried 'em all –
> The 'appy roads that take you o'er the world.
> Speakin' in general, I 'ave found them good . . .

Throughout, too, Kipling's way with the iambic pentameter is as varied as any comparable passage in Tennyson, partly because of caesurae, partly because the emphases of the speaking voice run over the metre's metronome. 'Sestina of the Tramp-Royal' isn't a great poem – even though it manages to modulate from the button-holing style of explanation to the poetic bravura of 'An', out at sea, be'eld the dock-lights die,/ An' met my mate – the wind that tramps the world!' – but it is a very good sestina.

And what it illustrates is the strength of not being poetic. Kipling's use of dialect is usually associated with the music hall – that is to say, a popular art form – whereas perhaps it would be more helpful and truer to classify it with modernism, with Stravinsky's use of jazz and Russian folk melodies, with Picasso's restless appropriation of African sculpture and everyday materials like the daily paper. Unquestionably, Kipling, though popular, was as prepared as Stravinsky or Picasso to flout conventional standards of beauty. Kipling's aesthetic position is the argument from authenticity:

> *Ah! What avails the classic bent*
> *And what the cultured word,*
> *Against the undoctored incident*
> *That actually occurred?*

(Note the extra 'undoctored' syllable in line 3.) This italicized quasi-manifesto from 'The Benefactors' attracts examples to itself from Kipling's entire *oeuvre*, where the 'beauty' of each example is the beauty of accuracy rather than the beauty of eloquence. For instance, the political background of the Marconi scandal is now almost irretrievably lost, so that 'Gehazi', once a topical poem, now survives as an unforgettable evocation of leprosy:

> The boils that shine and burrow,
> The sores that slough and bleed –

Four verbs that one can hardly bear to dwell on – so vivid that one almost flinches.

In this category, one can include the olfactory shock of 'the mud boils foul and blue'; the sticky candour of '"Snarleyow"' where a gun-carriage wheel is said to be 'juicy' after it has gone over a body; and the unpleasantly palpable details which Kipling relishes in 'Mandalay': the 'Beefy face an' grubby 'and' of housemaids in a London of 'gritty pavin'-stones', far from the 'sludgy, squdgy creek' back East. Kipling's poetry has a strong stomach and it hardly ever looks away. There is very little in the way of whiffling sensibility. Rather there is a determination to include the unaesthetic: 'breech-blocks jammed with mud'; 'the lid of the flesh-pot chattered high'; 'the ten-times fingering weed'; 'the club-footed vines'. Rather than the baby seal with its soap-bubble eye, seal culling means gloves 'stiff with frozen blood'. Barren, featureless, and therefore indescribable landscapes are not a problem for Kipling because he doesn't feel the constraint of literary decorum and takes his similes where and as he finds them: 'Old Aden, like a barrick-stove/ That no one's lit for years an' years.' He casts a cold eye on death, too – on 'the wide-eyed corpse', on 'Blanket-hidden bodies, flagless, followed by the flies', on ' 'Is carcase past rebellion, but 'is eyes inquirin' why'.

It would be easy to continue quoting in this heterogeneous way. Sounds and the sea, however, provide two conveniently unified anthologies of excellence. Perfectly captured sounds include: 'And the lisp of the split banana-frond/That talked us to sleep when we were small'; 'To hear the traffic slurring/Once more through London mud'; 'the sob of the questing lead!'; the 'snick' of a breech-bolt; 'the thresh of deep-sea rain'; 'the first dry rattle of new-drawn steel' at the battle of Edgehill.

The sea is an equally generous provider, bringing us 'wind-plaited sand-dunes' and 'rain-squalls' that 'lash and veer'. Kipling's beach is as real as Joyce's Sandymount Strand:

In the heel of the wind-bit pier,
Where the twisted weed was piled.

'Piled' somehow evokes very precisely the illusion of immense and slightly inept labour that is suggested by the accumulation of seaweed on a shore – as if it had been put there, deliberately, untidily, rather than accidentally. Kipling is good on the sea *solus* ('the drunken rollers comb') and in conjunction with ships: 'The shudder, the stumble, the swerve, as the star-stabbing bowsprit emerges'; 'the shouting of the back-stay in a gale'.

When it comes to the sinking of ships, Kipling surrenders everything to the task of seeing the object as in itself it really is: the most famous example occurs in 'The *Mary Gloster*':

Down by the head an' sinkin', her fires are drawn and cold,
And the water's splashin' hollow on the skin of the empty hold –
Churning an' choking and chuckling, quiet and scummy and dark –

In '"The Trade"', Kipling catches the aftermath: 'only whiffs of paraffin/Or creamy rings that fizz and fade'. 'The Destroyers' again consults the entrails of catastrophe: 'Till, streaked with ash and sleeked with oil,/The lukewarm whirlpools close!' Here, 'lukewarm' adds immeasurably to the reality of the scene. As an adjective, it is calculatedly unpoetic compared to the more obviously rhetorical lines which follow:

A shadow down the sickened wave
Long since her slayer fled.

Here we are recognizably in the presence of poetry, whereas with 'lukewarm' poetry was not a consideration.

In 'The King' (1894), Kipling shows himself fully aware of his aesthetic position which is completely counter to Arnold, who felt Victorian England to be intractably unpoetic – a supposition indubitably correct in his own case, as a glance at 'East London' and 'West London' will show. Kipling's allegiance is rather with Baudelaire and Eliot, poets determined to write in the present, with its gamps, galoshes, gaslights, spats, stove-pipe hats and area gates. Kipling's King is the spirit of

Romance – a figure generally considered to be incompatible with, say, the railway season ticket. Kipling's King brings up the 9.15 train, in the driver's cab, the 'unconsidered miracle'.

Kipling, then, is a modernist rather than the dated Edwardian of conventional criticism. Looked at thus, his poetry can surprise us with its affinities. Eliot, for instance, is indebted to 'The Long Trail' for the metre of 'Skimbleshanks' – the greatest modernist significantly taking the serious metric of Kipling and transposing it downwards to the frankly lighter mode. But more importantly Eliot is Kipling's debtor in 'The Hollow Men' and in the third of his 'Preludes':

> You dozed, and watched the night revealing
> The thousand sordid images
> Of which your soul was constituted;
> They flickered against the ceiling.

Kipling's 'Gentleman-Rankers' not only foreshadows Eliot's use of the nursery rhyme in 'The Hollow Men' ('We're poor little lambs who've lost our way,/Baa! Baa! Baa!') but also contributes:

> Every secret, self-revealing on the aching whitewashed ceiling.

When one reads 'Gertrude's Prayer', one looks back to Chaucer and to Ecclesiastes, but also ahead to Ezra Pound's *The Pisan Cantos* in their closing pages. The subject of both poems is irremediable error, for which a language drenched in contrition and self-denial is appropriate – so each poet chooses an impersonal, ritual dialect, a diction of hallowed simplicity, worn smooth with centuries of use, which yet avoids the taint of archaism, of mere quaint pageantry:

> The ant's a centaur in his dragon world.
> Pull down thy vanity, it is not man
> Made courage, or made order, or made grace,
>   Pull down thy vanity, I say pull down.
> Learn of the green world what can be thy place
> In scaled invention or true artistry,
> Pull down thy vanity,
>   Paquin pull down!

Pound's rhyme is more intermittent than Kipling's, but both men are masters of the refrain whose measured simplicity eventually amounts to what one can only call a scourged eloquence. 'Dayspring mishandled cometh not againe!'

Reading Kipling's poetry now is to realize how far ahead of his time his writing was. 'The Return' returns to a constant theme of Kipling's – the soldier's discontent in civvy street – and looks ahead to the laconic specificity of Auden. In 'Memorial for the City', Auden brings a scene alive with a single bizarre image: 'The soldiers fire, the mayor bursts into tears.' 'The Return' anticipates Auden's economical documentation of the war-zone:

> Towns without people, ten times took,
> An' ten times left an' burned at last;
> An' starvin' dogs that come to look
> For owners when a column passed . . .

Whose concentration camp is more vivid? Auden's or Kipling's? 'Barbed wire enclosed an arbitrary spot/Where bored officials lounged (one cracked a joke)/And sentries sweated for the day was hot . . .' I think Kipling's is less mannered and contrived: 'Be'ind the pegged barbed-wire strands./Beneath the tall electric light . . .' There are two words in the Kipling which expose Auden's effortful authenticity. They are 'pegged' and 'tall'.

I do not wish to overstate Kipling's modernism. It would be slightly fanciful, for instance, to insist on the *poésie pure* of 'McAndrew's Hymn' – the pure sound of catalogued technicalities like crosshead-gibs, the coupler-flange, the connecting-rod, the spindle-guide – since the poem is by way of being Kipling's earliest manifesto and fraught, therefore, with meaning. As a poem, it belongs with those others that declare the figure in Kipling's carpet – 'The Glory of the Garden', 'The Survival', and 'Alnaschar and the Oxen'. McAndrew is Kipling's lifelong subject. He is one of the Sons of Martha. He is an underdog – essential, but ignored by 'the passengers, wi' gloves an' canes'. In 'The Glory of the Garden', the lawns are not everything: 'the Glory of the Garden lies in more than meets the eye':

> For where the old thick laurels grow, along the thin red wall,
> You find the tool- and potting-sheds which are the heart of all;
> The cold-frames and the hot-houses, the dungpits and the tanks,
> The rollers, carts and drainpipes, with the barrows and the planks.

This is the metrical source, as it happens, for 'Growltiger's Last Stand'. How was it, then, that T. S. Eliot overlooked this vital connecting-rod? Eliot's selection of Kipling was made in 1941 and, in a sense, represents an aspect of the poet's war-work. France had capitulated, the evacuation at Dunkirk had taken place and Germany had begun what looked like a successful invasion of Russia. All this finds its reflection in Eliot's selection which draws heavily and understandably on Kipling's patriotic verse. As a result, Eliot's selection, though an enduring landmark, has some extraordinary omissions: the ballad 'The Gift of the Sea', the chilling and pitiless masterpiece 'A Death-Bed', 'My Boy Jack', 'A Nativity', the powerfully nostalgic 'Lichtenberg' whose refrain ('Riding in, in the rain') contains its own swallow of emotion, and 'Bridge-Guard in the Karroo'. This last poem, written in 1901, is one of Kipling's most characteristic masterpieces. Its territory is familiarly foreign. It deals with soldiers. Its narrative is easy to follow. It has none of the chilly parallelism of 'A Death-Bed' where the course of the First World War and the progress of a cancer patient towards certain death are juxtaposed with cold relish. The stamp of Kipling's authority is everywhere in 'Bridge-Guard in the Karroo' – from the beauty of the sunset ('Opal and ash-of-roses,/Cinnamon, umber, and dun') to the quiet desolation of the homesick guard:

> We slip through the broken panel
>   Of fence by the ganger's shed;
> We drop to the waterless channel
>   And the lean track overhead;
>
> We stumble on refuse of rations,
>   The beef and the biscuit-tins . . .

Kipling is our laureate of litter, our bard of homesickness, capable of capturing the very details of despair: 'the click of the restless girders/As steel contracts in the cold –'; 'A morsel of dry earth falling/From the flanks of the scarred ravine'. The 'hosts of heaven' themselves are seen 'Framed through the iron arches – /Banded and barred by the ties' – and remind one, yet again, of Pound:

> a sinistra la Torre
>   seen through a pair of breeches.

Perhaps it is appropriate to conclude with the coupling of two politically unpopular poets – with their beleaguered sympathies and their discriminating ears. However, the sceptic will respond, with some justice, that it is easy to justify 'Bridge-Guard in the Karroo' but where is the poetry in the famous, unexcludable 'If –'?

The case for 'If –' has never been made. Neither has the case against it. For admirers and detractors alike, I imagine, the verdict seems self-evident. Those who dislike Kipling on principle would frame their objections as follows: 'If –' is nothing more than the complacent aggregation of impossible precepts and as far from poetry as the average school song.

I agree that 'If –' is a test case. Personally, I feel the poem's power, but is that power the power of verse or the power of poetry? The advice is by and large sound, and line 8 ('And yet don't look too good, nor talk too wise') takes off the curse of complacency. What the sensitive reader responds to is not the particularities of advice but the impossibly stretched rhetorical structure. 'If –' is a single sentence, endlessly burdened by the weight of hypotheticals. The conclusion – 'you'll be a Man, my son!' – depends on more qualifications than it seems possible for one sentence to bear. The poem, then, mimics the moral difficulty posed by Kipling – and yet the successful negotiation of the impossibly cumbered sentence to its end demonstrates, in miniature, the possibility of achieving something genuinely difficult. As single-sentence poems go, it is one of the longest, and it possesses all the poetry of the lovingly deferred finale of Dvořák's Cello Concerto. The form tells as much as the substance – and is, indisputably, poetry of a high order.

CRAIG RAINE

Oxford, 30 December 1990

A Note on the Text

The text of this selection is taken from the *Definitive Edition* of Kipling's poetry, with five additional poems from *Early Verse by Rudyard Kipling* edited by Andrew Rutherford. Volume XXV of the Sussex edition of Kipling's work and Volume XXVIII of the Burwash edition of his work contain poems not included in the *Definitive Edition*, but I have chosen none of these.

The contents of the *Definitive Edition* (1940) are the same as *Verse, Inclusive Edition 1885–1932*, arranged and edited by Kipling himself, but with additional material authorized by his daughter.

All footnotes are Kipling's. Editorial notes can be found at the back of the book.

A Murder in the Compound

At the wall's foot a smear of fly-flecked red –
    Discoloured grass wherefrom the wild bees flee.
Across the pathway to the flower-bed,
    The dark stream struggles forward, lazily,
Blackened by that fierce fervour overhead
She does not heed, to whom the noontide glare
    And the flies' turmoil round her livid lips
Are less account than that green puddle where,
Just out of reach, the turbid water slips
Between the corn-ridge and the *siris*[1] trees . . .
    The crows are gathered now, and peer and glance
Athwart the branches, and no passer sees,
    When Life's last flicker leaves her countenance,
How, merrily, they drop down, one by one,
To that gay-tinted bundle in the sun.

'Way down the Ravi River'

I wandered by the riverside,
    To gaze upon the view,
And watched the Alligator glide
    After the dead Hindu,
Who stank and sank beneath the tide,
    Then rose and stank anew.

The evening dews were falling fast,
    The damp, unwholesome dew;
The river rippled 'neath the blast,
    The black crow roostward flew;
And swift the Alligator passed
    In chase of his Hindu.

1. Acacia.

I

And, from the margin of the tide
    I watched the twain that fled –
The Alligator, scaly-thighed,
    Close pressed the flying dead,
Who gazed, with eyeballs opened wide,
    Upward, but nothing said.

And many a time at eventide,
    As night comes on anew,
I think upon the riverside
    Where, gazing on the view,
I watched the Alligator glide
    After the dead Hindu.

Verse Heading to 'The "Kingdom" of Bombay'

Who are they that bluff and blow among the mud-banks of their harbour?
Making mock of Upper India where the High Gods live alway?
Grey rats of Prince's Dock – more dull than oysters of Colaba –
Apes of Apollo Bunder – yea, *bacilli* of Back Bay!

                                        Swinburne (adapted)

Verses on the Charleville Hotel, Mussoorie

A burning sun in cloudless skies
    And April dies,
A dusty mall – three sunsets splendid –
    And May is ended,
Grey mud beneath – grey cloud o'erhead
    And June is dead.
A little bill in late July
    And then we fly.

In Partibus

The 'buses run to Battersea,
*   The 'buses run to Bow,*
The 'buses run to Westbourne Grove,
*   And Notting Hill also;*
But I am sick of London Town,
*   From Shepherd's Bush to Bow.*

I see the smut upon my cuff,
   And feel him on my nose;
I cannot leave my window wide
   When gentle Zephyr blows,
Because he brings disgusting things,
   And drops 'em on my 'clo'es'.

The sky, a greasy soup-tureen,
   Shuts down atop my brow.
Yes, I have sighed for London Town
   And I have got it now:
And half of it is fog and filth,
   And half is fog and row.

And when I take my nightly prowl,
   'Tis passing good to meet
The pious Briton lugging home
   His wife and daughter sweet,
Through four packed miles of seething vice,
   Thrust out upon the street.

Earth holds no horror like to this
   In any land displayed,
From Suez unto Sandy Hook,
   From Calais to Port Said;
And 'twas to hide their heathendom
   The beastly fog was made.

I cannot tell when dawn is near,
　　Or when the day is done,
Because I always see the gas
　　And never see the sun,
And now, methinks, I do not care
　　A cuss for either one.

But stay, there was an orange, or
　　An aged egg its yolk;
It might have been a Pears' balloon
　　Or Barnum's latest joke:
I took it for the sun and wept
　　To watch it through the smoke.

It's Oh to see the morn ablaze
　　Above the mango-tope,
When homeward through the dewy cane
　　The little jackals lope,
And half Bengal heaves into view,
　　New-washed – with sunlight soap.

It's Oh for one deep whisky-peg
　　When Christmas winds are blowing,
When all the men you ever knew,
　　And all you've ceased from knowing,
Are 'entered for the Tournament,
　　And everything that's going'.

But I consort with long-haired things
　　In velvet collar-rolls,
Who talk about the Aims of Art,
　　And 'theories' and 'goals',
And moo and coo with womenfolk
　　About their blessed souls.

But that they call 'psychology'
　　Is lack of liver-pill,

And all that blights their tender souls
    Is eating till they're ill,
And their chief way of winning goals
    Consists of sitting still.

Its Oh to meet an Army man,
    Set up, and trimmed and taut,
Who does not spout hashed libraries
    Or think the next man's thought,
And walks as though he owned himself,
    And hogs his bristles short.

Hear now a voice across the seas
    To kin beyond my ken,
If ye have ever filled an hour
    With stories from my pen,
For pity's sake send some one here
    To bring me news of men!

The 'buses run to Islington,
    To Highgate and Soho,
To Hammersmith and Kew therewith,
    And Camberwell also,
But I can only murmur 'Bus!'
    From Shepherd's Bush to Bow.

Prelude

to *Departmental Ditties*

1885

I have eaten your bread and salt.
    I have drunk your water and wine.
The deaths ye died I have watched beside,
    And the lives ye led were mine.

Was there aught I did not share
  In vigil or toil or ease, –
One joy or woe that I did not know,
  Dear hearts across the seas?

I have written the tale of our life
  For a sheltered people's mirth,
In jesting guise – but ye are wise,
  And ye know what the jest is worth.

Army Headquarters

Old is the song that I sing –
  Old as my unpaid bills –
Old as the chicken that *khitmutgars*[1] bring
  Men at dâk-bungalows old as the Hills.

Ahasuerus Jenkins of the 'Operatic Own'
Was dowered with a tenor voice of *super*-Santley tone.
His views on equitation were, perhaps, a trifle queer.
He had no seat worth mentioning, but oh! he had an ear.

He clubbed his wretched company a dozen times a day;
He used to quit his charger in a parabolic way;
His method of saluting was the joy of all beholders;
But Ahasuerus Jenkins had a head upon his shoulders.

He took two months at Simla when the year was at the spring,
And underneath the deodars eternally did sing.
He warbled like a *bul-bul*[2] but particularly at
Cornelia Agrippina, who was musical and fat.

She controlled a humble husband, who, in turn, controlled a Dept
Where Cornelia Agrippina's human singing-birds were kept

1. Waiters. 2. Nightingale

6

From April to October on a plump retaining-fee,
Supplied, of course, *per mensem*, by the Indian Treasury.

Cornelia used to sing with him, and Jenkins used to play;
He praised unblushingly her notes, for he was false as they;
So when the winds of April turned the budding roses brown,
Cornelia told her husband: – 'Tom, you mustn't send him down.'

They haled him from his regiment, which didn't much regret him;
They found for him an office-stool, and on that stool they set him
To play with maps and catalogues three idle hours a day,
And draw his plump retaining-fee – which means his double pay.

Now, ever after dinner, when the coffee-cups are brought,
Ahasuerus waileth o'er the grand pianoforte;
And, thanks to fair Cornelia, his fame hath waxen great,
And Ahasuerus Jenkins is a Power in the State!

The Story of Uriah

'Now there were two men in one city;
the one rich, and the other poor.'

Jack Barrett went to Quetta
    Because they told him to.
He left his wife at Simla
    On three-fourths his monthly screw.
Jack Barrett died at Quetta
    Ere the next month's pay he drew.

Jack Barrett went to Quetta.
    He didn't understand
The reason of his transfer
    From the pleasant mountain-land.
The season was September,
    And it killed him out of hand.

Jack Barrett went to Quetta
   And there gave up the ghost,
Attempting two men's duty
   In that very healthy post;
And Mrs Barrett mourned for him
   Five lively months at most.

Jack Barrett's bones at Quetta
   Enjoy profound repose;
But I shouldn't be astonished
   If *now* his spirit knows
The reason for his transfer
   From the Himalayan snows.

And, when the Last Great Bugle Call
   Adown the Hurnai throbs,
And the last grim joke is entered
   In the big black Book of Jobs,
And Quetta graveyards give again
   Their victims to the air,
I shouldn't like to be the man
   Who sent Jack Barrett there.

The Post that Fitted

Though tangled and twisted the course of true love,
   This ditty explains,
No tangle's so tangled it cannot improve
   If the Lover has brains.

Ere the steamer bore him Eastward, Sleary was engaged to marry
An attractive girl at Tunbridge, whom he called 'my little Carrie'.
Sleary's pay was very modest; Sleary was the other way.
Who can cook a two-plate dinner on eight rupees a day?

Long he pondered o'er the question in his scantly furnished quarters –
Then proposed to Minnie Boffkin, eldest of Judge Boffkin's daughters.

Certainly an impecunious Subaltern was not a catch,
But the Boffkins knew that Minnie mightn't make another match.

So they recognized the business and, to feed and clothe the bride,
Got him made a Something Something somewhere on the Bombay
    side.
Anyhow, the billet carried pay enough for him to marry –
As the artless Sleary put it: – 'Just the thing for me and Carrie.'

Did he, therefore, jilt Miss Boffkin – impulse of a baser mind?
No! He started epileptic fits of an appalling kind.
[Of his *modus operandi* only this much I could gather: –
'Pears's shaving sticks will give you little taste and lots of lather.']

Frequently in public places his affliction used to smite
Sleary with distressing vigour – always in the Boffkins' sight.
Ere a week was over Minnie weepingly returned his ring,
Told him his 'unhappy weakness' stopped all thought of marrying.

Sleary bore the information with a chastened holy joy, –
Epileptic fits don't matter in Political employ, –
Wired three short words to Carrie – took his ticket, packed his kit -
Bade farewell to Minnie Boffkin in one last, long, lingering fit.

Four weeks later, Carrie Sleary read – and laughed until she wept –
Mrs Boffkin's warning letter on the 'wretched epilept' . . .
Year by year, in pious patience, vengeful Mrs Boffkin sits
Waiting for the Sleary babies to develop Sleary's fits.

The Last Department

Twelve hundred million men are spread
    About this Earth, and I and You
Wonder, when You and I are dead,
    'What will those luckless millions do?'

'None whole or clean,' we cry, 'or free from stain
Of favour.' Wait awhile, till we attain
   The Last Department where nor fraud nor fools,
Nor grade nor greed, shall trouble us again.

Fear, Favour, or Affection – what are these
To the grim Head who claims our services?
   I never knew a wife or interest yet
Delay that *pukka* step, miscalled 'decease';

When leave, long overdue, none can deny;
When idleness of all Eternity
   Becomes our furlough, and the marigold
Our thriftless, bullion-minting Treasury

Transferred to the Eternal Settlement,
Each in his strait, wood-scanted office pent,
   No longer Brown reverses Smith's appeals,
Or Jones records his Minute of Dissent.

And One, long since a pillar of the Court,
As mud between the beams thereof is wrought;
   And One who wrote on phosphates for the crops
Is subject-matter of his own Report.

These be the glorious ends whereto we pass –
Let Him who Is, go call on Him who Was;
   And He shall see the *mallie*[1] steals the slab
For curry-grinder, and for goats the grass.

A breath of wind, a Border bullet's flight,
A draught of water, or a horse's fright –
   The droning of the fat *Sheristadar*[2]
Ceases, the punkah stops and falls the night

---

1. The cemetery gardener.   2. Clerk of the Court.

For you or Me. Do those who live decline
The step that offers, or their work resign?
   Trust me, To-day's Most Indispensables,
Five hundred men can take your place or mine.

To the Unknown Goddess

Will you conquer my heart with your beauty, my soul going out from
    afar?
Shall I fall to your hand as a victim of crafty and cautious *shikar*?

Have I met you and passed you already, unknowing, unthinking, and
    blind?
Shall I meet you next season at Simla, O sweetest and best of your
    kind?

Does the P. & O. bear you to meward, or, clad in short frocks in the West,
Are you growing the charms that shall capture and torture the heart in
    my breast?

Will you stay in the Plains till September – my passion as warm as the day?
Will you bring me to book on the Mountains, or where the
    thermantidotes play?

When the light of your eyes shall make pallid the mean lesser lights I
    pursue,
And the charm of your presence shall lure me from love of the gay
    'thirteen-two',[1]

When the 'peg'[2] and the pigskin shall please not; when I buy me
    Calcutta-built clothes;
When I quit the Delight of Wild Asses, forswearing the swearing of oaths;

1. Polo-pony. 2. Whisky and soda.

As a deer to the hand of the hunter when I turn 'mid the gibes of my friends;
When the days of my freedom are numbered, and the life of the bachelor
    ends.

Ah, Goddess! child, spinster, or widow – as of old on Mars Hill when
    they raised
To the God that they knew not an altar – so I, a young Pagan, have praised

The Goddess I know not nor worship; yet, if half that men tell me be true,
You will come in the future, and therefore these verses are written to you.

Epigraph to *Pagett, M.P.*

> The toad beneath the harrow knows
> Exactly where each tooth-point goes;
> The butterfly upon the road
> Preaches contentment to that toad.

La Nuit Blanche

> A much-discerning Public hold
>   The Singer generally sings
>   Of personal and private things,
> And prints and sells his past for gold.
>
> Whatever I may here disclaim,
>   The very clever folk I sing to
>   Will most indubitably cling to
> Their pet delusion, just the same.

I had seen, as dawn was breaking
  And I staggered to my rest,
Tara Devi softly shaking
  From the Cart Road to the crest.

I had seen the spurs of Jakko
   Heave and quiver, swell and sink.
Was it Earthquake or tobacco,
   Day of Doom or Night of Drink?

In the full, fresh fragrant morning
   I observed a camel crawl,
Laws of gravitation scorning,
   On the ceiling and the wall.
Then I watched a fender walking,
   And I heard grey leeches sing,
And a red-hot monkey talking
   Did not seem the proper thing.

Then a Creature, skinned and crimson,
   Ran about the floor and cried,
And they said I had the 'jims' on,
   And they dosed me with bromide,
And they locked me in my bedroom –
   Me and one wee Blood-Red Mouse –
Though I said: – 'To give my head room
   'You had best unroof the house.'

But my words were all unheeded,
   Though I told the grave M.D.
That the treatment really needed
   Was a dip in open sea
That was lapping just below me,
   Smooth as silver, white as snow –
And it took three men to throw me
   When I found I could not go.

Half the night I watched the Heavens
   Fizz like '81 champagne –
Fly to sixes and to sevens,
   Wheel and thunder back again;

And when all was peace and order
  Save one planet nailed askew,
Much I wept because my warder
  Would not let me set it true.

After frenzied hours of waiting,
  When the Earth and Skies were dumb,
Pealed an awful voice dictating
  An interminable sum,
Changing to a tangled story –
  'What she said you said I said –'
Till the Moon arose in glory,
  And I found her . . . in my head;

Then a Face came, blind and weeping,
  And It couldn't wipe Its eyes,
And It muttered I was keeping
  Back the moonlight from the skies;
So I patted It for pity,
  But It whistled shrill with wrath,
And a huge, black Devil City
  Poured its peoples on my path.

So I fled with steps uncertain
  On a thousand-year-long race,
But the bellying of the curtain
  Kept me always in one place,
While the tumult rose and maddened
  To the roar of Earth on fire,
Ere it ebbed and sank and saddened
  To a whisper tense as wire.

In intolerable stillness
  Rose one little, little star,
And it chuckled at my illness,
  And it mocked me from afar;
And its brethren came and eyed me,
  Called the Universe to aid,

Till I lay, with naught to hide me,
  'Neath the Scorn of All Things Made.

Dun and saffron, robed and splendid
  Broke the solemn, pitying Day,
And I knew my pains were ended,
  And I turned and tried to pray;
But my speech was shattered wholly,
  And I wept as children weep,
Till the dawn-wind, softly, slowly,
  Brought to burning eyelids sleep.

The Lovers' Litany

Eyes of grey – a sodden quay,
Driving rain and falling tears,
As the steamer puts to sea
In a parting storm of cheers.
  Sing, for Faith and Hope are high –
  None so true as you and I –
  Sing the Lovers' Litany: –
  'Love like ours can never die!'

Eyes of black – a throbbing keel,
Milky foam to left and right;
Whispered converse near the wheel
In the brilliant tropic night.
  Cross that rules the southern Sky!
  Stars that sweep, and turn and fly
  Hear the Lovers' Litany: –
  'Love like ours can never die!'

Eyes of brown – a dusty plain
Split and parched with heat of June.
Flying hoof and tightened rein,
Hearts that beat the ancient tune.

Side by side the horses fly,
Frame we now the old reply
Of the Lovers' Litany: –
'Love like ours can never die!'

Eyes of blue – the Simla Hills
Silvered with the moonlight hoar;
Pleading of the waltz that thrills,
Dies and echoes round Benmore.
    'Mabel', 'Officers', 'Good-bye',
    Glamour, wine, and witchery –
    On my soul's sincerity,
    'Love like ours can never die!'

Maidens, of your charity,
Pity my most luckless state.
Four times Cupid's debtor I –
Bankrupt in quadruplicate.
    Yet, despite my evil case,
    An a maiden showed me grace,
    Four-and-forty times would I
    Sing the Lovers' Litany: –
    'Love like ours can never die!'

The Overland Mail

(*Foot-service to the Hills*)

In the Name of the Empress of India, make way,
    O Lords of the Jungle, wherever you roam,
The woods are astir at the close of the day –
    We exiles are waiting for letters from Home.
Let the robber retreat – let the tiger turn tail –
In the name of the Empress, the Overland Mail!

With a jingle of bells as the dusk gathers in,
    He turns to the footpath that heads up the hill –
The bags on his back and a cloth round his chin,
    And, tucked in his waistband, the Post Office bill: –
'Despatched on this date, as received by the rail,
'*Per* runner, two bags of the Overland Mail.'

Is the torrent in spate? He must ford it or swim.
    Has the rain wrecked the road? He must climb by the cliff.
Does the tempest cry halt? What are tempests to him?
    The service admits not a 'but' or an 'if'.
While the breath's in his mouth, he must bear without fail,
In the Name of the Empress, the Overland Mail.

From aloe to rose-oak, from rose-oak to fir,
    From level to upland, from upland to crest,
From rice-field to rock-ridge, from rock-ridge to spur,
    Fly the soft-sandalled feet, strains the brawny, brown chest.
From rail to ravine – to the peak from the vale –
Up, up through the night goes the Overland Mail.

There's a speck on the hillside, a dot on the road –
    A jingle of bells on the footpath below –
There's a scuffle above in the monkey's abode –
    The world is awake and the clouds are aglow.
For the great Sun himself must attend to the hail: –
'In the Name of the Empress, the Overland Mail!'

Epigraph to *The Ballad of Fisher's Boarding-House*

That night, when through the mooring-chains
    The wide-eyed corpse rolled free,
To blunder down by Garden Reach
    And rot at Kedgeree,
The tale the Hughli told the shoal
    The lean shoal told to me.

Possibilities

Ay, lay him 'neath the Simla pine –
  A fortnight fully to be missed,
  Behold, we lose our fourth at whist,
A chair is vacant where we dine.

His place forgets him; other men
  Have bought his ponies, guns, and traps.
  His fortune is the Great Perhaps
And that cool rest-house down the glen,

Whence he shall hear, as spirits may,
  Our mundane revel on the height,
  Shall watch each flashing *'rickshaw*-light
Sweep on to dinner, dance, and play.

Benmore shall woo him to the ball
  With lighted rooms and braying band;
  And he shall hear and understand
'Dream Faces' better than us all.

For, think you, as the vapours flee
  Across Sanjaolie after rain,
  His soul may climb the hill again
To each old field of victory.

Unseen, whom women held so dear,
  The strong man's yearning to his kind
  Shall shake at most the window-blind,
Or dull awhile the card-room's cheer.

In his own place of power unknown,
  His Light o' Love another's flame,
  His dearest pony galloped lame,
And he an alien and alone!

Yet may he meet with many a friend –
   Shrewd shadows, lingering long unseen
   Among us when '*God save the Queen*'
Shows even 'extras' have an end.

And, when we leave the heated room,
   And, when at four the lights expire,
   The crew shall gather round the fire
And mock our laughter in the gloom;

Talk as we talked, and they ere death –
   Flirt wanly, dance in ghostly wise,
   With ghosts of tunes for melodies,
And vanish at the morning's breath!

The Betrothed

'You must choose between me and your cigar.'
Breach of Promise Case, circa 1885

Open the old cigar-box, get me a Cuba stout,
For things are running crossways, and Maggie and I are out.

We quarrelled about Havanas – we fought o'er a good cheroot,
And *I* know she is exacting, and she says I am a brute.

Open the old cigar-box – let me consider a space;
In the soft blue veil of the vapour musing on Maggie's face.

Maggie is pretty to look at – Maggie's a loving lass,
But the prettiest cheeks must wrinkle, the truest of loves must pass.

There's peace in a Larranaga, there's calm in a Henry Clay;
But the best cigar in an hour is finished and thrown away –

Thrown away for another as perfect and ripe and brown –
But I could not throw away Maggie for fear o' the talk o' the town!

Maggie, my wife at fifty – grey and dour and old –
With never another Maggie to purchase for love or gold!

And the light of Days that have Been the dark of the Days that Are,
And Love's torch stinking and stale, like the butt of a dead cigar –

The butt of a dead cigar you are bound to keep in your pocket –
With never a new one to light tho' it's charred and black to the socket!

Open the old cigar-box – let me consider a while.
Here is a mild Manila – there is a wifely smile.

Which is the better portion – bondage bought with a ring,
Or a harem of dusky beauties, fifty tied in a string?

Counsellors cunning and silent – comforters true and tried,
And never a one of the fifty to sneer at a rival bride?

Thought in the early morning, solace in time of woes,
Peace in the hush of the twilight, balm ere my eyelids close,

This will the fifty give me, asking nought in return,
With only a *Suttee*'s passion – to do their duty and burn.

This will the fifty give me. When they are spent and dead,
Five times other fifties shall be my servants instead.

The furrows of far-off Java, the isles of the Spanish Main,
When they hear my harem is empty will send me my brides again.

I will take no heed to their raiment, nor food for their mouths withal,
So long as the gulls are nesting, so long as the showers fall.

I will scent 'em with best vanilla, with tea will I temper their hides,
And the Moor and the Mormon shall envy who read of the tale of my
        brides.

For Maggie has written a letter to give me my choice between
The wee little whimpering Love and the great god Nick o' Teen.

And I have been servant of Love for barely a twelvemonth clear,
But I have been Priest of Cabanas a matter of seven year;

And the gloom of my bachelor days is flecked with the cheery light
Of stumps that I burned to Friendship and Pleasure and Work and
        Fight.

And I turn my eyes to the future that Maggie and I must prove,
But the only light on the marshes is the Will-o'-the-Wisp of Love.

Will it see me safe through my journey or leave me bogged in the mire?
Since a puff of tobacco can cloud it, shall I follow the fitful fire?

Open the old cigar-box – let me consider anew –
Old friends, and who is Maggie that I should abandon *you*?

A million surplus Maggies are willing to bear the yoke;
And a woman is only a woman, but a good Cigar is a Smoke.

Light me another Cuba – I hold to my first-sworn vows.
If Maggie will have no rival, I'll have no Maggie for Spouse!

Christmas in India

Dim dawn behind the tamarisks – the sky is saffron-yellow –
   As the women in the village grind the corn,
And the parrots seek the river-side, each calling to his fellow
   That the Day, the staring Eastern Day, is born.
     O the white dust on the highway! O the stenches in the byway!
      O the clammy fog that hovers over earth!
     And at Home they're making merry 'neath the white and scarlet
       berry –
      What part have India's exiles in their mirth?

Full day behind the tamarisks – the sky is blue and staring –
   As the cattle crawl afield beneath the yoke,
And they bear One o'er the field-path, who is past all hope or caring,
   To the ghat below the curling wreaths of smoke.
     Call on Rama, going slowly, as ye bear a brother lowly –
      Call on Rama – he may hear, perhaps, your voice!
     With our hymn-books and our psalters we appeal to other altars,
      And to-day we bid 'good Christian men rejoice'!

High noon behind the tamarisks – the sun is hot above us –
  As at Home the Christmas Day is breaking wan.
They will drink our healths at dinner – those who tell us how they love
      us,
    And forget us till another year be gone!
      O the toil that knows no breaking! O the *Heimweh*, ceaseless, aching!
        O the black dividing Sea and alien Plain!
      Youth was cheap – wherefore we sold it. Gold was good – we
          hoped to hold it.
        And to-day we know the fullness of our gain!

Grey dusk behind the tamarisks – the parrots fly together –
  As the Sun is sinking slowly over Home;
And his last ray seems to mock us shackled in a lifelong tether
  That drags us back howe'er so far we roam.
      Hard her service, poor her payment – she in ancient, tattered
          raiment –
        India, she the grim Stepmother of our kind.
      If a year of life be lent her, if her temple's shrine we enter,
        The door is shut – we may not look behind.

Black night behind the tamarisks – the owls begin their chorus –
  As the conches from the temple scream and bray.
With the fruitless years behind us and the hopeless years before us,
  Let us honour, O my brothers, Christmas Day!
      Call a truce, then, to our labours – let us feast with friends and
          neighbours,
        And be merry as the custom of our caste;
      For if 'faint and forced the laughter', and if sadness follow after,
        We are richer by one mocking Christmas past.

The Grave of the Hundred Head

There's a widow in sleepy Chester
  Who weeps for her only son;
There's a grave on the Pabeng River,
  A grave that the Burmans shun;
And there's Subadar Prag Tewarri
  Who tells how the work was done.

A Snider squibbed in the jungle –
  Somebody laughed and fled,
And the men of the First Shikaris
  Picked up their Subaltern dead,
With a big blue mark on his forehead
  And the back blown out of his head.

Subadar Prag Tewarri,
  Jemadar Hira Lal,
Took command of the party,
  Twenty rifles in all,
Marched them down to the river
  As the day was beginning to fall.

They buried the boy by the river,
  A blanket over his face –
They wept for their dead Lieutenant,
  The men of an alien race –
They made a *samadh*[1] in his honour,
  A mark for his resting-place.

For they swore by the Holy Water,
  They swore by the salt they ate,
That the soul of Lieutenant Eshmitt Sahib
  Should go to his God in state,
With fifty file of Burmans
  To open him Heaven's Gate.

[1]. A memorial.

The men of the First Shikaris
  Marched till the break of day,
Till they came to the rebel village
  The village of Pabengmay –
A *jingal*[1] covered the clearing,
  Calthrops hampered the way.

Subadar Prag Tewarri,
  Bidding them load with ball,
Halted a dozen rifles
  Under the village wall;
Sent out a flanking-party
  With Jemadar Hira Lal.

The men of the First Shikaris
  Shouted and smote and slew,
Turning the grinning *jingal*
  On to the howling crew.
The Jemadar's flanking-party
  Butchered the folk who flew.

Long was the morn of slaughter,
  Long was the list of slain,
Five score heads were taken,
  Five score heads and twain;
And the men of the First Shikaris
  Went back to their grave again,

Each man bearing a basket
  Red as his palms that day,
Red as the blazing village –
  The village of Pabengmay.
And the '*drip-drip-drip*' from the baskets
  Reddened the grass by the way.

1. Native cannon.

They made a pile of their trophies
  High as a tall man's chin,
Head upon head distorted,
  Set in a sightless grin,
Anger and pain and terror
  Stamped on the smoke-scorched skin.

Subadar Prag Tewarri
  Put the head of the Boh
On top of the mound of triumph,
  The head of his son below –
With the sword and the peacock-banner
  That the world might behold and know.

Thus the *samadh* was perfect,
  Thus was the lesson plain
Of the wrath of the First Shikaris –
  The price of a white man slain;
And the men of the First Shikaris
  Went back into camp again.

Then a silence came to the river,
  A hush fell over the shore,
And Bohs that were brave departed,
  And Sniders squibbed no more;
  For the Burmans said
  That a white man's head
Must be paid for with heads five-score.

There's a widow in sleepy Chester
  Who weeps for her only son;
There's a grave on the Pabeng River,
  A grave that the Burmans shun;
And there's Subadar Prag Tewarri
  Who tells how the work was done.

from *Certain Maxims of Hafiz*

IV

The temper of chums, the love of your wife, and a new piano's
    tune –
Which of the three will you trust at the end of an Indian June?

XVI

My Son, if a maiden deny thee and scuffingly bid thee give o'er,
Yet lip meets with lip at the lastward. Get out! She has been there
    before.
They are pecked on the ear and the chin and the nose who are lacking
    in lore.

The Moon of Other Days

Beneath the deep verandah's shade,
    When bats begin to fly,
I sit me down and watch – alas!
    Another evening die.
Blood-red behind the sere *ferash*
    She rises through the haze.
Sainted Diana! can that be
    The Moon of Other Days?

Ah! shade of little Kitty Smith,
    Sweet Saint of Kensington!
Say, was it ever thus at Home
    The Moon of August shone,
When arm in arm we wandered long
    Through Putney's evening haze,
And Hammersmith was Heaven beneath
    The Moon of Other Days?

But Wandle's stream is Sutlej now,
   And Putney's evening haze
The dust that half a hundred kine
   Before my window raise.
Unkempt, unclean, athwart the mist
   The seething city looms,
In place of Putney's golden gorse
   The sickly *babul* blooms.

Glare down, old Hecate, through the dust,
   And bid the pie-dog yell,
Draw from the drain its typhoid-germ,
   From each bazar its smell;
Yea, suck the fever from the tank
   And sap my strength therewith;
Thank Heaven, you show a smiling face
   To little Kitty Smith!

from *One Viceroy Resigns*

LORD DUFFERIN TO LORD LANSDOWNE:

Perhaps you're right. I'll see you in the *Times* –
A quarter-column of eye-searing print,
A leader once a quarter – then a war;
The Strand a-bellow through the fog: – 'Defeat!'
' 'Orrible slaughter!' While you lie awake
And wonder. Oh, you'll wonder ere you're free!
I wonder now. The four years slide away
So fast, so fast, and leave me here alone.
Reay, Colvin, Lyall, Roberts, Buck, the rest,
Princes and Powers of Darkness, troops and trains,
(I *cannot* sleep in trains), land piled on land,
Whitewash and weariness, red rockets, dust,
White snows that mocked me, palaces – with draughts,
And Westland with the drafts he couldn't pay.

Poor Wilson reading his obituary
Before he died, and Hope, the man with bones,
And Aitchison a dripping mackintosh
At Council in the Rains, his grating 'Sirrr'
Half drowned by Hunter's silky: 'Bât, my lahd.'
Hunterian always: Marshal spinning plates
Or standing on his head; the Rent Bill's roar,
A hundred thousand speeches, much red cloth,
And Smiths thrice happy if I called them Jones,
(I can't remember half their names) or reined
My pony on the Mall to greet their wives.
More trains, more troops, more dust, and then all's done . . .
Four years, and I forget. If I forget,
How will *they* bear me in their minds? The North
Safeguarded – nearly (Roberts knows the rest),
A country twice the size of France annexed.
That stays at least. The rest may pass – may pass –
Your heritage – and I can teach you naught.
'High trust', 'vast honour', 'interests twice as vast',
'Due reverence to your Council' – keep to those.
I envy you the twenty years you've gained,
But not the five to follow. What's that? One!
Two! – Surely not so late. Good-night. *Don't* dream.

Sestina of
the Tramp-Royal

1896

Speakin' in general, I 'ave tried 'em all –
The 'appy roads that take you o'er the world.
Speakin' in general, I 'ave found them good
For such as cannot use one bed too long,
But must get 'ence, the same as I 'ave done,
An' go observin' matters till they die.

What do it matter where or 'ow we die,
So long as we've our 'ealth to watch it all –
The different ways that different things are done,
An' men an' women lovin' in this world;
Takin' our chances as they come along,
An' when they ain't, pretendin' they are good?

In cash or credit – no, it aren't no good;
You 'ave to 'ave the 'abit or you'd die,
Unless you lived your life but one day long,
Nor didn't prophesy nor fret at all,
But drew your tucker some'ow from the world,
An' never bothered what you might ha' done.

But, Gawd, what things are they I 'aven't done?
I've turned my 'and to most, an' turned it good,
In various situations round the world –
For 'im that doth not work must surely die;
But that's no reason man should labour all
'Is life on one same shift – life's none so long.

Therefore, from job to job I've moved along.
Pay couldn't 'old me when my time was done,
For something in my 'ead upset it all,
Till I 'ad dropped whatever 'twas for good,
An', out at sea, be'eld the dock-lights die,
An' met my mate – the wind that tramps the world!

It's like a book, I think, this bloomin' world,
Which you can read and care for just so long,
But presently you feel that you will die
Unless you get the page you're readin' done,
An' turn another – likely not so good;
But what you're after is to turn 'em all.

Gawd bless this world! Whatever she 'ath done –
Excep' when awful long – I've found it good.
So write, before I die, ''E liked it all!'

The Miracles

1894

I sent a message to my dear –
　A thousand leagues and more to Her –
The dumb sea-levels thrilled to hear,
　And Lost Atlantis bore to Her!

Behind my message hard I came,
　And nigh had found a grave for me;
But that I launched of steel and flame
　Did war against the wave for me.

Uprose the deep, in gale on gale,
　To bid me change my mind again –
He broke his teeth along my rail,
　And, roaring, swung behind again.

I stayed the sun at noon to tell
　My way across the waste of it;
I read the storm before it fell
　And made the better haste of it.

Afar, I hailed the land at night –
　The towers I built had heard of me –
And, ere my rocket reached its height,
　Had flashed my Love the word of me.

Earth sold her chosen men of strength
　(They lived and strove and died for me)
To drive my road a nation's length,
　And toss the miles aside for me.

I snatched their toil to serve my needs –
　Too slow their fleetest flew for me.
I tired twenty smoking steeds,
　And bade them bait a new for me.

I sent the Lightnings forth to see
   Where hour by hour She waited me.
Among ten million one was She,
   And surely all men hated me!

Dawn ran to meet me at my goal –
   Ah, day no tongue shall tell again!
And little folk of little soul
   Rose up to buy and sell again!

Song of the Wise Children

1902

When the darkened Fifties dip to the North,
   And frost and the fog divide the air,
And the day is dead at his breaking-forth,
   Sirs, it is bitter beneath the Bear!

Far to Southward they wheel and glance,
   The million molten spears of morn –
The spears of our deliverance
   That shine on the house where we were born.

Flying-fish about our bows,
   Flying sea-fires in our wake:
This is the road to our Father's House,
   Whither we go for our soul's sake!

We have forfeited our birthright,
   We have forsaken all things meet;
We have forgotten the look of light,
   We have forgotten the scent of heat.

They that walk with shaded brows,
   Year by year in a shining land,
They be men of our Father's House,
   They shall receive us and understand.

We shall go back by the boltless doors,
   To the life unaltered our childhood knew –
To the naked feet on the cool, dark floors,
     And the high-ceiled rooms that the Trade blows
        through:

To the trumpet-flowers and the moon beyond,
   And the tree-toad's chorus drowning all –
And the lisp of the split banana-frond
   That talked us to sleep when we were small.

The wayside magic, the threshold spells,
   Shall soon undo what the North has done –
Because of the sights and the sounds and the smells
   That ran with our youth in the eye of the sun.

And Earth accepting shall ask no vows,
   Nor the Sea our love, nor our lover the Sky.
When we return to our Father's House
   Only the English shall wonder why!

Buddha at Kamakura

1892

'And there is a Japanese idol at Kamakura.'

O ye who tread the Narrow Way
By Tophet-flare to Judgment Day,
Be gentle when 'the heathen' pray
   To Buddha at Kamakura!

To Him the Way, the Law, apart,
Whom Maya held beneath her heart,
Ananda's Lord, the Bodhisat,
   The Buddha of Kamakura.

For though He neither burns nor sees,
Nor hears ye thank your Deities,
Ye have not sinned with such as these,
   His children at Kamakura,

Yet spare us still the Western joke
When joss-sticks turn to scented smoke
The little sins of little folk
   That worship at Kamakura –

The grey-robed, gay-sashed butterflies
That flit beneath the Master's eyes.
He is beyond the Mysteries
   But loves them at Kamakura.

And whoso will, from Pride released,
Contemning neither creed nor priest,
May feel the Soul of all the East
   About him at Kamakura.

Yea, every tale Ananda heard,
Of birth as fish or beast or bird,
While yet in lives the Master stirred,
   The warm wind brings Kamakura.

Till drowsy eyelids seem to see
A-flower 'neath her golden *htee*
The Shwe-Dagon flare easterly
   From Burma to Kamakura,

And down the loaded air there comes
The thunder of Thibetan drums,

And droned – '*Om mane padme hum's*'[1]
  A world's-width from Kamakura.

Yet Brahmans rule Benares still,
Buddh-Gaya's ruins pit the hill,
And beef-fed zealots threaten ill
  To Buddha and Kamakura.

A tourist-show, a legend told,
A rusting bulk of bronze and gold,
So much, and scarce so much, ye hold
  The meaning of Kamakura?

But when the morning prayer is prayed,
Think, ere ye pass to strife and trade,
Is God in human image made
  No nearer than Kamakura?

The Sea-Wife

1893

There dwells a wife by the Northern Gate,
  And a wealthy wife is she;
She breeds a breed of roving men
  And casts them over sea.

And some are drowned in deep water,
  And some in sight o' shore,
And word goes back to the weary wife
  And ever she sends more.

For since that wife had gate or gear,
  Or hearth or garth or field,
She willed her sons to the white harvest,
  And that is a bitter yield.

1. The Buddhist invocation.

34

She wills her sons to the wet ploughing,
 To ride the horse of tree;
And syne her sons come back again
 Far-spent from out the sea.

The good wife's sons come home again
 With little into their hands,
But the lore of men that have dealt with men
 In the new and naked lands;

But the faith of men that have brothered men
 By more than easy breath,
And the eyes of men that have read with men
 In the open books of Death.

Rich are they, rich in wonders seen,
 But poor in the goods of men;
So what they have got by the skin of their teeth
 They sell for their teeth again.

And whether they lose to the naked life
 Or win to their hearts' desire,
They tell it all to the weary wife
 That nods beside the fire.

Her hearth is wide to every wind
 That makes the white ash spin;
And tide and tide and 'tween the tides
 Her sons go out and in;

(Out with great mirth that do desire
 Hazard of trackless ways –
In with content to wait their watch
 And warm before the blaze);

And some return by failing light,
 And some in waking dream,
For she hears the heels of the dripping ghosts
 That ride the rough roof-beam.

Home, they come home from all the ports,
　　The living and the dead;
The good wife's sons come home again
　　For her blessing on their head!

The Broken Men

1902

For things we never mention,
　　For Art misunderstood –
For excellent intention
　　That did not turn to good;
From ancient tales' renewing,
　　From clouds we would not clear –
Beyond the Law's pursuing
　　We fled, and settled here.

We took no tearful leaving,
　　We bade no long good-byes.
Men talked of crime and thieving,
　　Men wrote of fraud and lies.
To save our injured feelings
　　'Twas time and time to go –
Behind was dock and Dartmoor,
　　Ahead lay Callao!

The widow and the orphan
　　That pray for ten per cent,
They clapped their trailers on us
　　To spy the road we went.
They watched the foreign sailings
　　(They scan the shipping still),
And that's your Christian people
　　Returning good for ill!

36

God bless the thoughtful islands
    Where never warrants come;
God bless the just Republics
    That give a man a home,
That ask no foolish questions,
    But set him on his feet;
And save his wife and daughters
    From the workhouse and the street!

On church and square and market
    The noonday silence falls;
You'll hear the drowsy mutter
    Of the fountain in our halls.
Asleep amid the yuccas
    The city takes her ease –
Till twilight brings the land-wind
    To the clicking jalousies.

Day long the diamond weather,
    The high, unaltered blue –
The smell of goats and incense
    And the mule-bells tinkling through.
Day long the warder ocean
    That keeps us from our kin,
And once a month our levée
    When the English mail comes in.

You'll find us up and waiting
    To treat you at the bar;
You'll find us less exclusive
    Than the average English are.
We'll meet you with a carriage,
    Too glad to show you round,
But – we do not lunch on steamers,
    For they are English ground.

We sail o' nights to England
   And join our smiling Boards –
Our wives go in with Viscounts
   And our daughters dance with Lords,
But behind our princely doings,
   And behind each coup we make,
We feel there's Something Waiting,
   And – we meet It when we wake.

Ah, God! One sniff of England –
   To greet our flesh and blood –
To hear the traffic slurring
   Once more through London mud!
Our towns of wasted honour –
   Our streets of lost delight!
How stands the old Lord Warden?
   Are Dover's cliffs still white?

Gethsemane

1914–18

The Garden called Gethsemane
   In Picardy it was,
And there the people came to see
   The English soldiers pass.
We used to pass – we used to pass
   Or halt, as it might be,
And ship our masks in case of gas
   Beyond Gethsemane.

The Garden called Gethsemane,
   It held a pretty lass,
But all the time she talked to me
   I prayed my cup might pass.

The officer sat on the chair,
   The men lay on the grass,
And all the time we halted there
   I prayed my cup might pass.

It didn't pass – it didn't pass –
   It didn't pass from me.
I drank it when we met the gas
   Beyond Gethsemane!

The Song of the Banjo

1894

You couldn't pack a Broadwood half a mile –
   You mustn't leave a fiddle in the damp –
You couldn't raft an organ up the Nile,
   And play it in an Equatorial swamp.
I travel with the cooking-pots and pails –
   I'm sandwiched 'tween the coffee and the pork –
And when the dusty column checks and tails,
   You should hear me spur the rearguard to a walk!

     With my '*Pilly-willy-winky-winky-popp!*'
       [Oh, it's any tune that comes into my head!]
     So I keep 'em moving forward till they drop;
       So I play 'em up to water and to bed.

In the silence of the camp before the fight,
   When it's good to make your will and say your prayer,
You can hear my *strumpty-tumpty* overnight,
   Explaining ten to one was always fair.
I'm the Prophet of the Utterly Absurd,
   Of the Patently Impossible and Vain –
And when the Thing that Couldn't has occurred,
   Give me time to change my leg and go again.

With my '*Tumpa-tumpa-tumpa-tumpa-tump!*'
   In the desert where the dung-fed camp-smoke curled.
There was never voice before us till I led our lonely chorus,
   I – the war-drum of the White Man round the world!

By the bitter road the Younger Son must tread,
   Ere he win to hearth and saddle of his own, –
'Mid the riot of the shearers at the shed,
   In the silence of the herder's hut alone –
In the twilight, on a bucket upside down,
   Hear me babble what the weakest won't confess –
I am Memory and Torment – I am Town!
   I am all that ever went with evening dress!

   With my '*Tunka-tunka-tunka-tunka-tunk!*'
     [So the lights – the London Lights – grow near and plain!]
   So I rowel 'em afresh towards the Devil and the Flesh,
     Till I bring my broken rankers home again.

In desire of many marvels over sea,
   Where the new-raised tropic city sweats and roars,
I have sailed with Young Ulysses from the quay
   Till the anchor rumbled down on stranger shores.
He is blooded to the open and the sky,
   He is taken in a snare that shall not fail,
He shall hear me singing strongly, till he die,
   Like the shouting of a backstay in a gale.

   With my '*Hya! Heeya! Heeya! Hullah! Haul!*'
     [Oh, the green that thunders aft along the deck!]
   Are you sick o' towns and men? You must sign and sail again,
     For it's 'Johnny Bowlegs, pack your kit and trek!'

Through the gorge that gives the stars at noon-day clear –
   Up the pass that packs the scud beneath our wheel –
Round the bluff that sinks her thousand fathom sheer –
   Down the valley with our guttering brakes asqueal:

Where the trestle groans and quivers in the snow,
   Where the many-shedded levels loop and twine,
Hear me lead my reckless children from below
   Till we sing the Song of Roland to the pine!

    With my '*Tinka-tinka-tinka-tinka-tink!*'
     [Oh, the axe has cleared the mountain, croup and crest!]
     And we ride the iron stallions down to drink,
      Through the cañons to the waters of the West!

And the tunes that meant so much to you alone –
   Common tunes that make you choke and blow your nose –
Vulgar tunes that bring the laugh that brings the groan –
   I can rip your very heartstrings out with those;
With the feasting, and the folly, and the fun –
   And the lying, and the lusting, and the drink,
And the merry play that drops you, when you're done,
   To the thoughts that burn like irons if you think.

    With my '*Plunka-lunka-lunka-lunka-lunk!*'
     Here's a trifle on account of pleasure past,
     Ere the wit that made you win gives you eyes to see your sin
      And – the heavier repentance at the last!

Let the organ moan her sorrow to the roof –
   I have told the naked stars the Grief of Man!
Let the trumpet snare the foeman to the proof –
   I have known Defeat, and mocked it as we ran!
My bray ye may not alter nor mistake
   When I stand to jeer the fatted Soul of Things,
But the Song of Lost Endeavour that I make,
   Is it hidden in the twanging of the strings?

    With my '*Ta-ra-rara-rara-ra-ra-rrrp!*'
     [Is it naught to you that hear and pass me by?]
     But the word – the word is mine, when the order moves the line
      And the lean, locked ranks go roaring down to die!

The grandam of my grandam was the Lyre –
  [Oh, the blue below the little fisher-huts!]
That the Stealer stooping beachward filled with fire,
  Till she bore my iron head and ringing guts!
By the wisdom of the centuries I speak –
  To the tune of yestermorn I set the truth –
I, the joy of life unquestioned – I, the Greek –
  I, the everlasting Wonder-song of Youth!

  With my *'Tinka-tinka-tinka-tinka-tink!'*
    [What d'ye lack, my noble masters! What d'ye lack?]
  So I draw the world together link by link:
    Yea, from Delos up to Limerick and back!

The Spies' March

1913

'The outbreak is in full swing and our death-rate would
sicken Napoleon . . . Dr M— died last week, and C— on
Monday, but some more medicines are coming . . . We
don't seem to be able to check it at all . . . Villages
panicking badly . . . In some places not a living soul . . .
But at any rate the experience gained may come in
useful, so I am keeping my notes written up to date in
case of accidents . . . Death is a queer chap to live with
for steady company.'
      – *Extract from a private letter from Manchuria*

There are no leaders to lead us to honour, and yet without leaders we
    sally;
Each man reporting for duty alone, out of sight, out of reach, of his
    fellow.
There are no bugles to call the battalions, and yet without bugle we
    rally
From the ends of the earth to the ends of the earth, to follow the
    Standard of Yellow!
      Fall in! O fall in! O fall in!

Not where the squadrons mass,
    Not where the bayonets shine,
Not where the big shell shout as they pass
    Over the firing-line;
Not where the wounded are,
    Not where the nations die,
Killed in the cleanly game of war –
    That is no place for a spy!
O Princes, Thrones and Powers, your work is less than ours –
    Here is no place for a spy!

Trained to another use,
    We march with colours furled,
Only concerned when Death breaks loose
    On a front of half a world.
Only for General Death
    The Yellow Flag may fly,
While we take post beneath –
    That is the place for a spy.
Where Plague has spread his pinions over Nations and Dominions –
    Then will be work for a spy!

The dropping shots begin,
    The single funerals pass,
Our skirmishers run in,
    The corpses dot the grass!
The howling towns stampede,
    The tainted hamlets die.
Now it is war indeed –
    Now there is room for a spy!
O Peoples, Kings and Lands, we are waiting your commands –
    What is the work for a spy?
            (Drums) – *Fear is upon us, spy!*

'Go where his pickets hide –
    Unmask the shape they take,
Whether a gnat from the waterside,
    Or a stinging fly in the brake,

43

Or filth of the crowded street,
  Or a sick rat limping by,
Or a smear of spittle dried in the heat –
  That is the work for a spy!
          (Drums) – *Death is upon us, spy!*

'What does he next prepare?
  Whence will he move to attack? –
By water, earth or air? –
  How can we head him back?
Shall we starve him out if we burn
  Or bury his food-supply?
Slip through his lines and learn –
  That is the work for a spy!
          (Drums) – *Get to your business, spy!*

'Does he feint or strike in force?
  Will he charge or ambuscade?
What is it checks his course?
  Is he beaten or only delayed?
How long will the lull endure?
  Is he retreating? Why?
Crawl to his camp and make sure –
  That is the work for a spy!
          (Drums) – *Fetch us our answer, spy!*

'Ride with him girth to girth
  Wherever the Pale Horse wheels.
Wait on his councils, ear to earth,
  And show what the dust reveals.
For the smoke of our torment rolls
  Where the burning corpses lie;
What do we care for men's bodies or souls?
  Bring us deliverance, spy!'

The Explorer

1898

'There's no sense in going further – it's the edge of cultivation,'
  So they said, and I believed it – broke my land and sowed my crop –
Built my barns and strung my fences in the little border station
  Tucked away below the foothills where the trails run out and stop:

Till a voice, as bad as Conscience, rang interminable changes
  On one everlasting Whisper day and night repeated – so:
'Something hidden. – Go and find it. – Go and look behind the Ranges –
  'Something lost behind the Ranges. Lost and waiting for you. Go!'

So I went, worn out of patience; never told my nearest neighbours –
  Stole away with pack and ponies – left 'em drinking in the town;
And the faith that moveth mountains didn't seem to help my labours
  As I faced the sheer main-ranges, whipping up and leading down.

March by march I puzzled through 'em, turning flanks and dodging
      shoulders,
  Hurried on in hope of water, headed back for lack of grass;
Till I camped above the tree-line – drifted snow and naked boulders –
  Felt free air astir to windward – knew I'd stumbled on the Pass.

'Thought to name it for the finder: but that night the Norther found
      me –
  Froze and killed the plains-bred ponies; so I called the camp Despair
(It's the Railway Gap to-day, though). Then my Whisper waked to
      hound me: –
  'Something lost behind the Ranges. – Over yonder! – Go you there!'

Then I knew, the while I doubted – knew His Hand was certain o'er
      me.
  Still – it might be self-delusion – scores of better men had died –
I could reach the township living, but . . . He knows what terror tore
      me . . .
  But I didn't . . . but I didn't. I went down the other side,

Till the snow ran out in flowers, and the flowers turned to aloes,
  And the aloes sprung to thickets and a brimming stream ran by;
But the thickets dwined to thorn-scrub, and the water drained to shallows,
  And I dropped again on desert – blasted earth, and blasting sky . . .

I remember lighting fires; I remember sitting by 'em;
  I remember seeing faces, hearing voices, through the smoke;
I remember they were fancy – for I threw a stone to try 'em.
  'Something lost behind the Ranges' was the only word they spoke.

I remember going crazy. I remember that I knew it
  When I heard myself hallooing to the funny folk I saw.
'Very full of dreams that desert, but my two legs took me through it . . .
  And I used to watch 'em moving with the toes all black and raw.

But at last the country altered – White Man's country past disputing –
  Rolling grass and open timber, with a hint of hills behind –
There I found me food and water, and I lay a week recruiting.
  Got my strength and lost my nightmares. Then I entered on my
    find.

Thence I ran my first rough survey – chose my trees and blazed and
    ringed 'em –
  Week by week I pried and sampled – week by week my findings
    grew.
Saul he went to look for donkeys, and by God he found a kingdom!
  But by God, who sent His Whisper, I had struck the worth of two!

Up along the hostile mountains, where the hair-poised snowslide
    shivers –
  Down and through the big fat marshes that the virgin ore-bed
    stains,
Till I heard the mile-wide mutterings of unimagined rivers,
  And beyond the nameless timber saw illimitable plains!

'Plotted sites of future cities, traced the easy grades between 'em;
  Watched unharnessed rapids wasting fifty thousand head an hour;

Counted leagues of water-frontage through the axe-ripe woods that
     screen 'em –
  Saw the plant to feed a people – up and waiting for the power!

Well I know who'll take the credit – all the clever chaps that followed –
  Came, a dozen men together – never knew my desert-fears;
Tracked me by the camps I'd quitted, used the water-holes I'd hollowed.
  They'll go back and do the talking. *They'll* be called the Pioneers!

They will find my sites of townships – not the cities that I set there.
  They will rediscover rivers – not my rivers heard at night.
By my own old marks and bearings they will show me how to get
     there,
  By the lonely cairns I builded they will guide my feet aright.

Have I named one single river? Have I claimed one single acre?
  Have I kept one single nugget – (barring samples)? No, not I!
Because my price was paid me ten times over by my Maker.
  But you wouldn't understand it. You go up and occupy.

Ores you'll find there; wood and cattle; water-transit sure and steady
  (That should keep the railway-rates down), coal and iron at your
     doors.
God took care to hide that country till He judged His people ready,
  Then He chose me for His Whisper, and I've found it, and it's
     yours!

Yes, your 'Never-never country' – yes, your 'edge of cultivation'
  And 'no sense in going further' – till I crossed the range to see.
God forgive me! No, *I* didn't. It's God's present to our nation.
  Anybody might have found it, but – His Whisper came to Me!

The Pro-Consuls

(LORD MILNER)

The overfaithful sword returns the user
His heart's desire at price of his heart's blood.
The clamour of the arrogant accuser
Wastes that one hour we needed to make good.
This was foretold of old at our outgoing;
This we accepted who have squandered, knowing,
The strength and glory of our reputations,
At the day's need, as it were dross, to guard
The tender and new-dedicate foundations
Against the sea we fear – not man's award.

They that dig foundations deep,
　Fit for realms to rise upon,
Little honour do they reap
　Of their generation,
Any more than mountains gain
Stature till we reach the plain.

With no veil before their face
　Such as shroud or sceptre lend –
Daily in the market-place,
　Of one height to foe and friend –
They must cheapen self to find
Ends uncheapened for mankind.

Through the night when hirelings rest,
　Sleepless they arise, alone,
The unsleeping arch to test
　And the o'er-trusted corner-stone,
'Gainst the need, they know, that lies
Hid behind the centuries.

Not by lust of praise or show,
　　Not by Peace himself betrayed –
Peace herself must they forgo
　　Till that peace be fitly made;
And in single strength uphold
Wearier hands and hearts acold.

On the stage their act hath framed
　　For thy sports, O Liberty!
Doubted are they, and defamed
　　By the tongues their act set free,
While they quicken, tend and raise
Power that must their power displace.

Lesser men feign greater goals,
　　Failing whereof they may sit
Scholarly to judge the souls
　　That go down into the Pit,
And, despite its certain clay,
Heave a new world toward the day.

These at labour make no sign,
　　More than planets, tides or years
Which discover God's design,
　　Not our hopes and not our fears;
Nor in aught they gain or lose
Seek a triumph or excuse!

For, so the Ark be borne to Zion, who
Heeds how they perished or were paid that bore it?
For, so the Shrine abide, what shame – what pride –
If we, the priests, were bound or crowned before it?

The Runners

Indian Frontier, *1904*

('A Sahibs' War' – *Traffics and Discoveries*)

    News!
What is the word that they tell now – now – now!
The little drums beating in the bazaars?
    They beat (among the buyers and the sellers)
        '*Nimrud – ah, Nimrud!*
        God sends a gnat against Nimrud!'
Watchers, O Watchers a thousand!

    News!
At the edge of the crops – now – now – where the well-wheels are halted,
One prepares to loose the bullocks and one scrapes his hoe,
    They beat (among the sowers and the reapers)
        '*Nimrud – ah, Nimrud!*
        God prepares an ill day for Nimrud!'
Watchers, O Watchers ten thousand.

    News!
By the fires of the camps – now – now – where the travellers meet,
Where the camels come in and the horses, their men conferring,
    They beat (among the packmen and the drivers)
        '*Nimrud – ah, Nimrud!*
        Thus it befell last noon to Nimrud!'
Watchers, O Watchers an hundred thousand!

    News!
Under the shadow of the border-peels – now – now – now!
In the rocks of the passes where the expectant shoe their horses,
    They beat (among the rifles and the riders)
        '*Nimrud – ah, Nimrud!*
        Shall we go up against Nimrud?'
Watchers, O Watchers a thousand thousand!

News!
Bring out the heaps of grain – open the account-books again!
Drive forward the well-bullocks against the taxable harvest!
Eat and lie under the trees – pitch the police-guarded fairgrounds,
  O dancers!
Hide away the rifles and let down the ladders from the watch-towers!
  They beat (among all the peoples)
    '*Now – now – now!*
    God has reserved the Sword for Nimrud!
    God has given Victory to Nimrud!
    Let us abide under Nimrud!'
  O Well-disposed and Heedful, an hundred thousand thousand!

The Sea and the Hills

1902

Who hath desired the Sea? – the sight of salt water unbounded –
The heave and the halt and the hurl and the crash of the comber-
  wind-hounded?
The sleek-barrelled swell before storm, grey, foamless, enormous, and
  growing –
Stark calm on the lap of the Line or the crazy-eyed hurricane blowing –
His Sea in no showing the same – his Sea and the same 'neath each
  showing:
    His Sea as she slackens or thrills?
So and no otherwise – so and no otherwise – hillmen desire their Hills!

Who hath desired the Sea? – the immense and contemptuous surges?
The shudder, the stumble, the swerve, as the star-stabbing bowsprit
  emerges?
The orderly clouds of the Trades, the ridged, roaring sapphire
  thereunder –
Unheralded cliff-haunting flaws and the headsail's low-volleying
  thunder –

His Sea in no wonder the same – his Sea and the same through each
    wonder:
        His Sea as she rages or stills?
So and no otherwise – so and no otherwise – hillmen desire their Hills.

Who hath desired the Sea? Her menaces swift as her mercies?
The in-rolling walls of the fog and the silver-winged breeze that disperses?
The unstable mined berg going South and the calvings and groans
    that declare it –
White water half-guessed overside and the moon breaking timely to
    bare it –
His Sea as his fathers have dared – his Sea as his children shall dare it:
       His Sea as she serves him or kills?
So and no otherwise – so and no otherwise – hillmen desire their Hills.

Who hath desired the Sea? Her excellent loneliness rather
Than forecourts of kings, and her outermost pits than the streets where
    men gather
Inland, among dust, under trees – inland where the slayer may slay
    him –
Inland, out of reach of her arms, and the bosom whereon he must lay
    him –
His Sea from the first that betrayed – at the last that shall never betray
    him:
       His Sea that his being fulfils?
So and no otherwise – so and no otherwise – hillmen desire their Hills.

McAndrew's Hymn

1893

Lord, Thou hast made this world below the shadow of a dream,
An', taught by time, I tak' it so – exceptin' always Steam.
From coupler-flange to spindle-guide I see Thy Hand, O God –
Predestination in the stride o' yon connectin'-rod.
John Calvin might ha' forged the same – enormous, certain, slow –
Ay, wrought it in the furnace-flame –my 'Institutio'.

I cannot get my sleep to-night; old bones are hard to please;
I'll stand the middle watch up here – alone wi' God an' these
My engines, after ninety days o' race an' rack an' strain
Through all the seas of all Thy world, slam-bangin' home again.
Slam-bang too much – they knock a wee – the crosshead-gibs are
    loose,
But thirty thousand mile o' sea has gied them fair excuse . . .
Fine, clear an' dark – a full-draught breeze, wi' Ushant out o' sight,
An' Ferguson relievin' Hay. Old girl, ye'll walk to-night!
His wife's at Plymouth . . . Seventy – One – Two – Three since he
    began –
Three turns for Mistress Ferguson . . . and who's to blame the man?
There's none at any port for me, by drivin' fast or slow,
Since Elsie Campbell went to Thee, Lord, thirty years ago.
(The year the *Sarah Sands* was burned. Oh, roads we used to tread,
Fra' Maryhill to Pollokshaws – fra' Govan to Parkhead!)
Not but they're ceevil on the Board. Ye'll hear Sir Kenneth say:
'Good morrn, McAndrew! Back again? An' how's your bilge to-day?'
Miscallin' technicalities but handin' me my chair
To drink Madeira wi' three Earls – the auld Fleet Engineer
That started as a boiler-whelp – when steam and he were low.
I mind the time we used to serve a broken pipe wi' tow!
Ten pound was all the pressure then – Eh! Eh! – a man wad drive;
An' here, our workin' gauges give one hunder sixty-five!
We're creepin' on wi' each new rig – less weight an' larger power;
There'll be the loco-boiler next an' thirty mile an hour!
Thirty an' more. What I ha' seen since ocean-steam began
Leaves me na doot for the machine: but what about the man?
The man that counts, wi' all his runs, one million mile o' sea:
Four time the span from earth to moon . . . How far, O Lord, from
    Thee
That wast beside him night an' day? Ye mind my first typhoon?
It scoughed the skipper on his way to jock wi' the saloon.
Three feet were on the stokehold-floor – just slappin' to an' fro –
An' cast me on a furnace-door. I have the marks to show.
Marks! I ha' marks o' more than burns – deep in my soul an' black,
An' times like this, when things go smooth, my wickudness comes
    back.

The sins o' four an' forty years, all up an' down the seas,
Clack an' repeat like valves half-fed . . . Forgie's our trespasses!
Nights when I'd come on deck to mark, wi' envy in my gaze,
The couples kittlin' in the dark between the funnel-stays;
Years when I raked the Ports wi' pride to fill my cup o' wrong –
Judge not, O Lord, my steps aside at Gay Street in Hong-Kong!
Blot out the wastrel hours of mine in sin when I abode –
Jane Harrigan's an' Number Nine, The Reddick an' Grant Road!
An' waur than all – my crownin' sin – rank blasphemy an' wild.
I was not four and twenty then – Ye wadna judge a child?
I'd seen the tropics first that run – new fruit, new smells, new air –
How could I tell – blind-fou wi' sun – the Deil was lurkin' there?
By day like playhouse-scenes the shore slid past our sleepy eyes;
By night those soft, lasceevious stars leered from those velvet skies,
In port (we used no cargo-steam) I'd daunder down the streets –
An ijjit grinnin' in a dream – for shells an' parrakeets,
An' walkin'-sticks o' carved bamboo an' blowfish stuffed an' dried –
Fillin' my bunk wi' rubbishry the Chief put overside.
Till, off Sambawa Head, Ye mind, I heard a land-breeze ca',
Milk-warm wi' breath o' spice an' bloom: 'McAndrew, come awa'!'
Firm, clear an' low – no haste, no hate – the ghostly whisper went,
Just statin' eevidential facts beyon' all argument:
'Your mither's God's a graspin' deil, the shadow o' yoursel',
'Got out o' books by meenisters clean daft on Heaven an' Hell.
'They mak' him in the Broomielaw, o' Glasgie cold an' dirt,
'A jealous, pridefu' fetich, lad, that's only strong to hurt.
'Ye'll not go back to Him again an' kiss His red-hot rod,
'But come wi' Us' (Now, who were *They?*) 'an' know the Leevin' God,
'That does not kipper souls for sport or break a life in jest,
'But swells the ripenin' cocoanuts an' ripes the woman's breast.'
An' there it stopped – cut off – no more – that quiet, certain voice –
For me, six months o' twenty-four, to leave or take at choice.
'Twas on me like a thunderclap – it racked me through an' through –
Temptation past the show o' speech, unnameable an' new –
The Sin against the Holy Ghost? . . . An' under all, our screw.

That storm blew by but left behind her anchor-shiftin' swell.
Thou knowest all my heart an' mind, Thou knowest, Lord, I fell –

Third on the *Mary Gloster* then, and first that night in Hell!
Yet was Thy Hand beneath my head, about my feet Thy Care –
Fra' Deli clear to Torres Strait, the trial o' despair,
But when we touched the Barrier Reef Thy answer to my prayer! . . .
We dared na run that sea by night but lay an' held our fire,
An' I was drowsin' on the hatch – sick – sick wi' doubt an' tire:
'Better the sight of eyes that see than wanderin' o' desire!'
Ye mind that word? Clear as our gongs – again, an' once again,
When rippin' down through coral-trash ran out our moorin'-chain:
An', by Thy Grace, I had the Light to see my duty plain.
Light on the engine-room – no more – bright as our carbons burn.
I've lost it since a thousand times, but never past return!

Obsairve! Per annum we'll have here two thousand souls aboard –
Think not I dare to justify myself before the Lord,
But – average fifteen hunder souls safe-borne fra' port to port –
I *am* o' service to my kind. Ye wadna blame the thought?
Maybe they steam from Grace to Wrath – to sin by folly led –
It isna mine to judge their path – their lives are on my head.
Mine at the last – when all is done it all comes back to me,
The fault that leaves six thousand ton a log upon the sea.
We'll tak' one stretch – three weeks an' odd by ony road ye steer –
Fra' Cape Town east to Wellington – ye need an engineer.
Fail there – ye've time to weld your shaft – ay, eat it, ere ye're spoke;
Or make Kerguelen under sail – three jiggers burned wi' smoke!
An' home again – the Rio run: it's no child's play to go
Steamin' to bell for fourteen days o' snow an' floe an' blow.
The bergs like kelpies overside that girn an' turn an' shift
Whaur, grindin' like the Mills o' God, goes by the big South drift.
(Hail, Snow and Ice that praise the Lord. I've met them at their work,
An' wished we had anither route or they anither kirk.)
Yon's strain, hard strain, o' head an' hand, for though Thy Power
      brings
All skill to naught, Ye'll understand a man must think o' things.
Then, at the last, we'll get to port an' hoist their baggage clear –
The passengers, wi' gloves an' canes – an' this is what I'll hear:
'Well, thank ye for a pleasant voyage. The tender's comin' now.'
While I go testin' follower-bolts an' watch the skipper bow.

They've words for every one but me – shake hands wi' half the crew,
Except the dour Scots engineer, the man they never knew.
An' yet I like the wark for all we've dam'-few pickin's here –
No pension, an' the most we'll earn's four hunder pound a year.
Better myself abroad? Maybe. *I'd* sooner starve than sail
Wi' such as call a snifter-rod *ross* . . . French for nightingale.
Commeesion on my stores? Some do; but I cannot afford
To lie like stewards wi' patty-pans. I'm older than the Board.
A bonus on the coal I save? Ou ay, the Scots are close,
But when I grudge the strength Ye gave I'll grudge their food to *those*.
(There's bricks that I might recommend – an' clink the fire-bars cruel.
No! Welsh – Wangarti at the worst – an' damn all patent fuel!)
Inventions? Ye must stay in port to mak' a patent pay.
My Deeferential Valve-Gear taught me how that business lay.
I blame no chaps wi' clearer heads for aught they make or sell.
I found that I could not invent an' look to these as well.
So, wrestled wi' Apollyon – Nah! – fretted like a bairn –
But burned the workin'-plans last run, wi' all I hoped to earn.
Ye know how hard an Idol dies, an' what that meant to me –
E'en tak' it for a sacrifice acceptable to Thee . . .
Below there! Oiler! What's your wark? Ye find it runnin' hard?
Ye needn't swill the cup wi' oil – this isn't the Cunard!
Ye thought? Ye are not paid to think. Go, sweat that off again!
Tck! Tck! It's deeficult to sweer nor tak' The Name in vain!
Men, ay, an women, call me stern. Wi' these to oversee,
Ye'll note I've little time to burn on social repartee.
The bairns see what their elders miss; they'll hunt me to an' fro,
Till for the sake of – well, a kiss – I tak' 'em down below.
That minds me of our Viscount loon – Sir Kenneth's kin – the
    chap
Wi' Russia-leather tennis-shoon an' spar-decked yachtin'-cap.
I showed him round last week, o'er all – an' at the last says he:
'Mister McAndrew, don't you think steam spoils romance at sea?'
Damned ijjit! I'd been doon that morn to see what ailed the
    throws,
Manholin', on my back – the cranks three inches off my nose.
Romance! Those first-class passengers they like it very well,
Printed an' bound in little books; but why don't poets tell?

I'm sick of all their quirks an' turns – the loves an' doves they
    dream –
Lord, send a man like Robbie Burns to sing the Song o' Steam!
To match wi Scotia's noblest speech yon orchestra sublime
Whaurto – uplifted like the Just – the tail-rods mark the time.
The crank-throws give the double-bass, the feed-pump sobs an'
    heaves,
An' now the main eccentrics start their quarrel on the sheaves:
Her time, her own appointed time, the rocking link-head bides,
Till – hear that note? – the rod's return whings glimmerin' through
    the guides.
They're all awa'! True beat, full power, the clangin' chorus goes
Clear to the tunnel where they sit, my purrin' dynamoes.
Interdependence absolute, foreseen, ordained, decreed,
To work, Ye'll note, at ony tilt an' every rate o' speed.
Fra' skylight-lift to furnace-bars, backed, bolted, braced an' stayed,
An' singin' like the Mornin' Stars for joy that they are made;
While, out o' touch o' vanity, the sweatin' thrust-block says:
'Not unto us the praise, or man – not unto us the praise!'
Now, a' together, hear them lift their lesson – theirs an' mine:
'Law, Orrder, Duty an' Restraint, Obedience, Discipline!'
Mill, forge an' try-pit taught them that when roarin' they arose,
An' whiles I wonder if a soul was gied them wi' the blows.
Oh for a man to weld it then, in one trip-hammer strain,
Till even first-class passengers could tell the meanin' plain!
But no one cares except mysel' that serve an' understand
My seven thousand horse-power here. Eh, Lord! They're grand –
    they're grand!
Uplift am I? When first in store the new-made beasties stood,
Where Ye cast down that breathed the Word declarin' all things
    good?
Not so! O' that warld-liftin' joy no after-fall could vex,
Ye've left a glimmer still to cheer the Man – the Arrtifex!
That holds, in spite o' knock and scale, o' friction, waste an' slip,
An' by that light – now, mark my word – we'll build the Perfect
    Ship.
I'll never last to judge her lines or take her curve – not I.
But I ha' lived an' I ha' worked. Be thanks to Thee, Most High!

An' I ha' done what I ha' done – judge Thou if ill or well –
Always Thy Grace preventin' me . . .
                    Losh! Yon's the 'Stand-by' bell.
Pilot so soon? His flare it is. The mornin'-watch is set.
Well, God be thanked, as I was sayin', I'm no Pelagian yet.
Now I'll tak' on . . .
   'Morrn, Ferguson. Man, have ye ever thought
What your good leddy costs in coal? . . . I'll burn 'em down to port.

The Mary Gloster

1894

I've paid for your sickest fancies; I've humoured your crackedest
    whim –
Dick, it's your daddy, dying; you've got to listen to him!
Good for a fortnight, am I? The doctor told you? He lied.
I shall go under by morning, and – Put that nurse outside.
'Never seen death yet, Dickie? Well, now is your time to learn,
And you'll wish you held my record before it comes to your turn.
Not counting the Line and the Foundry, the Yards and the village, too,
I've made myself and a million; but I'm damned if I made you.
Master at two-and-twenty, and married at twenty-three –
Ten thousand men on the pay-roll, and forty freighters at sea!
Fifty years between 'em, and every year of it fight,
And now I'm Sir Anthony Gloster, dying, a baronite:
For I lunched with his Royal 'Ighness – what was it the papers had?
'Not least of our merchant-princes'. Dickie, that's me, your dad!
I didn't begin with askings. *I* took my job and I stuck;
I took the chances they wouldn't, an' now they're calling it luck.
Lord, what boats I've handled – rotten and leaky and old –
Ran 'em, or – opened the bilge-cock, precisely as I was told.
Grub that 'ud bind you crazy, and crews that 'ud turn you grey,
And a big fat lump of insurance to cover the risk on the way.
The others they dursn't do it; they said they valued their life
(They've served me since as skippers). *I* went, and I took my wife.

Over the world I drove 'em, married at twenty-three,
And your mother saving the money and making a man of me.
I was content to be master, but she said there was better behind;
She took the chances I wouldn't, and I followed your mother blind.
She egged me to borrow the money, an' she helped me to clear the
     loan,
When we bought half-shares in a cheap 'un and hoisted a flag of our
     own.
Patching and coaling on credit, and living the Lord knew how,
We started the Red Ox freighters – we've eight-and-thirty now.
And those were the days of clippers, and the freights were clipper-
     freights,
And we knew we were making our fortune, but she died in Macassar
     Straits –
By the Little Paternosters, as you come to the Union Bank –
And we dropped her in fourteen fathom: I pricked it off where she
     sank.
Owners we were, full owners, and the boat was christened for her,
And she died in the *Mary Gloster*. My heart, how young we were!
So I went on a spree round Java and well-nigh ran her ashore,
But your mother came and warned me and I wouldn't liquor no more:
Strict I stuck to my business, afraid to stop or I'd think,
Saving the money (she warned me), and letting the other men drink.
And I met M'Cullough in London (I'd saved five 'undred then),
And 'tween us we started the Foundry – three forges and twenty men.
Cheap repairs for the cheap 'uns. It paid, and the business grew;
For I bought me a steam-lathe patent, and that was a gold mine too.
'Cheaper to build 'em than buy 'em,' *I* said, but M'Cullough he shied,
And we wasted a year in talking before we moved to the Clyde.
And the Lines were all beginning, and we all of us started fair,
Building our engines like houses and staying the boilers square.
But M'Cullough 'e wanted cabins with marble and maple and all,
And Brussels an' Utrecht velvet, and baths and a Social Hall,
And pipes for closets all over, and cutting the frames too light,
But M'Cullough he died in the Sixties, and – Well, I'm dying
     to-night . . .
I knew – *I* knew what was coming, when we bid on the *Byfleet*'s keel –
They piddled and piffled with iron. I'd given my orders for steel!

Steel and the first expansions. It paid, I tell you, it paid,
When we came with our nine-knot freighters and collared the long-run
    trade!
And they asked me how I did it, and I gave 'em the Scripture text,
'You keep your light so shining a little in front o' the next!'
They copied all they could follow, but they couldn't copy my mind,
And I left 'em sweating and stealing a year and a half behind.
Then came the armour-contracts, but that was M'Cullough's side;
He was always best in the Foundry, but better, perhaps, he died.
I went through his private papers; the notes was plainer than print;
And I'm no fool to finish if a man'll give me a hint.
(I remember his widow was angry.) So I saw what his drawings meant,
And I started the six-inch rollers, and it paid me sixty per cent.
Sixty per cent *with* failures, and more than twice we could do,
And a quarter-million to credit, and I saved it all for you!
I thought – it doesn't matter – you seemed to favour your ma,
But you're nearer forty than thirty, and I know the kind you are.
Harrer an' Trinity College! I ought to ha' sent you to sea –
But I stood you an education, an' what have you done for me?
The things I knew was proper you wouldn't thank me to give,
And the things I knew was rotten you said was the way to live.
For you muddled with books and pictures, an' china an' etchin's an' fans,
And your rooms at college was beastly – more like a whore's than a
    man's;
Till you married that thin-flanked woman, as white and as stale as a
    bone,
An' she gave you your social nonsense; but where's that kid o' your
    own?
I've seen your carriages blocking the half o' the Cromwell Road,
But never the doctor's brougham to help the missus unload.
(So there isn't even a grandchild, an' the Gloster family's done.)
Not like your mother, she isn't. *She* carried her freight each run.
But they died, the pore little beggars! At sea she had 'em – they died.
Only you, an' you stood it. You haven't stood much beside.
Weak, a liar, and idle, and mean as a collier's whelp
Nosing for scraps in the galley. No help – my son was no help!
So he gets three 'undred thousand, in trust and the interest paid.
I wouldn't give it you, Dickie – you see, I made it in trade.

You're saved from soiling your fingers, and if you have no child,
It all comes back to the business. 'Gad, won't your wife be wild!
'Calls and calls in her carriage, her 'andkerchief up to 'er eye:
'Daddy! dear daddy's dyin'!' and doing her best to cry.
Grateful? Oh, yes, I'm grateful, but keep her away from here.
Your mother 'ud never ha' stood 'er, and, anyhow, women are
          queer . . .
There's women will say I've married a second time. Not quite!
But give pore Aggie a hundred, and tell her your lawyers'll fight.
She was the best o' the boiling – you'll meet her before it ends.
I'm in for a row with the mother – I'll leave you settle my friends.
For a man he must go with a woman, which women don't
          understand –
Or the sort that say they can see it they aren't the marrying brand.
But I wanted to speak o' your mother that's Lady Gloster still;
I'm going to up and see her, without its hurting the will.
Here! Take your hand off the bell-pull. Five thousand's waiting for
          you,
If you'll only listen a minute, and do as I bid you do.
They'll try to prove me crazy, and, if you bungle, they can;
And I've only you to trust to! (O God, why ain't it a man?)
There's some waste money on marbles, the same as M'Cullough tried –
Marbles and mausoleums – but I call that sinful pride.
There's some ship bodies for burial – we've carried 'em, soldered and
          packed;
Down in their wills they wrote it, and nobody called *them* cracked.
But me – I've too much money, and people might . . . All my fault:
It come o' hoping for grandsons and buying that Wokin' vault . . .
I'm sick o' the 'ole dam' business. I'm going back where I came.
Dick, you're the son o' my body, and you'll take charge o' the same!
I want to lie by your mother, ten thousand mile away,
And they'll want to send me to Woking; and that's where you'll earn
          your pay.
I've thought it out on the quiet, the same as it ought to be done –
Quiet, and decent, and proper – an' here's your orders, my son.
You know the Line? You don't, though. You write to the Board, and
          tell
Your father's death has upset you an' you're goin' to cruise for a spell,

An' you'd like the *Mary Gloster* – I've held her ready for this –
They'll put her in working order and you'll take her out as she is.
Yes, it was money idle when I patched her and laid her aside
(Thank God, I can pay for my fancies!) – the boat where your mother
  died,
By the Little Paternosters, as you come to the Union Bank,
We dropped her – I think I told you – and I pricked it off where she
  sank.
['Tiny she looked on the grating – that oily, treacly sea –]
'Hundred and Eighteen East, remember, and South just Three.
Easy bearings to carry – Three South – Three to the dot;
But I gave McAndrew a copy in case of dying – or not.
And so you'll write to McAndrew, he's Chief of the Maori Line;
They'll give him leave, if you ask 'em and say it's business o' mine.
I built three boats for the Maoris, an' very well pleased they were,
An' I've known Mac since the Fifties, and Mac knew me – and her.
After the first stroke warned me I sent him the money to keep
Against the time you'd claim it, committin' your dad to the deep;
For you are the son o' my body, and Mac was my oldest friend,
I've never asked 'im to dinner, but he'll see it out to the end.
Stiff-necked Glasgow beggar! I've heard he's prayed for my soul,
But he couldn't lie if you paid him, and he'd starve before he stole.
He'll take the *Mary* in ballast – you'll find her a lively ship;
And you'll take Sir Anthony Gloster, that goes on 'is wedding-trip,
Lashed in our old deck-cabin with all three port-holes wide,
The kick o' the screw beneath him and the round blue seas outside!
Sir Anthony Gloster's carriage – our 'ouse-flag flyin' free –
Ten thousand men on the pay-roll and forty freighters at sea!
He made himself and a million, but this world is a fleetin' show,
And he'll go to the wife of 'is bosom the same as he ought to go –
By the heel of the Paternosters – there isn't a chance to mistake –
And Mac'll pay you the money soon as the bubbles break!
Five thousand for six weeks' cruising, the staunchest freighter
  afloat,
And Mac he'll give you your bonus the minute I'm out o' the boat!
He'll take you round to Macassar, and you'll come back alone;
He knows what I want o' the *Mary* . . . I'll do what I please with
  my own.

Your mother 'ud call it wasteful, but I've seven-and-thirty more;
I'll come in my private carriage and bid it wait at the door . . .
For my son 'e was never a credit: 'e muddled with books and art,
And 'e lived on Sir Anthony's money and 'e broke Sir Anthony's heart.
There isn't even a grandchild, and the Gloster family's done –
The only one you left me – O mother, the only one!
Harrer and Trinity College – me slavin' early an' late –
An' he thinks I'm dying crazy, and you're in Macassar Strait!
Flesh o' my flesh, my dearie, for ever an' ever amen,
That first stroke come for a warning. I ought to ha' gone to you then.
But – cheap repairs for a cheap 'un – the doctors said I'd do.
Mary, why didn't *you* warn me? I've allus heeded to you,
Excep' – I know – about women; but you are a spirit now;
An', wife, they was only women, and I was a man. That's how.
An' a man 'e must go with a woman, as you *could* not understand;
But I never talked 'em secrets. I paid 'em out o' hand.
Thank Gawd, I can pay for my fancies! Now what's five thousand to
     me,
For a berth off the Paternosters in the haven where I would be?
I believe in the Resurrection, if I read my Bible plain,
But I wouldn't trust 'em at Wokin'; we're safer at sea again.
For the heart it shall go with the treasure – go down to the sea in ships.
I'm sick of the hired women. I'll kiss my girl on her lips!
I'll be content with my fountain. I'll drink from my own well,
And the wife of my youth shall charm me – an' the rest can go to Hell!
(Dickie, *he* will, that's certain.) I'll lie in our standin'-bed,
An' Mac'll take her in ballast – an' she trims best by the head . . .
Down by the head an' sinkin', her fires are drawn and cold,
And the water's splashin' hollow on the skin of the empty hold –
Churning an' choking and chuckling, quiet and scummy and dark –
Full to her lower hatches and risin' steady. Hark!
That was the after-bulkhead . . . She's flooded from stem to stern . . .
'Never seen death yet, Dickie? . . . Well, now is your time to learn!

The Ballad of the Bolivar

1890

Seven men from all the world back to Docks again,
Rolling down the Ratcliffe Road drunk and raising Cain.
Give the girls another drink 'fore we sign away –
We that took the Bolivar *out across the Bay!*

We put out from Sunderland loaded down with rails;
　We put back to Sunderland 'cause our cargo shifted;
We put out from Sunderland – met the winter gales –
　Seven days and seven nights to The Start we drifted.

　　　Racketing her rivets loose, smoke-stack white as snow,
　　　All the coals adrift adeck, half the rails below,
　　　Leaking like a lobster-pot, steering like a dray –
　　　Out we took the *Bolivar*, out across the Bay!

One by one the Lights came up, winked and let us by;
　Mile by mile we waddled on, coal and fo'c'sle short;
Met a blow that laid us down, heard a bulkhead fly;
　Left The Wolf behind us with a two-foot list to port.

　　　Trailing like a wounded duck, working out her soul;
　　　Clanging like a smithy-shop after every roll;
　　　Just a funnel and a mast lurching through the spray –
　　　So we threshed the *Bolivar* out across the Bay!

Felt her hog and felt her sag, betted when she'd break;
　Wondered every time she raced if she'd stand the shock;
Heard the seas like drunken men pounding at her strake;
　Hoped the Lord 'ud keep His thumb on the plummer-block!

　　　Banged against the iron decks, bilges choked with coal;
　　　Flayed and frozen foot and hand, sick of heart and soul;
　　　'Last we prayed she'd buck herself into Judgment Day –
　　　Hi! we cursed the *Bolivar* knocking round the Bay!

O her nose flung up to sky, groaning to be still –
    Up and down and back we went, never time for breath;
Then the money paid at Lloyds' caught her by the keel,
    And the stars ran round and round dancin' at our death!

        Aching for an hour's sleep, dozing off between:
        'Heard the rotten rivets draw when she took it green;
        'Watched the compass chase its tail like a cat at play –
        That was on the *Bolivar*, south across the Bay!

Once we saw between the squalls, lyin' head to swell –
    Mad with work and weariness, wishin' they was we –
Some damned Liner's lights go by like a grand hotel;
    'Cheered her from the *Bolivar* swampin' in the sea.

        Then a greybeard cleared us out, then the skipper laughed;
        'Boys, the wheel has gone to Hell – rig the winches aft!
        'Yoke the kicking rudder-head – get her under way!'
        So we steered her, pully-haul, out across the Bay!

Just a pack o' rotten plates puttied up with tar,
In we came, an' time enough, 'cross Bilbao Bar.
Overloaded, undermanned, meant to founder, we
Euchred God Almighty's storm, bluffed the Eternal Sea!

Seven men from all the world back to town again,
Rollin' down the Ratcliffe Road drunk and raising Cain:
Seven men from out of Hell. Ain't the owners gay,
Cause we took the Bolivar *safe across the Bay?*

The Destroyers

1898

The strength of twice three thousand horse
  That seeks the single goal;
The line that holds the rending course,
  The hate that swings the whole:
The stripped hulls, slinking through the gloom,
  At gaze and gone again –
The Brides of Death that wait the groom –
  The Choosers of the Slain!

Offshore where sea and skyline blend
  In rain, the daylight dies;
The sullen, shouldering swells attend
  Night and our sacrifice.
Adown the stricken capes no flare –
  No mark on spit or bar, –
Girdled and desperate we dare
  The blindfold game of war.

Nearer the up-flung beams that spell
  The council of our foes;
Clearer the barking guns that tell
  Their scattered flank to close.
Sheer to the trap they crowd their way
  From ports for this unbarred.
Quiet, and count our laden prey,
  The convoy and her guard!

On shoal with scarce a foot below,
  Where rock and islet throng,
Hidden and hushed we watch them throw
  Their anxious lights along.
Not here, not here your danger lies –
  (Stare hard, O hooded eyne!)

66

Save where the dazed rock-pigeons rise
   The lit cliffs give no sign.

Therefore – to break the rest ye seek,
   The Narrow Seas to clear –
Hark to the siren's whimpering shriek –
   The driven death is here!
Look to your van a league away, –
   What midnight terror stays
The bulk that checks against the spray
   Her crackling tops ablaze?

Hit, and hard hit! The blow went home,
   The muffled, knocking stroke –
The steam that overruns the foam –
   The foam that thins to smoke –
The smoke that clokes the deep aboil –
   The deep that chokes her throes
Till, streaked with ash and sleeked with oil,
   The lukewarm whirlpools close!

A shadow down the sickened wave
   Long since her slayer fled:
But hear their chattering quick-fires rave
   Astern, abeam, ahead!
Panic that shells the drifting spar –
   Loud waste with none to check –
Mad fear that rakes a scornful star
   Or sweeps a consort's deck.

Now, while their silly smoke hangs thick,
   Now ere their wits they find,
Lay in and lance them to the quick –
   Our gallied whales are blind!
Good luck to those that see the end,
   Good-bye to those that drown –
For each his chance as chance shall send –
   And God for all! *Shut down!*

The strength of twice three thousand horse
  That serve the one command;
The hand that heaves the headlong force,
  The hate that backs the hand:
The doom-bolt in the darkness freed,
  The mine that splits the main;
The white-hot wake, the 'wildering speed –
  The Choosers of the Slain!

White Horses

1897

Where run your colts at pasture?
  Where hide your mares to breed?
'Mid bergs about the Ice-cap
  Or wove Sargasso weed;
By chartless reef and channel,
  Or crafty coastwise bars,
But most the ocean-meadows
  All purple to the stars!

Who holds the rein upon you?
  The latest gale let free.
What meat is in your mangers?
  The glut of all the sea.
'Twixt tide and tide's returning
  Great store of newly dead, –
The bones of those that faced us,
  And the hearts of those that fled.

Afar, off-shore and single,
  Some stallion, rearing swift,
Neighs hungry for new fodder,
  And calls us to the drift:

Then down the cloven ridges –
  A million hooves unshod –
Break forth the mad White Horses
  To seek their meat from God!

Girth-deep in hissing water
  Our furious vanguard strains –
Through mist of mighty tramplings
  Roll up the fore-blown manes –
A hundred leagues to leeward,
  Ere yet the deep is stirred,
The groaning rollers carry
  The coming of the herd!

Whose hand may grip your nostrils –
  Your forelock who may hold?
E'en they that use the broads with us –
  The riders bred and bold,
That spy upon our matings,
  That rope us where we run –
They know the strong White Horses
  From father unto son.

We breathe about their cradles,
  We race their babes ashore,
We snuff against their thresholds,
  We nuzzle at their door;
By day with stamping squadrons,
  By night in whinnying droves,
Creep up the wise White Horses,
  To call them from their loves.

And come they for your calling?
  No wit of man may save.
They hear the loosed White Horses
  Above their fathers' grave;

And, kin to those we crippled,
 And, sons of those we slew,
Spur down the wild white riders
 To school the herds anew.

What service have ye paid them,
 O jealous steeds and strong?
Save we that throw their weaklings,
 Is none dare work them wrong;
While thick around the homestead
 Our snow-backed leaders graze –
A guard behind their plunder,
 And a veil before their ways.

With march and countermarchings –
 With weight of wheeling hosts –
Stray mob or bands embattled –
 We ring the chosen coasts:
And, careless of our clamour
 That bids the stranger fly,
At peace within our pickets
 The wild white riders lie.
 .   .   .   .   .

Trust ye the curdled hollows –
 Trust ye the neighing wind –
Trust ye the moaning groundswell –
 Our herds are close behind!
To bray your foeman's armies –
 To chill and snap his sword –
Trust ye the wild White Horses,
 The Horses of the Lord!

The Derelict

1894

'And reports the derelict *Margaret Pollock* still at sea.' –
Shipping News

I was the staunchest of our fleet
Till the sea rose beneath my feet
Unheralded, in hatred past all measure.
Into his pits he stamped my crew,
Buffeted, blinded, bound and threw,
Bidding me eyeless wait upon his pleasure.

Man made me, and my will
Is to my maker still,
Whom now the currents con, the rollers steer –
Lifting forlorn to spy
Trailed smoke along the sky,
Falling afraid lest any keel come near!

Wrenched as the lips of thirst,
Wried, dried, and split and burst,
Bone-bleached my decks, wind-scoured to the graining;
And, jarred at every roll,
The gear that was my soul
Answers the anguish of my beams' complaining.

For life that crammed me full,
Gangs of the prying gull
That shriek and scrabble on the riven hatches.
For roar that dumbed the gale,
My hawse-pipes' guttering wail,
Sobbing my heart out through the uncounted watches.

Blind in the hot blue ring
Through all my points I swing –
Swing and return to shift the sun anew.

Blind in my well-known sky
　　I hear the stars go by,
Mocking the prow that cannot hold one true.

　　White on my wasted path
　　Wave after wave in wrath
Frets 'gainst his fellow, warring where to send me.
　　Flung forward, heaved aside,
　　Witless and dazed I bide
The mercy of the comber that shall end me.

　　North where the bergs careen,
　　The spray of seas unseen
Smokes round my head and freezes in the falling.
　　South where the corals breed,
　　The footless, floating weed
Folds me and fouls me, strake on strake upcrawling.

　　I that was clean to run
　　My race against the sun —
Strength on the deep — am bawd to all disaster;
　　Whipped forth by night to meet
　　My sister's careless feet,
And with a kiss betray her to my master.

　　Man made me, and my will
　　Is to my maker still —
To him and his, our peoples at their pier:
　　Lifting in hope to spy
　　Trailed smoke along the sky,
Falling afraid lest any keel come near!

The Song of Diego Valdez

1902

The God of Fair Beginnings
    Hath prospered here my hand –
The cargoes of my lading,
    And the keels of my command.
For out of many ventures
    That sailed with hope as high,
My own have made the better trade,
    And Admiral am I.

To me my King's much honour,
    To me my people's love –
To me the pride of Princes
    And power all pride above;
To me the shouting cities,
    To me the mob's refrain: –
'Who knows not noble Valdez
    'Hath never heard of Spain.'

But I remember comrades –
    Old playmates on new seas –
Whenas we traded orpiment
    Among the savages –
A thousand leagues to south'ard
    And thirty years removed –
They knew not noble Valdez,
    But me they knew and loved.

Then they that found good liquor,
    They drank it not alone,
And they that found fair plunder,
    They told us every one,

About our chosen islands
   Or secret shoals between,
When, weary from far voyage,
   We gathered to careen.

There burned our breaming-fagots
   All pale along the shore:
There rose our worn pavilions –
   A sail above an oar:
As flashed each yearning anchor
   Through mellow seas afire,
So swift our careless captains
   Rowed each to his desire.

Where lay our loosened harness?
   Where turned our naked feet?
Whose tavern 'mid the palm-trees?
   What quenchings of what heat?
Oh, fountain in the desert!
   Oh, cistern in the waste!
Oh, bread we ate in secret!
   Oh, cup we spilled in haste!

The youth new-taught of longing,
   The widow curbed and wan,
The goodwife proud at season,
   And the maid aware of man –
All souls unslaked, consuming,
   Defrauded in delays,
Desire not more their quittance
   Than I those forfeit days!

I dreamed to wait my pleasure
   Unchanged my spring would bide:
Wherefore, to wait my pleasure,
   I put my spring aside
Till, first in face of Fortune,
   And last in mazed disdain,

I made Diego Valdez
  High Admiral of Spain.

Then walked no wind 'neath Heaven
  Nor surge that did not aid –
I dared extreme occasion,
  Nor ever one betrayed.
They wrought a deeper treason –
  (Led seas that served my needs!)
They sold Diego Valdez
  To bondage of great deeds.

The tempest flung me seaward,
  And pinned and bade me hold
The course I might not alter –
  And men esteemed me bold!
The calms embayed my quarry,
  The fog-wreath sealed his eyes;
The dawn-wind brought my topsails –
  And men esteemed me wise!

Yet, 'spite my tyrant triumphs,
  Bewildered, dispossessed –
My dream held I before me –
  My vision of my rest;
But, crowned by Fleet and People,
  And bound by King and Pope –
Stands here Diego Valdez
  To rob me of my hope.

No prayer of mine shall move him.
  No word of his set free
The Lord of Sixty Pennants
  And the Steward of the Sea.
His will can loose ten thousand
  To seek their loves again –
But not Diego Valdez,
  High Admiral of Spain.

There walks no wind 'neath Heaven
    Nor wave that shall restore
The old careening riot
    And the clamorous, crowded shore –
The fountain in the desert,
    The cistern in the waste,
The bread we ate in secret,
    The cup we spilled in haste.

Now call I to my Captains –
    For council fly the sign –
Now leap their zealous galleys,
    Twelve-oared, across the brine.
To me the straiter prison,
    To me the heavier chain –
To me Diego Valdez,
    High Admiral of Spain!

The Second Voyage

1903

We've sent our little Cupids all ashore –
    They were frightened, they were tired, they were cold.
Our sails of silk and purple go to store,
    And we've cut away our mast of beaten gold.
            (Foul weather!)
Oh, 'tis hemp and singing pine for to stand against the brine,
    But Love he is our master as of old!

The sea has shorn our galleries away,
    The salt has soiled our gilding past remede;
Our paint is flaked and blistered by the spray,
    Our sides are half a fathom furred in weed.
            (Foul weather!)
And the Doves of Venus fled and the petrels came instead,
    But Love he was our master at our need!

'Was Youth would keep no vigil at the bow,
  'Was Pleasure at the helm too drunk to steer –
We've shipped three able quartermasters now.
  Men call them Custom, Reverence, and Fear.
          (Foul weather!)
They are old and scarred and plain, but we'll run no risk again
  From any Port o' Paphos mutineer!

We seek no more the tempest for delight,
  We skirt no more the indraught and the shoal –
We ask no more of any day or night
  Than to come with least adventure to our goal.
          (Foul weather!)
What we find we needs must brook, but we do not go to look
  Nor tempt the Lord our God that saved us whole.

Yet, caring so, not overmuch we care
  To brace and trim for every foolish blast,
If the squall be pleased to sweep us unaware,
  He may bellow off to leeward like the last.
          (Foul weather!)
We will blame it on the deep (for the watch must have their sleep),
  And Love can come and wake us when 'tis past.

Oh, launch them down with music from the beach,
  Oh, warp them out with garlands from the quays –
Most resolute – a damsel unto each –
  New prows that seek the old Hesperides!
          (Foul weather!)
Though we know their voyage is vain, yet we see our path again
  In the saffroned bridesails scenting all the seas!
          (Foul weather!)

The Oldest Song

'For before Eve was Lilith.' – *Old Tale*

'These were never your true love's eyes.
  Why do you feign that you love them?
You that broke from their constancies,
  And the wide calm brows above them!

This was never your true love's speech.
  Why do you thrill when you hear it?
You that have ridden out of its reach
  The width of the world or near it!

This was never your true love's hair, –
  You that chafed when it bound you
Screened from knowledge or shame or care,
  In the night that it made around you!'

'All these things I know, I know.
  And that's why my heart is breaking!'
'Then what do you gain by pretending so?'
  'The joy of an old wound waking.'

The Long Trail

There's a whisper down the field where the year has shot her yield,
  And the ricks stand grey to the sun,
Singing: 'Over then, come over, for the bee has quit the clover,
  'And your English summer's done.'

    You have heard the beat of the off-shore wind,
    And the thresh of the deep-sea rain;
    You have heard the song – how long? how long?
    Pull out on the trail again!

78

Ha' done with the Tents of Shem, dear lass,
We've seen the seasons through,
And it's time to turn on the old trail, our own trail, the out trail,
Pull out, pull out, on the Long Trail – the trail that is always new!

It's North you may run to the rime-ringed sun
　Or South to the blind Horn's hate;
Or East all the way into Mississippi Bay,
　Or West to the Golden Gate –
　　Where the blindest bluffs hold good, dear lass,
　　And the wildest tales are true,
　　And the men bulk big on the old trail, our own trail, the out trail,
　　And life runs large on the Long Trail – the trail that is always
　　　new.

The days are sick and cold, and the skies are grey and old,
　And the twice-breathed airs blow damp;
And I'd sell my tired soul for the bucking beam-sea roll
　Of a black Bilbao tramp,
　　With her load-line over her hatch, dear lass,
　　And a drunken Dago crew,
　　And her nose held down on the old trail, our own trail, the out
　　　trail
　　From Cadiz south on the Long Trail – the trail that is always
　　　new.

There be triple ways to take, of the eagle or the snake,
　Or the way of a man with a maid;
But the sweetest way to me is a ship's upon the sea
　In the heel of the North-East Trade.
　　Can you hear the crash on her bows, dear lass,
　　And the drum of the racing screw,
　　As she ships it green on the old trail, our own trail, the out
　　　trail,
　　As she lifts and 'scends on the Long Trail – the trail that is
　　　always new?

See the shaking funnels roar, with the Peter at the fore,
   And the fenders grind and heave,
And the derricks clack and grate, as the tackle hooks the crate,
   And the fall-rope whines through the sheave;
      It's 'Gang-plank up and in,' dear lass,
      It's 'Hawsers warp her through!'
      And it's 'All clear aft' on the old trail, our own trail, the out trail,
      We're backing down on the Long Trail – the trail that is always new.

O the mutter overside, when the port-fog holds us tied,
   And the sirens hoot their dread,
When foot by foot we creep o'er the hueless, viewless deep
   To the sob of the questing lead!
      It's down by the Lower Hope, dear lass,
      With the Gunfleet Sands in view,
      Till the Mouse swings green on the old trail, our own trail, the
         out trail,
      And the Gull Light lifts on the Long Trail – the trail that is
         always new.

O the blazing tropic night, when the wake's a welt of light
   That holds the hot sky tame,
And the steady fore-foot snores through the planet-powdered floors
   Where the scared whale flukes in flame!
      Her plates are flaked by the sun, dear lass,
      And her ropes are taut with the dew,
      For we're booming down on the old Trail, our own trail, the out
         trail,
      We're sagging south on the Long Trail – the trail that is always new.

Then home, get her home, where the drunken rollers comb,
   And the shouting seas drive by,
And the engines stamp and ring, and the wet bows reel and swing,
   And the Southern Cross rides high!
      Yes, the old lost stars wheel back, dear lass,
      That blaze in the velvet blue.
      They're all old friends on the old trail, our own trail, the out trail,
      They're God's own guides on the Long Trail – the trail that is
         always new.

Fly forward, O my heart, from the Foreland to the Start –
   We're steaming all too slow,
And it's twenty thousand mile to our little lazy isle
   Where the trumpet-orchids blow!
     You have heard the call of the off-shore wind
     And the voice of the deep-sea rain;
     You have heard the song – how long? – how long?
     Pull out on the trail again!

The Lord knows what we may find, dear lass,
And The Deuce knows what we may do –
But we're back once more on the old trail, our own trail, the out trail,
We're down, hull-down, on the Long Trail – the trail that is always
    new!

from *The Song of the Dead*

Hear now the Song of the Dead – in the North by the torn berg-edges –
They that look still to the Pole, asleep by their hide-stripped sledges.
Song of the Dead in the South – in the sun by their skeleton horses,
Where the warrigal whimpers and bays through the dust of the sere river-
    courses.

Song of the Dead in the East – in the heat-rotted jungle-hollows,
Where the dog-ape barks in the kloof – in the brake of the buffalo-wallows.
Song of the Dead in the West – in the Barrens, the pass that betrayed
    them,
Where the wolverine tumbles their packs from the camp and the grave-
    mound they made them;
        Hear now the Song of the Dead!

I

We were dreamers, dreaming greatly, in the man-stifled town;
We yearned beyond the sky-line where the strange roads go down.
Came the Whisper, came the Vision, came the Power with the Need.
Till the Soul that is not man's soul was lent us to lead.

As the deer breaks – as the steer breaks – from the herd where they
    graze,
In the faith of little children we went on our ways.
Then the wood failed – then the food failed – then the last water
    dried –
In the faith of little children we lay down and died.
On the sand-drift – on the veldt-side – in the fern-scrub we lay,
That our sons might follow after by the bones on the way.
Follow after – follow after! We have watered the root,
And the bud has come to blossom that ripens for fruit!
Follow after – we are waiting, by the trails that we lost,
For the sounds of many footsteps, for the tread of a host.
Follow after – follow after – for the harvest is sown:
By the bones about the wayside ye shall come to your own!

The Deep-Sea Cables

The wrecks dissolve above us; their dust drops down from afar –
Down to the dark, to the utter dark, where the blind white sea-snakes
    are.
There is no sound, no echo of sound, in the deserts of the deep,
Or the great grey level plains of ooze where the shell-burred cables creep.

Here in the womb of the world – here on the tie-ribs of earth
   Words, and the words of men, flicker and flutter and beat –
Warning, sorrow, and gain, salutation and mirth –
   For a Power troubles the Still that has neither voice nor feet.

They have wakened the timeless Things; they have killed their father
    Time;
   Joining hands in the gloom, a league from the last of the sun.
Hush! Men talk to-day o'er the waste of the ultimate slime,
   And a new Word runs between: whispering, 'Let us be one!'

The Native-Born

1894

We've drunk to the Queen – God bless her! –
  We've drunk to our mothers' land;
We've drunk to our English brother,
  (But he does not understand);
We've drunk to the wide creation,
  And the Cross swings low for the morn,
Last toast, and of Obligation,
  A health to the Native-born!

They change their skies above them,
  But not their hearts that roam!
We learned from our wistful mothers
  To call old England 'home';
We read of the English skylark,
  Of the spring in the English lanes,
But we screamed with the painted lories
  As we rode on the dusty plains!

They passed with their old-world legends –
  Their tales of wrong and dearth –
Our fathers held by purchase,
  But we by the right of birth;
Our heart's where they rocked our cradle,
  Our love where we spent our toil,
And our faith and our hope and our honour
  We pledge to our native soil!

I charge you charge your glasses –
  I charge you drink with me
To the men of the Four New Nations,
  And the Islands of the Sea –

To the last least lump of coral
  That none may stand outside,
And our own good pride shall teach us
  To praise our comrade's pride.

To the hush of the breathless morning
  On the thin, tin, crackling roofs,
To the haze of the burned back-ranges
  And the dust of the shoeless hoofs –
To the risk of a death by drowning,
  To the risk of a death by drouth –
To the men of a million acres,
  To the Sons of the Golden South!

To the Sons of the Golden South (Stand up!),
  And the life we live and know,
Let a fellow sing o' the little things he cares about,
If a fellow fights for the little things he cares about
  With the weight of a single blow!

To the smoke of a hundred coasters,
  To the sheep on a thousand hills,
To the sun that never blisters,
  To the rain that never chills –
To the land of the waiting springtime,
  To our five-meal, meat-fed men,
To the tall, deep-bosomed women,
  And the children nine and ten!

And the children nine and ten (Stand up!),
  And the life we live and know,
Let a fellow sing o' the little things he cares about,
If a fellow fights for the little things he cares about
  With the weight of a two-fold blow!

To the far-flung, fenceless prairie
  Where the quick, cloud-shadows trail,

To our neighbour's barn in the offing
   And the line of the new-cut rail;
To the plough in her league-long furrow
   With the grey Lake gulls behind –
To the weight of a half-year's winter
   And the warm wet western wind!

To the home of the floods and thunder,
   To her pale dry healing blue –
To the lift of the great Cape combers,
   And the smell of the baked Karroo.
To the growl of the sluicing stamp-head –
   To the reef and the water-gold,
To the last and the largest Empire,
   To the map that is half unrolled!

To our dear dark foster-mothers,
   To the heathen songs they sung –
To the heathen speech we babbled
   Ere we came to the white man's tongue.
To the cool of our deep verandahs –
   To the blaze of our jewelled main,
To the night, to the palms in the moonlight,
   And the fire-fly in the cane!

To the hearth of Our People's People –
   To her well-ploughed windy sea,
To the hush of our dread high-altar
   Where The Abbey makes us We.
To the grist of the slow-ground ages,
   To the gain that is yours and mine –
To the Bank of the Open Credit,
   To the Power-house of the Line!

We've drunk to the Queen – God bless her!
   We've drunk to our mothers' land;
We've drunk to our English brother
   (And we hope he'll understand).

We've drunk as much as we're able,
    And the Cross swings low for the morn;
Last toast – and your foot on the table! –
    A health to the Native-born!

A health to the Native-born (Stand up!),
    We're six white men arow,
All bound to sing o' the little things we care about,
All bound to fight for the little things we care about
    With the weight of a six-fold blow!
By the might of our Cable-tow (Take hands!),
    From the Orkneys to the Horn
All round the world (and a little loop to pull it by),
All round the world (and a little strap to buckle it).
    A health to the Native-born!

The Last of the Light Brigade

1891

There were thirty million English who talked of England's might,
There were twenty broken troopers who lacked a bed for the night.
They had neither food nor money, they had neither service nor trade;
They were only shiftless soldiers, the last of the Light Brigade.

They felt that life was fleeting; they knew not that art was long,
That though they were dying of famine, they lived in deathless song.
They asked for a little money to keep the wolf from the door;
And the thirty million English sent twenty pounds and four!

They laid their heads together that were scarred and lined and grey;
Keen were the Russian sabres, but want was keener than they;
And an old Troop-Sergeant muttered, 'Let us go to the man who writes
The things on Balaclava the kiddies at school recites.'

They went without bands or colours, a regiment ten-file strong,
To look for the Master-singer who had crowned them all in his song;
And, waiting his servant's order, by the garden gate they stayed,
A desolate little cluster, the last of the Light Brigade.

They strove to stand to attention, to straighten the toil-bowed back;
They drilled on an empty stomach, the loose-knit files fell slack;
With stooping of weary shoulders, in garments tattered and frayed,
They shambled into his presence, the last of the Light Brigade.

The old Troop-Sergeant was spokesman, and 'Beggin' your pardon,'
    he said,
'You wrote o' the Light Brigade, sir. Here's all that isn't dead.
An' it's all come true what you wrote, sir, regardin' the mouth of hell;
For we're all of us nigh to the workhouse, an' we thought we'd call an'
    tell.

'No, thank you, we don't want food, sir; but couldn't you take an' write
A sort of "to be continued" and "see next page" o' the fight?
We think that someone has blundered, an' couldn't you tell 'em how?
You wrote we were heroes once, sir. Please, write we are starving now.'

The poor little army departed, limping and lean and forlorn.
And the heart of the Master-singer grew hot with 'the scorn of scorn'.
And he wrote for them wonderful verses that swept the land like flame,
Till the fatted souls of the English were scourged with the thing called
    Shame.

O thirty million English that babble of England's might,
Behold there are twenty heroes who lack their food to-night;
Our children's children are listening to 'honour the charge they made – '
And we leave to the streets and the workhouse the charge of the Light
    Brigade!

Bridge-Guard in the Karroo

1901

'. . . and will supply details of the Blood River Bridge.'
District Orders: Lines of Communication –
South African War

Sudden the desert changes,
    The raw glare softens and clings,
Till the aching Oudtshoorn ranges
    Stand up like the thrones of Kings –

Ramparts of slaughter and peril –
    Blazing, amazing, aglow –
'Twixt the sky-line's belting beryl
    And the wine-dark flats below.

Royal the pageant closes,
    Lit by the last of the sun –
Opal and ash-of-roses,
    Cinnamon, umber, and dun.

The twilight swallows the thicket,
    The starlight reveals the ridge.
The whistle shrills to the picket –
    We are changing guard on the bridge.

(Few, forgotten and lonely,
    Where the empty metals shine –
No, not combatants – only
    Details guarding the line.)

We slip through the broken panel
    Of fence by the ganger's shed;
We drop to the waterless channel
    And the lean track overhead;

88

We stumble on refuse of rations,
   The beef and the biscuit-tins;
We take our appointed stations,
   And the endless night begins.

We hear the Hottentot herders
   As the sheep click past to the fold –
And the click of the restless girders
   As the steel contracts in the cold –

Voices of jackals calling
   And, loud in the hush between,
A morsel of dry earth falling
   From the flanks of the scarred ravine.

And the solemn firmament marches,
   And the hosts of heaven rise
Framed through the iron arches –
   Banded and barred by the ties,

Till we feel the far track humming,
   And we see her headlight plain,
And we gather and wait her coming –
   The wonderful north-bound train.

(Few, forgotten and lonely,
   Where the white car-windows shine –
No, not combatants – only
   Details guarding the line.)

Quick, ere the gift escape us!
   Out of the darkness we reach
For a handful of week-old papers
   And a mouthful of human speech.

And the monstrous heaven rejoices,
   And the earth allows again
Meetings, greetings, and voices
   Of women talking with men.

So we return to our places,
    As out on the bridge she rolls;
And the darkness covers our faces,
    And the darkness re-enters our souls.

More than a little lonely
    Where the lessening tail-lights shine.
No – not combatants – only
    Details guarding the line!

My Boy Jack

1914–18

'Have you news of my boy Jack?'
    Not this tide.
'When d'you think that he'll come back?'
    Not with this wind blowing, and this tide.

'Has any one else had word of him?'
    Not this tide.
For what is sunk will hardly swim,
    Not with this wind blowing, and this tide.

'Oh, dear, what comfort can I find?'
    None this tide,
    Nor any tide,
Except he did not shame his kind –
    Not even with that wind blowing, and that tide.

Then hold your head up all the more,
    This tide,
    And every tide;
Because he was the son you bore,
    And gave to that wind blowing and that tide!

A Nativity

1914–18

The Babe was laid in the Manger
  Between the gentle kine –
All safe from cold and danger –
  'But it was not so with mine,
            (With mine!   With mine!)
'Is it well with the child, is it well?'
  The waiting mother prayed.
'For I know not how he fell,
  And I know not where he is laid.'

A Star stood forth in Heaven;
  The Watchers ran to see
The Sign of the Promise given –
  'But there comes no sign to me.
            (To me!   To me!)
'*My* child died in the dark.
  Is it well with the child, is it well?
There was none to tend him or mark,
  And I know not how he fell.'

The Cross was raised on high;
  The Mother grieved beside –
'But the Mother saw Him die
  And took Him when He died.
            (He died!   He died!)
'Seemly and undefiled
  His burial-place was made –
Is it well, is it well with the child?
  For I know not where he is laid.'

On the dawning of Easter Day
  Comes Mary Magdalene;
But the Stone was rolled away,
  And the Body was not within –

(Within!   Within!)
'Ah, who will answer my word?'
   The broken mother prayed.
'They have taken away my Lord,
   And I know not where He is laid.'

.   .   .   .   .

'*The Star stands forth in Heaven.*
   The Watchers watch in vain
For Sign of the Promise given
   Of peace on Earth again –
                                (Again!   Again!)
'But I know for Whom he fell' –
   The steadfast mother smiled,
'Is it well with the child – is it well?
   It is well – it is well with the child!'

Dirge of Dead Sisters

1902

(*For the Nurses who died in the South African War*)

Who recalls the twilight and the rangèd tents in order
   (Violet peaks uplifted through the crystal evening air?)
And the clink of iron teacups and the piteous, noble laughter,
   And the faces of the Sisters with the dust upon their hair?

(Now and not hereafter, while the breath is in our nostrils,
   Now and not hereafter, ere the meaner years go by –
Let us now remember many honourable women,
   Such as bade us turn again when we were like to die.)

Who recalls the morning and the thunder through the foothills,
   (Tufts of fleecy shrapnel strung along the empty plains?)
And the sun-scarred Red-Cross coaches creeping guarded to the culvert,
   And faces of the Sisters looking gravely from the trains?

(When the days were torment and the nights were clouded terror,
  When the Powers of Darkness had dominion on our soul –
When we fled consuming through the Seven Hells of Fever,
  These put out their hands to us and healed and made us whole.)

Who recalls the midnight by the bridge's wrecked abutment,
  (Autumn rain that rattled like a Maxim on the tin?)
And the lightning-dazzled levels and the streaming, straining wagons,
  And the faces of the Sisters as they bore the wounded in?

(Till the pain was merciful and stunned us into silence –
  When each nerve cried out on God that made the misused clay;
When the Body triumphed and the last poor shame departed –
  These abode our agonies and wiped the sweat away.)

Who recalls the noontide and the funerals through the market,
  (Blanket-hidden bodies, flagless, followed by the flies?)
And the footsore firing-party, and the dust and stench and staleness,
  And the faces of the Sisters and the glory in their eyes?

(Bold behind the battle, in the open camp all-hallowed,
  Patient, wise, and mirthful in the ringed and reeking town,
These endured unresting till they rested from their labours –
  Little wasted bodies, ah, so light to lower down!)

Yet their graves are scattered and their names are clean forgotten,
  Earth shall not remember, but the Waiting Angel knows
Them that died at Uitvlugt when the plague was on the city –
  Her that fell at Simon's Town [1] in service on our foes.

Wherefore we they ransomed, while the breath is in our nostrils,
  Now and not hereafter – ere the meaner years go by –
Praise with love and worship many honourable women,
  Those that gave their lives for us when we were like to die!

1. Mary Kingsley.

The Vampire
1897

A fool there was and he made his prayer
(Even as you and I!)
To a rag and a bone and a hank of hair
(We called her the woman who did not care)
But the fool he called her his lady fair –
(Even as you and I!)

Oh, the years we waste and the tears we waste
And the work of our head and hand
Belong to the woman who did not know
(And now we know that she never could know)
And did not understand!

A fool there was and his goods he spent
(Even as you and I!)
Honour and faith and a sure intent
(And it wasn't the least what the lady meant)
But a fool must follow his natural bent
(Even as you and I!)

Oh, the toil we lost and the spoil we lost
And the excellent things we planned
Belong to the woman who didn't know why
(And now we know that she never knew why)
And did not understand!

The fool was stripped to his foolish hide
(Even as you and I!)
Which she might have seen when she threw him aside –
(But it isn't on record the lady tried)
So some of him lived but the most of him died –
(Even as you and I!)

And it isn't the shame and it isn't the blame
That stings like a white-hot brand –
It's coming to know that she never knew why
(Seeing, at last, she could never know why)
And never could understand!

The English Flag

1891

Above the portico a flag-staff, bearing the Union Jack,
remained fluttering in the flames for some time, but
ultimately when it fell the crowds rent the air with
shouts, and seemed to see significance in the incident.
Daily Papers

Winds of the World, give answer! They are whimpering to and fro –
And what should they know of England who only England know? –
The poor little street-bred people that vapour and fume and brag,
They are lifting their heads in the stillness to yelp at the English Flag!

Must we borrow a clout from the Boer – to plaster anew with dirt?
An Irish liar's bandage, or an English coward's shirt?
We may not speak of England; her Flag's to sell or share.
What is the Flag of England? Winds of the World, declare!

The North Wind blew: – 'From Bergen my steel-shod vanguards go;
'I chase your lazy whalers home from the Disko floe.
'By the great North Lights above me I work the will of God,
'And the liner splits on the ice-field or the Dogger fills with cod.

'I barred my gates with iron, I shuttered my doors with flame,
'Because to force my ramparts your nutshell navies came.
'I took the sun from their presence, I cut them down with my blast.
'And they died, but the Flag of England blew free ere the spirit passed.

'The lean white bear hath seen it in the long, long Arctic nights,
'The musk-ox knows the standard that flouts the Northern Lights:
'What is the Flag of England? Ye have but my bergs to dare,
'Ye have but my drifts to conquer. Go forth, for it is there!'

The South Wind sighed: – 'From the Virgins my mid-sea course was
    ta'en
'Over a thousand islands lost in an idle main,
'Where the sea-egg flames on the coral and the long-backed breakers
    croon
'Their endless ocean legends to the lazy, locked lagoon.

'Strayed amid lonely islets, mazed amid outer keys,
'I waked the palms to laughter – I tossed the scud in the breeze.
'Never was isle so little, never was sea so lone,
'But over the scud and the palm-trees an English flag was flown.

'I have wrenched it free from the halliards to hang for a wisp on the
    Horn;
'I have chased it north to the Lizard – ribboned and rolled and torn;
'I have spread its folds o'er the dying, adrift in a hopeless sea;
'I have hurled it swift on the slaver, and seen the slave set free.

'My basking sunfish know it, and wheeling albatross,
'Where the lone wave fills with fire beneath the Southern Cross.
'What is the Flag of England? Ye have but my reefs to dare,
'Ye have but my seas to furrow. Go forth, for it is there!'

The East Wind roared: – 'From the Kuriles, the Bitter Seas, I come,
'And me men call the Home-Wind, for I bring the English home.
'Look – look well to your shipping! By the breath of my mad typhoon
'I swept your close-packed Praya and beached your best at Kowloon!

'The reeling junks behind me and the racing seas before,
'I raped your richest roadstead – I plundered Singapore!
'I set my hand on the Hoogli; as a hooded snake she rose;
'And I flung your stoutest streamers to roost with the startled crows.

'Never the lotos closes, never the wild-fowl wake,
'But a soul goes out on the East Wind that died for England's sake –
'Man or woman or suckling, mother or bride or maid –
'Because on the bones of the English the English Flag is stayed.

'The desert-dust hath dimmed it, the flying wild-ass knows,
'The scared white leopard winds it across the taintless snows.
'What is the Flag of England? Ye have but my sun to dare,
'Ye have but my sands to travel. Go forth, for it is there!'

The West Wind called: – 'In squadrons the thoughtless galleons fly
'That bear the wheat and cattle lest street-bred people die.
'They make my might their porter, they make my house their path,
'Till I loose my neck from their rudder and whelm them all in my
      wrath.

'I draw the gliding fog-bank as a snake is drawn from the hole.
'They bellow one to the other, the frighted ship-bells toll;
'For day is a drifting terror till I raise the shroud with my breath,
'And they see strange bows above them and the two go locked to death.

'But whether in calm or wrack-wreath, whether by dark or day,
'I heave them whole to the conger or rip their plates away,
'First of the scattered legions, under a shrieking sky,
'Dipping between the rollers, the English Flag goes by.

'The dead dumb fog hath wrapped it – the frozen dews have kissed –
'The naked stars have seen it, a fellow-star in the mist.
'What is the Flag of England? Ye have but my breath to dare,
'Ye have but my waves to conquer. Go forth, for it is there!'

When Earth's Last Picture is Painted

1892

(L'Envoi to *The Seven Seas*)

When Earth's last picture is painted and the tubes are twisted and dried,
When the oldest colours have faded, and the youngest critic has died,
We shall rest, and, faith, we shall need it – lie down for an æon or two,
Till the Master of All Good Workmen shall put us to work anew.

And those that were good shall be happy: they shall sit in a golden chair;
They shall splash at a ten-league canvas with brushes of comets' hair.
They shall find real saints to draw from – Magdalene, Peter, and Paul;
They shall work for an age at a sitting and never be tired at all!

And only The Master shall praise us, and only The Master shall blame;
And no one shall work for money, and no one shall work for fame,
But each for the joy of the working, and each, in his separate star,
Shall draw the Thing as he sees It for the God of Things as They are!

'Cleared'

1890

(*In memory of the Parnell Commission*)

Help for a patriot distressed, a spotless spirit hurt,
Help for an honourable clan sore trampled in the dirt!
From Queenstown Bay to Donegal, oh, listen to my song,
The honourable gentlemen have suffered grievous wrong.

Their noble names were mentioned – Oh, the burning black disgrace! –
By a brutal Saxon paper in an Irish shooting-case;
They sat upon it for a year, then steeled their heart to brave it,
And 'coruscating innocence' the learned Judges gave it.

'CLEARED'

Bear witness, Heaven, of that grim crime beneath the surgeon's knife,
The 'honourable gentlemen' deplored the loss of life!
Bear witness of those chanting choirs that burke and shirk and snigger,
No man laid hand upon the knife or finger to the trigger!

Cleared in the face of all mankind beneath the winking skies,
Like phœnixes from Phœnix Park (and what lay there) they rise!
Go shout it to the emerald seas – give word to Erin now,
Her honourable gentlemen are cleared – and this is how: –

They only paid the Moonlighter his cattle-hocking price,
They only helped the murderer with counsel's best advice,
But – sure it keeps their honour white – the learned Court believes
They never give a piece of plate to murderers and thieves.

They never told the ramping crowd to card a woman's hide,
They never marked a man for death – what fault of theirs he died? –
They only said 'intimidate', and talked and went away –
By God, the boys that did the work were braver men than they!

Their sin it was that fed the fire – small blame to them that heard –
The boys get drunk on rhetoric, and madden at a word –
They knew whom they were talking at, if they were Irish too,
The gentlemen that lied in Court, they knew, and well they knew!

They only took the Judas-gold from Fenians out of jail,
They only fawned for dollars on the blood-dyed Clan-na-Gael.
If black is black or white is white, in black and white it's down,
They're only traitors to the Queen and rebels to the Crown.

'Cleared', honourable gentlemen! Be thankful it's no more: –
The widow's curse is on your house, the dead are at your door.
On you the shame of open shame; on you from North to South
The hand of every honest man flat-heeled across your mouth.

'Less black than we were painted'? – Faith, no word of black was said;
The lightest touch was human blood, and that, you know, runs red.
It's sticking to your fist to-day for all your sneer and scoff,
And by the Judge's well-weighed word you cannot wipe it off.

99

Hold up those hands of innocence – go, scare your sheep together,
The blundering, tripping tups that bleat behind the old bell-wether;
And if they snuff the taint and break to find another pen,
Tell them it's tar that glistens so, and daub them yours again!

'The charge is old'? – As old as Cain – as fresh as yesterday;
Old as the Ten Commandments – have ye talked those laws away?
If words are words or death is death, or powder sends the ball,
You spoke the words that sped the shot – the curse be on you all!

'Our friends believe'? Of course they do – as sheltered women may;
But have they seen the shrieking soul ripped from the quivering clay?
They! – If their own front door is shut, they'll swear the whole world's
      warm;
What do they know of dread of death or hanging fear of harm?

The secret half a county keeps, the whisper in the lane,
The shriek that tells the shot went home behind the broken pane,
The dry blood crisping in the sun that scares the honest bees,
And shows the boys have heard your talk – what do they know of these?

But you – you know – ay, ten times more; the secrets of the dead,
Black terror on the country-side by word and whisper bred,
The mangled stallion's scream at night, the tail-cropped heifer's low.
Who set the whisper going first? You know, and well you know!

My soul! I'd sooner lie in jail for murder plain and straight,
Pure crime I'd done with my own hand for money, lust, or hate
Than take a seat in Parliament by fellow felons cheered,
While one of those 'not provens' proved me cleared as you are cleared.

Cleared – you that 'lost' the League accounts – go, guard our honour
      still,
Go, help to make our country's laws that broke God's law at will –
One hand stuck out behind the back, to signal 'strike again';
The other on your dress-shirt-front to show your heart is clane.

If black is black or white is white, in black and white it's down,
You're only traitors to the Queen and rebels to the Crown.
If print is print or words are words, the learned Court perpends: –
We are not ruled by murderers, but only – by their friends.

from *The Ballad of East and West*

1889

Oh, East is East, and West is West, and never the twain shall meet,
Till Earth and Sky stand presently at God's great Judgment Seat;
But there is neither East nor West, Border, nor Breed, nor Birth,
When two strong men stand face to face, though they come from the ends
    of the earth!

Gehazi

1915

Whence comest thou, Gehazi,
  So reverend to behold,
In scarlet and in ermines
  And chain of England's gold?
'From following after Naaman
  To tell him all is well,
Whereby my zeal hath made me
  A Judge in Israel.'

Well done, well done, Gehazi!
  Stretch forth thy ready hand.
Thou barely 'scaped from judgment,
  Take oath to judge the land
Unswayed by gift of money
  Or privy bribe, more base,
Of knowledge which is profit
  In any market-place.

GEHAZI

Search out and probe, Gehazi,
    As thou of all canst try,
The truthful, well-weighed answer
    That tells the blacker lie –
The loud, uneasy virtue,
    The anger feigned at will,
To overbear a witness
    And make the Court keep still.

Take order now, Gehazi,
    That no man talk aside
In secret with his judges
    The while his case is tried.
Lest he should show them – reason
    To keep a matter hid,
And subtly lead the questions
    Away from what he did.

Thou mirror of uprightness,
    What ails thee at thy vows?
What means the risen whiteness
    Of the skin between thy brows?
The boils that shine and burrow,
    The sores that slough and bleed –
The leprosy of Naaman
    On thee and all thy seed?
        Stand up, stand up, Gehazi,
            Draw close thy robe and go,
        Gehazi, Judge in Israel,
            A leper white as snow!

The Ballad of the King's Mercy

1889

Abdhur Rahman, the Durani Chief, of him is the story told.
His mercy fills the Khyber hills – his grace is manifold;
He has taken toll of the North and the South – his glory reacheth far,
And they tell the tale of his charity from Balkh to Kandahar.

Before the old Peshawur Gate, where Kurd and Kafir meet,
The Governor of Kabul dealt the Justice of the Street,
And that was strait as running noose and swift as plunging knife,
Tho' he who held the longer purse might hold the longer life.
There was a hound of Hindustan had struck a Yusufzai,
Wherefore they spat upon his face and led him out to die.
It chanced the King went forth that hour when throat was bared to
      knife;
The Kafir grovelled under-hoof and clamoured for his life.

Then said the King: 'Have hope, O friend! Yea, Death disgraced is
      hard.
'Much honour shall be thine'; and called the Captain of the Guard,
Yar Khan, a bastard of the Blood, so city-babble saith,
And he was honoured of the King – the which is salt to Death;
And he was son of Daoud Shah, the Reiver of the Plains,
And blood of old Durani Lords ran fire in his veins;
And 'twas to tame an Afghan pride nor Hell nor Heaven could bind,
The King would make him butcher to a yelping cur of Hind.

'Strike!' said the King. 'King's blood art thou – his death shall be his
      pride!'
Then louder, that the crowd might catch: 'Fear not – his arms are
      tied!'
Yar Khan drew clear the Khyber knife, and struck, and sheathed again.
'O man, thy will is done,' quoth he; 'A King this dog hath slain.'

Abdhur Rahman, the Durani Chief, to the North and the South is sold.
The North and the South shall open their mouth to a Ghilzai flag
unrolled,
When the big guns speak to the Khyber peak, and his dog-Heratis fly:
Ye have heard the song – How long? How long? Wolves of the
Abazai!

That night before the watch was set, when all the streets were clear,
The Governor of Kabul spoke: 'My King, hast thou no fear?
'Thou knowest – thou hast heard,' – his speech died at his master's face.
And grimly said the Afghan King: 'I rule the Afghan race.
'My path is mine – see thou to thine. To-night upon thy bed
'Think who there be in Kabul now that clamour for thy head.'

That night when all the gates were shut to City and to throne,
Within a little garden-house the King lay down alone.
Before the sinking of the moon, which is the Night of Night,
Yar Khan came softly to the King to make his honour white.
(The children of the town had mocked beneath his horse's hoofs,
The harlots of the town had hailed him 'butcher!' from their roofs.)

But as he groped against the wall, two hands upon him fell,
The King behind his shoulder spake: 'Dead man, thou dost not well!
''Tis ill to jest with Kings by day and seek a boon by night;
'And that thou bearest in thy hand is all too sharp to write.
'But three days hence, if God be good, and if thy strength remain,
'Thou shalt demand one boon of me and bless me in thy pain.
'For I am merciful to all, and most of all to thee.
'My butcher of the shambles, rest – no knife hast thou for me!'

Abdhur Rahman, the Durani Chief, holds hard by the South and the
North;
But the Ghilzai knows, ere the melting snows, when the swollen banks
break forth,
When the red-coats crawl to the sungar wall, and his Usbeg lances fail:
Ye have heard the song – How long? How long? Wolves of the Zukka
Kheyl!

They stoned him in the rubbish-field when dawn was in the sky,
According to the written word, 'See that he do not die.'
They stoned him till the stones were piled above him on the plain,
And those the labouring limbs displaced they tumbled back again.
One watched beside the dreary mound that veiled the battered thing,
And him the King with laughter called the Herald of the King.

It was upon the second night, the night of Ramazan,
The watcher leaning earthward heard the message of Yar Khan.
From shattered breast through shrivelled lips broke forth the rattling
      breath,
'Creature of God, deliver me from agony of Death.'

They sought the King among his girls, and risked their lives thereby:
'Protector of the Pitiful, give orders that he die!'
'Bid him endure until the day,' a lagging answer came;
'The night is short, and he can pray and learn to bless my name.'

Before the dawn three times he spoke, and on the day once more:
'Creature of God, deliver me, and bless the King therefor!'

They shot him at the morning prayer, to ease him of his pain,
And when he heard the matchlocks clink, he blessed the King again.

Which thing the singers made a song for all the world to sing
So that the Outer Seas may know the mercy of the King.

    Abdhur Rahman, the Durani Chief, of him is the story told,
    He had opened his mouth to the North and the South, they have stuffed
        his mouth with gold.
    Ye know the truth of his tender ruth – and sweet his favours are:
    Ye have heard the song – How long? How long? – from Balkh to
        Kandahar.

The Ballad of Boh Da Thone
1888

(*Burma War, 1883–85*)

This is the ballad of Boh Da Thone,
Erst a Pretender to Theebaw's throne,
Who harried the District of Alalone:
How he met with his fate and the V.P.P.[1]
At the hand of Harendra Mukerji,
Senior Gomashta, G.B.T.[2]

Boh Da Thone was a warrior bold:
His sword and his rifle were bossed with gold,

And the Peacock Banner his henchman bore
Was stiff with bullion but stiffer with gore.

He shot at the strong and he slashed at the weak
From the Salween scrub to the Chindwin teak:

He crucified noble, he scarified mean,
He filled old ladies with kerosene:

While over the water the papers cried,
'The patriot fights for his countryside!'

But little they cared for the Native press,
The worn white soldiers in khaki dress,

Who tramped through the jungle and camped in the byre,
Who died in the swamp and were tombed in the mire,

Who gave up their lives, at the Queen's Command,
For the Pride of their Race and the Peace of the Land.

Now, first of the foemen of Boh Da Thone
Was Captain O'Neil of the Black Tyrone,

1. Value Payable Post: Collect on Delivery.
2. Head Clerk, Government Bullock Train.

And his was a Company, seventy strong,
Who hustled that dissolute Chief along.

There were lads from Galway and Louth and Meath
Who went to their death with a joke in their teeth,

And worshipped with fluency, fervour, and zeal
The mud on the boot-heels of 'Crook' O'Neil.

But ever a blight on their labours lay,
And ever their quarry would vanish away,

Till the sun-dried boys of the Black Tyrone
Took a brotherly interest in Boh Da Thone,

And, sooth, if pursuit in possession ends,
The Boh and his trackers were best of friends.

The word of a scout – a march by night –
A rush through the mist – a scattering fight –

A volley from cover – a corpse in the clearing –
A glimpse of a loin-cloth and heavy jade earring –

The flare of a village – the tally of slain –
And . . . the Boh was abroad on the raid again!

They curse their luck, as the Irish will,
They gave him credit for cunning and skill,

They buried their dead, they bolted their beef,
And started anew on the track of the thief,

Till, in place of the 'Kalends of Greece', men said,
'When Crook and his darlings come back with the head.'

They had hunted the Boh from the hills to the plain –
He doubled and broke for the hills again:

They had crippled his power for rapine and raid,
They had routed him out of his pet stockade,

And at last, they came, when the Daystar tired,
To a camp deserted – a village fired.

A black cross blistered the morning-gold,
But the body upon it was stark and cold.

The wind of the dawn went merrily past,
The high grass bowed her plumes to the blast,

And out of the grass, on a sudden, broke
A spirtle of fire, a whorl of smoke –

And Captain O'Neil of the Black Tyrone
Was blessed with a slug in the ulnar-bone –
The gift of his enemy Boh Da Thone.

(Now a slug that is hammered from telegraph-wire
Is a thorn in the flesh and a rankling fire.)

    .   .   .   .   .   .

The shot-wound festered – as shot-wounds may
In a steaming barrack at Mandalay.

The left arm throbbed, and the Captain swore,
'I'd like to be after the Boh once more!'

The fever held him – the Captain said,
'I'd give a hundred to look at his head!'

The Hospital punkahs creaked and whirred,
But Babu Harendra (Gomashta) heard.

He thought of the cane-brake, green and dank,
That girdled his home by the Dacca tank.

He thought of his wife and his High School son,
He thought – but abandoned the thought – of a gun.

His sleep was broken by visions dread
Of a shining Boh with a silver head.

He kept his counsel and went his way,
And swindled the cartmen of half their pay.

    .   .   .   .   .   .

And the months went on, as the worst must do,
And the Boh returned to the raid anew.

But the Captain had quitted the long-drawn strife,
And in far Simoorie had taken a wife;

And she was a damsel of delicate mould,
With hair like the sunshine and heart of gold,

And little she knew the arms that embraced
Had cloven a man from the brow to the waist:

And little she knew that the loving lips
Had ordered a quivering life's eclipse,

Or the eye that lit at her lightest breath
Had glared unawed in the Gates of Death.

(For these be matters a man would hide,
As a general rule, from an innocent Bride.)

And little the Captain thought of the past,
And, of all men, Babu Harendra last.

   .   .   .   .   .   .

But slow, in the sludge of the Kathun road,
The Government Bullock Train toted its load.

Speckless and spotless and shining with *ghi*,
In the rearmost cart sat the Babu-jee;

And ever a phantom before him fled
Of a scowling Boh with a silver head.

Then the lead-cart stuck, though the coolies slaved,
And the cartmen flogged and the escort raved,

And out of the jungle, with yells and squeals,
Pranced Boh Da Thone, and his gang at his heels!

Then belching blunderbuss answered back
The Snider's snarl and the carbine's crack,

And the blithe revolver began to sing
To the blade that twanged on the locking-ring,

And the brown flesh blued where the bayonet kissed,
As the steel shot back with a wrench and a twist,

And the great white oxen with onyx eyes
Watched the souls of the dead arise,

And over the smoke of the fusillade
The Peacock Banner staggered and swayed.

The Babu shook at the horrible sight,
And girded his ponderous loins for flight,

But Fate had ordained that the Boh should start
On a lone-hand raid of the rearmost cart,

And out of that cart, with a bellow of woe,
The Babu fell – flat on the top of the Boh!

For years had Harendra served the State,
To the growth of his purse and the girth of his *pêt*.[1]

There were twenty stone, as the tally-man knows,
On the broad of the chest of this best of Bohs.

And twenty stone from a height discharged
Are bad for a Boh with a spleen enlarged.

Oh, short was the struggle – severe was the shock –
He dropped like a bullock – he lay like a block;

And the Babu above him, convulsed with fear,
Heard the labouring life-breath hissed out in his ear.

And thus in a fashion undignified
The princely pest of the Chindwin died.

  .   .   .   .   .   .

Turn now to Simoorie, where, all at his ease,
The Captain is petting the Bride on his knees,

Where the *whit* of the bullet, the wounded man's scream
Are mixed as the mist of some devilish dream –

Forgotten, forgotten the sweat of the shambles
Where the hill-daisy blooms and the grey monkey gambols,

1. Stomach.

From the sword-belt set free and released from the steel,
The Peace of the Lord is on Captain O'Neil!

Up the hill to Simoorie – most patient of drudges –
The bags on his shoulder, the mail-runner trudges.

'For Captain O'Neil Sahib. One hundred and ten
'Rupees to collect on delivery.'
                              Then

(Their breakfast was stopped while the screw-jack and hammer
Tore waxcloth, split teak-wood, and chipped out the dammer;[1])

Open-eyed, open-mouthed, on the napery's snow,
With a crash and a thud, rolled – the Head of the Boh!

And gummed to the scalp was a letter which ran: –
                    'IN FIELDING FORCE SERVICE
                        'Encampment,
                           '10th Jan.

'Dear Sir, – I have honour to send, as you said,
'For final approval (see under) Boh's Head;

'Was took by myself in most bloody affair.
'By High Education brought pressure to bear.

'Now violate Liberty, time being bad,
'To mail V.P.P. (rupees hundred) Please add

'Whatever Your Honour can pass. Price of Blood
'Much cheap at one hundred, and children want food.

'So trusting Your Honour will somewhat retain
'True love and affection for Govt. Bullock Train,

'And show awful kindness to satisfy me,
                 'I am,
                    'Graceful Master,
                       'Your
                          'H. MUKERJI.'

1. Native sealing wax.

· · · · · · ·

As the rabbit is drawn to the rattlesnake's power,
As the smoker's eye fills at the opium hour,

As a horse reaches up to the manger above,
As the waiting ear yearns for the whisper of love,

From the arms of the Bride, iron-visaged and slow,
The Captain bent down to the Head of the Boh.

And e'en as he looked on the Thing where It lay
'Twixt the winking new spoons and the napkins' array,

The freed mind fled back to the long-ago days –
The hand-to-hand scuffle – the smoke and the blaze –

The forced march at night and the quick rush at dawn –
The banjo at twilight, the burial ere morn –

The stench of the marshes – the raw, piercing smell
When the overhand stabbing-cut silenced the yell –

The oaths of his Irish that surged when they stood
Where the black crosses hung o'er the Kuttamow flood.

As a derelict ship drifts away with the tide
The Captain went out on the Past from his Bride,

Back, back, through the springs to the chill of the year,
When he hunted the Boh from Maloon to Tsaleer.

As the shape of a corpse dimmers up through deep water,
In his eye lit the passionless passion of slaughter,

And men who had fought with O'Neil for the life
Had gazed on his face with less dread than his wife.

For she who had held him so long could not hold him –
Though a four-month Eternity should have controlled him! –

But watched the twin Terror – the head turned to head –
The scowling, scarred Black, and the flushed savage Red –

The spirit that changed from her knowing and flew to
Some grim hidden Past she had never a clue to.

But It knew as It grinned, for he touched it unfearing,
And muttered aloud, 'So you kept that jade earring!'

Then nodded, and kindly, as friend nods to friend,
'Old man, you fought well, but you lost in the end.'

   .   .   .   .   .   .

The visions departed, and Shame followed Passion: –
'He took what I said in this horrible fashion?

'*I'll* write to Harendra!' With language unsainted
The Captain came back to the Bride . . . who had fainted.

   .   .   .   .   .   .

And this is a fiction? No. Go to Simoorie
And look at their baby, a twelve-month old Houri,

A pert little, Irish-eyed Kathleen Mavournin –
She's always about on the Mall of a mornin' –

And you'll see, if her right shoulder-strap is displaced,
This: *Gules* upon *argent*, a Boh's Head, *erased*!

The Feet of the Young Men

1897

Now the Four-way Lodge is opened, now the Hunting Winds are
    loose –
  Now the Smokes of Spring go up to clear the brain;
Now the Young Men's hearts are troubled for the whisper of the
    Trues,
  Now the Red Gods make their medicine again!
Who hath seen the beaver busied? Who hath watched the black-tail
    mating?
  Who hath lain alone to hear the wild-goose cry?
Who hath worked the chosen water where the ouananiche is waiting,
  Or the sea-trout's jumping-crazy for the fly?

He must go – go – go away from here!
On the other side the world he's overdue.
'Send your road is clear before you when the old Spring-fret comes o'er
you,
And the Red Gods call for you!

So for one the wet sail arching through the rainbow round the bow,
And for one the creak of snow-shoes on the crust;
And for one the lakeside lilies where the bull-moose waits the cow,
And for one the mule-train coughing in the dust.
Who hath smelt wood-smoke at twilight? Who hath heard the birch-log
burning?
Who is quick to read the noises of the night?
Let him follow with the others, for the Young Men's feet are turning
To the camps of proved desire and known delight!

Let him go – go, etc.

I

Do you know the blackened timber – do you know that racing stream
With the raw, right-angled log-jam at the end;
And the bar of sun-warmed shingle where a man may bask and dream
To the click of shod canoe-poles round the bend?
It is there that we are going with our rods and reels and traces,
To a silent, smoky Indian that we know –
To a couch of new-pulled hemlock, with the starlight on our faces,
For the Red Gods call us out and we must go!

They must go – go, etc.

II

Do you know the shallow Baltic where the seas are steep and short,
Where the bluff, lee-boarded fishing-luggers ride?
Do you know the joy of threshing leagues to leeward of your port
On a coast you've lost the chart of overside?

It is there that I am going, with an extra hand to bale her –
　　Just one able 'long-shore loafer that I know.
He can take his chance of drowning, while I sail and sail and sail her,
　　For the Red Gods call me out and I must go!

He must go – go, etc.

III

Do you know the pile-built village where the sago-dealers trade –
　　Do you know the reek of fish and wet bamboo?
Do you know the steaming stillness of the orchid-scented glade
　　When the blazoned, bird-winged butterflies flap through?
It is there that I am going with my camphor, net, and boxes,
　　To a gentle, yellow pirate that I know –
To my little wailing lemurs, to my palms and flying-foxes,
　　For the Red Gods call me out and I must go!

He must go – go, etc.

IV

Do you know the world's white roof-tree – do you know that windy
　　rift
　　Where the baffling mountain-eddies chop and change?
Do you know the long day's patience, belly-down on frozen drift,
　　While the head of heads is feeding out of range?
It is there that I am going, where the boulders and the snow lie,
　　With a trusty, nimble tracker that I know.
I have sworn an oath, to keep it on the Horns of Ovis Poli,
　　And the Red Gods call me out and I must go!

He must go – go, etc.

Now the Four-way Lodge is opened – now the Smokes of Council
　　rise –
　　Pleasant smokes, ere yet 'twixt trail and trail they choose –
Now the girths and ropes are tested: now they pack their last supplies:
　　Now our Young Men go to dance before the Trues!

Who shall meet them at those altars – who shall light them to that
    shrine?
  Velvet-footed, who shall guide them to their goal?
Unto each the voice and vision: unto each his spoor and sign –
Lonely mountain in the Northland, misty sweat-bath 'neath the Line –
  And to each a man that knows his naked soul!

White or yellow, black or copper, he is waiting, as a lover,
  Smoke of funnel, dust of hooves, or beat of train –
Where the high grass hides the horseman or the glaring flats discover –
Where the steamer hails the landing, or the surf-boat brings the rover –
Where the rails run out in sand-drift . . . Quick! ah, heave the camp-kit
  over,
  For the Red Gods make their medicine again!

    And we go – go – go away from here!
      On the other side the world we're overdue!
    'Send the road is clear before you when the old Spring-fret comes
        o'er you,
      And the Red Gods call for you!

The Truce of the Bear
1898

Yearly, with tent and rifle, our careless white men go
By the Pass called Muttianee, to shoot in the vale below.
Yearly by Muttianee he follows our white men in –
Matun, the old blind beggar, bandaged from brow to chin.

Eyeless, noseless, and lipless – toothless, broken of speech,
Seeking a dole at the doorway he mumbles his tale to each;
Over and over the story, ending as he began:
'Make ye no truce with Adam-zad – the Bear that walks like a Man!

'There was a flint in my musket – pricked and primed was the pan,
When I went hunting Adam-zad – the Bear that stands like a Man.

I looked my last on the timber, I looked my last on the snow,
When I went hunting Adam-zad fifty summers ago!

'I knew his times and his seasons, as he knew mine, that fed
By night in the ripened maizefield and robbed my house of bread.
I knew his strength and cunning, as he knew mine, that crept
At dawn to the crowded goat-pens and plundered while I slept.

'Up from his stony playground – down from his well-digged lair –
Out on the naked ridges ran Adam-zad the Bear –
Groaning, grunting, and roaring, heavy with stolen meals,
Two long marches to northward, and I was at his heels!

'Two long marches to northward, at the fall of the second night,
I came on mine enemy Adam-zad all panting from his flight.
There was a charge in the musket – pricked and primed was the pan –
My finger crooked on the trigger – when he reared up like a man.

'Horrible, hairy, human, with paws like hands in prayer,
Making his supplication rose Adam-zad the Bear!
I looked at the swaying shoulders, at the paunch's swag and swing,
And my heart was touched with pity for the monstrous, pleading thing.

'Touched with pity and wonder, I did not fire then . . .
I have looked no more on women – I have walked no more with men.
Nearer he tottered and nearer, with paws like hands that pray –
From brow to jaw that steel-shod paw, it ripped my face away!

'Sudden, silent, and savage, searing as flame the blow –
Faceless I fell before his feet, fifty summers ago.
I heard him grunt and chuckle – I heard him pass to his den.
He left me blind to the darkened years and the little mercy of men.

'Now ye go down in the morning with guns of the newer style,
That load (I have felt) in the middle and range (I have heard) a mile?
Luck to the white man's rifle, that shoots so fast and true,
But – pay, and I lift my bandage and show what the Bear can do!'

(Flesh like slag in the furnace, knobbed and withered and grey –
Matun, the old blind beggar, he gives good worth for his pay.)
'Rouse him at noon in the bushes, follow and press him hard –
Not for his raging and roarings flinch ye from Adam-zad.

'But (pay, and I put back the bandage) *this* is the time to fear,
When he stands up like a tired man, tottering near and near;
When he stands up as pleading, in wavering, man-brute guise,
When he veils the hate and cunning of his little, swinish eyes;

'When he shows as seeking quarter, with paws like hands in prayer,
That is the time of peril – the time of the Truce of the Bear!'

Eyeless, noseless, and lipless, asking a dole at the door,
Matun, the old blind beggar, he tells it o'er and o'er;
Fumbling and feeling the rifles, warming his hands at the flame,
Hearing our careless white men talk of the morrow's game;

Over and over the story, ending as he began: –
'*There is no truce with Adam-zad, the Bear that looks like a Man!*'

A Death-Bed

1918

'This is the State above the Law.
    The State exists for the State alone.'
[*This is a gland at the back of the jaw,
    And an answering lump by the collar-bone.*]

Some die shouting in gas or fire;
    Some die silent, by shell and shot.
Some die desperate, caught on the wire;
    Some die suddenly. This will not.

'Regis suprema voluntas Lex'
    [*It will follow the regular course of – throats.*]

Some die pinned by the broken decks,
  Some die sobbing between the boats.

Some die eloquent, pressed to death
  By the sliding trench, as their friends can hear.
Some die wholly in half a breath.
  Some – give trouble for half a year.

'There is neither Evil nor Good in life
  Except as the needs of the State ordain.'
[*Since it is rather too late for the knife,*
  All we can do is to mask the pain.]

Some die saintly in faith and hope –
  One died thus in a prison-yard –
Some die broken by rape or the rope;
  Some die easily. This dies hard.

'I will dash to pieces who bar my way.
  Woe to the traitor! Woe to the weak!'
[*Let him write what he wishes to say.*
  It tires him out if he tries to speak.]

Some die quietly. Some abound
  In loud self-pity. Others spread
Bad morale through the cots around . . .
  This is a type that is better dead.

'The war was forced on me by my foes.
  All that I sought was the right to live.'
[*Don't be afraid of a triple dose;*
  The pain will neutralize half we give.

Here are the needles. See that he dies
  While the effects of the drug endure . . .
What is the question he asks with his eyes? –
  Yes, All-Highest, to God, be sure.]

'Before a Midnight Breaks in Storm'

1903

Before a midnight breaks in storm,
  Or herded sea in wrath,
Ye know what wavering gusts inform
  The greater tempest's path;
    Till the loosed wind
    Drive all from mind,
Except Distress, which, so will prophets cry,
O'ercame them, houseless, from the unhinting sky.

Ere rivers league against the land
  In piratry of flood,
Ye know what waters steal and stand
  Where seldom water stood.
    Yet who will note,
    Till fields afloat,
And washen carcass and the returning well,
Trumpet what these poor heralds strove to tell?

Ye know who use the Crystal Ball
  (To peer by stealth on Doom),
The Shade that, shaping first of all,
  Prepares an empty room.
    Then doth It pass
    Like breath from glass,
But, on the extorted Vision bowed intent,
No man considers why It came or went.

Before the years reborn behold
  Themselves with stranger eye,
And the sport-making Gods of old,
  Like Samson slaying, die,

Many shall hear
    The all-pregnant sphere,
Bow to the birth and sweat, but – speech denied –
Sit dumb or – dealt in part – fall weak and wide.

Yet instant to fore-shadowed need
    The eternal balance swings;
That wingèd men the Fates may breed
    So soon as Fate hath wings.
        These shall possess
        Our littleness,
And in the imperial task (as worthy) lay
Up our lives' all to piece one giant Day.

The Bell Buoy

1896

They christened my brother of old –
    And a saintly name he bears –
They gave him his place to hold
    At the head of the belfry-stairs,
    Where the minster-towers stand
And the breeding kestrels cry.
    Would I change with my brother a league inland?
(*Shoal! 'Ware shoal!*) Not I!

In the flush of the hot June prime,
    O'er sleek flood-tides afire,
I hear him hurry the chime
    To the bidding of checked Desire;
    Till the sweated ringers tire
And the wild bob-majors die.
    Could I wait for my turn in the godly choir?
(*Shoal! 'Ware shoal!*) Not I!

When the smoking scud is blown –
   When the greasy wind-rack lowers –
Apart and at peace and alone,
   He counts the changeless hours.
   He wars with darkling Powers
(I war with a darkling sea);
   Would he stoop to my work in the gusty mirk?
(*Shoal! 'Ware shoal!*) Not he!

There was never a priest to pray,
   There was never a hand to toll,
When they made me guard of the bay,
   And moored me over the shoal.
   I rock, I reel, and I roll –
My four great hammers ply –
   Could I speak or be still at the Church's will?
(*Shoal! 'Ware shoal!*) Not I!

The landward marks have failed,
   The fog-bank glides unguessed,
The seaward lights are veiled,
   The spent deep feigns her rest:
   But my ear is laid to her breast,
I lift to the swell – I cry!
   Could I wait in sloth on the Church's oath?
(*Shoal! 'Ware shoal!*) Not I!

At the careless end of night
   I thrill to the nearing screw;
I turn in the clearing light
   And I call to the drowsy crew;
   And the mud boils foul and blue
As the blind bow backs away.
   Will they give me their thanks if they clear the banks?
(*Shoal! 'Ware shoal!*) Not they!

The beach-pools cake and skim,
   The bursting spray-heads freeze,

I gather on crown and rim
    The grey, grained ice of the seas,
    Where, sheathed from bitt to trees,
The plunging colliers lie.
    Would I barter my place for Church's grace?
(*Shoal! 'Ware shoal!*) Not I!

Through the blur of the whirling snow,
    Or the black of the inky sleet,
The lanterns gather and grow,
    And I look for the homeward fleet.
    Rattle of block and sheet –
'Ready about – stand by!'
    Shall I ask them a fee ere they fetch the quay?
(*Shoal! 'Ware shoal!*) Not I!

I dip and I surge and I swing
    In the rip of the racing tide,
By the gates of doom I sing,
    On the horns of death I ride.
    A ship-length overside,
Between the course and the sand,
    Fretted and bound I bide
        Peril whereof I cry.
Would I change with my brother a league inland?
(*Shoal! 'Ware shoal!*) Not I!

Mesopotamia

1917

They shall not return to us, the resolute, the young,
    The eager and whole-hearted whom we gave:
But the men who left them thriftily to die in their own dung,
    Shall they come with years and honour to the grave?

They shall not return to us, the strong men coldly slain
    In sight of help denied from day to day:
But the men who edged their agonies and chid them in their pain,
    Are they too strong and wise to put away?

Our dead shall not return to us while Day and Night divide –
    Never while the bars of sunset hold.
But the idle-minded overlings who quibbled while they died,
    Shall they thrust for high employments as of old?

Shall we only threaten and be angry for an hour?
    When the storm is ended shall we find
How softly but how swiftly they have sidled back to power
    By the favour and contrivance of their kind?

Even while they soothe us, while they promise large amends,
    Even while they make a show of fear,
Do they call upon their debtors, and take counsel with their friends,
    To confirm and re-establish each career?

Their lives cannot repay us – their death could not undo –
    The shame that they have laid upon our race.
But the slothfulness that wasted and the arrogance that slew,
    Shall we leave it unabated in its place?

The Islanders

1902

No doubt but ye are the People – your throne is above the King's.
Whoso speaks in your presence must say acceptable things:
Bowing the head in worship, bending the knee in fear –
Bringing the word well smoothen – such as a King should hear.

Fenced by your careful fathers, ringed by your leaden seas,
Long did ye wake in quiet and long lie down at ease;

Till ye said of Strife, 'What is it?' of the Sword, 'It is far from our
    ken';
Till ye made a sport of your shrunken hosts and a toy of your armèd
    men.
Ye stopped your ears to the warning – ye would neither look nor heed –
Ye set your leisure before their toil and your lusts above their need.
Because of your witless learning and your beasts of warren and chase,
Ye grudged your sons to their service and your fields for their
    camping-place.
Ye forced them glean in the highways the straw for the bricks they
    brought;
Ye forced them follow in byways the craft that ye never taught.
Ye hampered and hindered and crippled; ye thrust out of sight and
    away
Those that would serve you for honour and those that served you for
    pay.
Then were the judgments loosened; then was your shame revealed,
At the hands of a little people, few but apt in the field.
Yet ye were saved by a remnant (and your land's long-suffering star),
When your strong men cheered in their millions while your striplings
    went to the war.
Sons of the sheltered city – unmade, unhandled, unmeet –
Ye pushed them raw to the battle as ye picked them raw from the
    street.
And what did ye look they should compass? Warcraft learned in a
    breath,
Knowledge unto occasion at the first far view of Death?
So? And ye train your horses and the dogs ye feed and prize?
How are the beasts more worthy than the souls, your sacrifice?
But ye said, 'Their valour shall show them'; but ye said, 'The end is
    close.'
And ye sent them comfits and pictures to help them harry your foes:
And ye vaunted your fathomless power, and ye flaunted your iron
    pride,
Ere – ye fawned on the Younger Nations for the men who could shoot
    and ride!
Then ye returned to your trinkets; then ye contented your souls
With the flannelled fools at the wicket or the muddied oafs at the goals.

Given to strong delusion, wholly believing a lie,
Ye saw that the land lay fenceless, and ye let the months go by
Waiting some easy wonder, hoping some saving sign –
Idle – openly idle – in the lee of the forespent Line.
Idle – except for your boasting – and what is your boasting worth
If ye grudge a year of service to the lordliest life on earth?
Ancient, effortless, ordered, cycle on cycle set,
Life so long untroubled, that ye who inherit forget
It was not made with the mountains, it is not one with the deep.
Men, not gods, devised it. Men, not gods, must keep.
Men, not children, servants, or kinsfolk called from afar,
But each man born in the Island broke to the matter of war.
Soberly and by custom taken and trained for the same,
Each man born in the Island entered at youth to the game –
As it were almost cricket, not to be mastered in haste,
But after trial and labour, by temperance, living chaste.
As it were almost cricket – as it were even your play,
Weighed and pondered and worshipped, and practised day and day.
So ye shall bide sure-guarded when the restless lightnings wake
In the womb of the blotting war-cloud, and the pallid nations quake.
So, at the haggard trumpets, instant your soul shall leap
Forthright, accoutred, accepting – alert from the wells of sleep.
So at the threat ye shall summon – so at the need ye shall send
Men, not children or servants, tempered and taught to the end;
Cleansed of servile panic, slow to dread or despise,
Humble because of knowledge, mighty by sacrifice . . .
But ye say, 'It will mar our comfort.' Ye say, 'It will minish our trade.'
Do ye wait for the spattered shrapnel ere ye learn how a gun is laid?
For the low, red glare to southward when the raided coast-towns
    burn?
(Light ye shall have on that lesson, but little time to learn.)
Will ye pitch some white pavilion, and lustily even the odds,
With nets and hoops and mallets, with rackets and bats and rods?
Will the rabbit war with your foemen – the red deer horn them for hire?
Your kept cock-pheasant keep you? – he is master of many a shire.
Arid, aloof, incurious, unthinking, unthanking, gelt,
Will ye loose your schools to flout them till their brow-beat columns
    melt?

Will ye pray them or preach them, or print them, or ballot them back
  from your shore?
Will your workmen issue a mandate to bid them strike no more?
Will ye rise and dethrone your rulers? (Because ye were idle both?
Pride by Insolence chastened? Indolence purged by Sloth?)
No doubt but ye are the People; who shall make you afraid?
Also your gods are many; no doubt but your gods shall aid.
Idols of greasy altars built for the body's ease;
Proud little brazen Baals and talking fetishes;
Teraphs of sept and party and wise wood-pavement gods –
These shall come down to the battle and snatch you from under the
  rods?
From the gusty, flickering gun-roll with viewless salvoes rent,
And the pitted hail of the bullets that tell not whence they were sent.
When ye are ringed as with iron, when ye are scourged as with whips,
When the meat is yet in your belly, and the boast is yet on your lips;
When ye go forth at mornings and the noon beholds you broke,
Ere ye lie down at even, your remnant, under the yoke?

No doubt but ye are the People – absolute, strong, and wise;
Whatever your heart has desired ye have not withheld from your eyes.
On your own heads, in your own hands, the sin and the saving lies!

The White Man's Burden

1899

(The United States and the Philippine Islands)

Take up the White Man's burden –
  Send forth the best ye breed –
Go bind your sons to exile
  To serve your captives' need;
To wait in heavy harness
  On fluttered folk and wild –
Your new-caught, sullen peoples,
  Half devil and half child.

Take up the White Man's burden –
   In patience to abide,
To veil the threat of terror
   And check the show of pride;
By open speech and simple,
   An hundred times made plain,
To seek another's profit,
   And work another's gain.

Take up the White Man's burden –
   The savage wars of peace –
Fill full the mouth of Famine
   And bid the sickness cease;
And when your goal is nearest
   The end for others sought,
Watch Sloth and heathen Folly
   Bring all your hope to nought.

Take up the White Man's burden –
   No tawdry rule of kings,
But toil of serf and sweeper –
   The tale of common things.
The ports ye shall not enter,
   The roads ye shall not tread,
Go make them with your living,
   And mark them with your dead!

Take up the White Man's burden –
   And reap his old reward:
The blame of those ye better,
   The hate of those ye guard –
The cry of hosts ye humour
   (Ah, slowly!) toward the light: –
'Why brought ye us from bondage,
   'Our loved Egyptian night?'

Take up the White Man's burden –
   Ye dare not stoop to less –
Nor call too loud on Freedom
   To cloak your weariness;
By all ye cry or whisper,
   By all ye leave or do,
The silent, sullen peoples
   Shall weigh your Gods and you.

Take up the White Man's burden –
   Have done with childish days –
The lightly proffered laurel,
   The easy, ungrudged praise.
Comes now, to search your manhood
   Through all the thankless years,
Cold-edged with dear-bought wisdom,
   The judgment of your peers!

A Song at Cock-Crow

1918

'Ille autem iterum negavit.'

The first time that Peter denièd his Lord
He shrank from the cudgel, the scourge and the cord,
But followed far off to see what they would do,
Till the cock crew – till the cock crew –
After Gethsemane, till the cock crew!

The first time that Peter denièd his Lord
'Twas only a maid in the palace who heard,
As he sat by the fire and warmed himself through.
Then the cock crew! Then the cock crew!
('Thou also art one of them.') Then the cock crew!

The first time that Peter denièd his Lord
He had neither the Throne, nor the Keys nor the Sword –
A poor silly fisherman, what could he do,
When the cock crew – when the cock crew –
But weep for his wickedness when the cock crew?

    .   .   .   .   .   .

The next time that Peter denièd his Lord
He was Fisher of Men, as foretold by the Word,
With the Crown on his brow and the Cross on his shoe,
When the cock crew – when the cock crew –
In Flanders and Picardy when the cock crew!

The next time that Peter denièd his Lord
'Twas Mary the Mother in Heaven Who heard,
And She grieved for the maidens and wives that they slew
When the cock crew – when the cock crew –
At Tirmonde and Aerschott when the cock crew!

The next time that Peter denièd his Lord
The Babe in the Manger awakened and stirred,
And He stretched out His arms for the playmates He knew –
When the cock crew – when the cock crew –
But the waters had covered them when the cock crew!

The next time that Peter denièd his Lord
'Twas Earth in her agony waited his word,
But he sat by the fire and naught would he do,
Though the cock crew – though the cock crew –
Over all Christendom, though the cock crew!

The last time that Peter denièd his Lord,
The Father took from him the Keys and the Sword,
And the Mother and Babe brake his Kingdom in two,
When the cock crew – when the cock crew –
(Because of his wickedness) when the cock crew!

Recessional

1897

God of our fathers, known of old,
   Lord of our far-flung battle-line,
Beneath whose awful Hand we hold
   Dominion over palm and pine –
Lord God of Hosts, be with us yet,
Lest we forget – lest we forget!

The tumult and the shouting dies;
   The Captains and the Kings depart:
Still stands Thine ancient sacrifice,
   An humble and a contrite heart.
Lord God of Hosts, be with us yet,
Lest we forget – lest we forget!

Far-called, our navies melt away;
   On dune and headland sinks the fire:
Lo, all our pomp of yesterday
   Is one with Nineveh and Tyre!
Judge of the Nations, spare us yet,
Lest we forget – lest we forget!

If, drunk with sight of power, we loose
   Wild tongues that have not Thee in awe,
Such boastings as the Gentiles use,
   Or lesser breeds without the Law –
Lord God of Hosts, be with us yet,
Lest we forget – lest we forget!

For heathen heart that puts her trust
   In reeking tube and iron shard,
All valiant dust that builds on dust,
   And guarding, calls not Thee to guard,
For frantic boast and foolish word –
Thy mercy on Thy People, Lord!

The Three-Decker

1894

'The three-volume novel is extinct.'

Full thirty foot she towered from waterline to rail.
It took a watch to steer her, and a week to shorten sail;
But, spite all modern notions, I've found her first and best –
The only certain packet for the Islands of the Blest.

Fair held the breeze behind us – 'twas warm with lovers' prayers.
We'd stolen wills for ballast and a crew of missing heirs.
They shipped as Able Bastards till the Wicked Nurse confessed,
And they worked the old three-decker to the Islands of the Blest.

By ways no gaze could follow, a course unspoiled of Cook,
Per Fancy, fleetest in man, our titled berths we took,
With maids of matchless beauty and parentage unguessed,
And a Church of England parson for the Islands of the Blest.

We asked no social questions – we pumped no hidden shame –
We never talked obstetrics when the Little Stranger came:
We left the Lord in Heaven, we left the fiends in Hell.
We weren't exactly Yussufs, but – Zuleika didn't tell.

No moral doubt assailed us, so when the port we neared,
The villain had his flogging at the gangway, and we cheered.
'Twas fiddle in the foc's'le – 'twas garlands on the mast,
For every one got married, and I went ashore at last.

I left 'em all in couples a-kissing on the decks.
I left the lovers loving and the parents signing cheques.
In endless English comfort, by county-folk caressed,
I left the old three-decker at the Islands of the Blest! . . .

That route is barred to steamers: you'll never lift again
Our purple-painted headlands or the lordly keeps of Spain.
They're just beyond your skyline, howe'er so far you cruise
In a ram-you-damn-you liner with a brace of bucking screws.

Swing round your aching searchlight – 'twill show no haven's peace.
Ay, blow your shrieking sirens at the deaf, grey-bearded seas!
Boom out the dripping oil-bags to skin the deep's unrest –
And you aren't one knot nearer to the Islands of the Blest.

But when you're threshing, crippled, with broken bridge and rail,
At a drogue of dead convictions to hold you head to gale,
Calm as the Flying Dutchman, from truck to taffrail dressed,
You'll see the old three-decker for the Islands of the Blest.

You'll see her tiering canvas in sheeted silver spread;
You'll hear the long-drawn thunder 'neath her leaping figure-head;
While far, so far above you, her tall poop-lanterns shine
Unvexed by wind or weather like the candles round a shrine!

Hull down – hull down and under – she dwindles to a speck,
With noise of pleasant music and dancing on her deck.
All's well – all's well aboard her – she's left you far behind,
With a scent of old-world roses through the fog that ties you blind.

Her crews are babes or madmen? Her port is all to make?
You're manned by Truth and Science, and you steam for steaming's
   sake?
Well, tinker up your engines – you know your business best –
She's taking tired people to the Islands of the Blest!

The Conundrum of the Workshops

1890

When the flush of a new-born sun fell first on Eden's green and gold,
Our father Adam sat under the Tree and scratched with a stick in the
   mould;
And the first rude sketch that the world had seen was joy to his mighty
   heart,
Till the Devil whispered behind the leaves, 'It's pretty, but is it Art?'

Wherefore he called to his wife, and fled to fashion his work anew –
The first of his race who cared a fig for the first, most dread review;
And he left his lore to the use of his sons – and that was a glorious gain
When the Devil chuckled 'Is it Art?' in the ear of the branded Cain.

They builded a tower to shiver the sky and wrench the stars apart,
Till the Devil grunted behind the bricks: 'It's striking, but is it Art?'
The stone was dropped at the quarry-side and the idle derrick swung,
While each man talked of the aims of Art, and each in an alien tongue.

They fought and they talked in the North and the South; they talked
    and they fought in the West,
Till the waters rose on the pitiful land, and the poor Red Clay had
    rest –
Had rest till that dank blank-canvas dawn when the Dove was preened
    to start,
And the Devil bubbled below the keel: 'It's human, but is it Art?'

The tale is as old as the Eden Tree – and new as the new-cut tooth –
For each man knows ere his lip-thatch grows he is master of Art and
    Truth;
And each man hears as the twilight nears, to the beat of his dying
    heart,
The Devil drum on the darkened pane: 'You did it, but was it Art?'

We have learned to whittle the Eden Tree to the shape of a surplice-
    peg,
We have learned to bottle our parents twain in the yelk of an addled
    egg,
We know that the tail must wag the dog, for the horse is drawn by the
    cart;
But the Devil whoops, as he whooped of old: 'It's clever, but is it Art?'

When the flicker of London sun falls faint on the Club-room's green
    and gold,
The sons of Adam sit them down and scratch with their pens in the
    mould –

They scratch with their pens in the mould of their graves, and the ink
    and the anguish start,
For the Devil mutters behind the leaves: 'It's pretty, but is it Art?'

Now, if we could win to the Eden Tree where the Four Great Rivers flow,
And the Wreath of Eve is red on the turf as she left it long ago,
And if we could come when the sentry slept and softly scurry through,
By the favour of God we might know as much – as our father Adam knew!

The Benefactors

Ah! What avails the classic bent
    And what the cultured word,
Against the undoctored incident
    That actually occurred?

And what is Art whereto we press
    Through paint and prose and rhyme –
When Nature in her nakedness
    Defeats us every time?

It is not learning, grace nor gear,
    Nor easy meat and drink,
But bitter pinch of pain and fear
    That makes creation think.

When in this world's unpleasing youth
    Our godlike race began,
The longest arm, the sharpest tooth,
    Gave man control of man;

Till, bruised and bitten to the bone
    And taught by pain and fear,
He learned to deal the far-off stone,
    And poke the long, safe spear.

So tooth and nail were obsolete
　　As means against a foe,
Till, bored by uniform defeat,
　　Some genius built the bow.

Then stone and javelin proved as vain
　　As old-time tooth and nail;
Till, spurred anew by fear and pain,
　　Man fashioned coats of mail.

Then was there safety for the rich
　　And danger for the poor,
Till someone mixed a powder which
　　Redressed the scale once more.

Helmet and armour disappeared
　　With sword and bow and pike,
And, when the smoke of battle cleared,
　　All men were armed alike . . .

And when ten million such were slain
　　To please one crazy king,
Man, schooled in bulk by fear and pain,
　　Grew weary of the thing;

And, at the very hour designed
　　To enslave him past recall,
His tooth-stone-arrow-gun-shy mind
　　Turned and abolished all.

All Power, each Tyrant, every Mob
　　Whose head has grown too large,
Ends by destroying its own job
　　And works its own discharge;

And Man, whose mere necessities
　　Move all things from his path,
Trembles meanwhile at their decrees,
　　And deprecates their wrath!

The Craftsman

Once, after long-drawn revel at The Mermaid,
He to the overbearing Boanerges
Jonson, uttered (if half of it were liquor,
        Blessed be the vintage!)

Saying how, at an alehouse under Cotswold,
He had made sure of his very Cleopatra
Drunk with enormous, salvation-contemning
        Love for a tinker.

How, while he hid from Sir Thomas's keepers,
Crouched in a ditch and drenched by the midnight
Dews, he had listened to gipsy Juliet
        Rail at the dawning.

How at Bankside, a boy drowning kittens
Winced at the business; whereupon his sister –
Lady Macbeth aged seven – thrust 'em under,
        Sombrely scornful.

How on a Sabbath, hushed and compassionate –
She being known since her birth to the townsfolk –
Stratford dredged and delivered from Avon
        Dripping Ophelia.

So, with a thin third finger marrying
Drop to wine-drop domed on the table,
Shakespeare opened his heart till the sunrise
        Entered to hear him.

London waked and he, imperturbable,
Passed from waking to hurry after shadows . . .
Busied upon shows of no earthly importance?
        Yes, but he knew it!

Samuel Pepys

1933

Like as the Oak whose roots descend
　　Through earth and stillness seeking food
Most apt to furnish in the end
　　That dense, indomitable wood

Which, felled, may arm a seaward flank
　　Of Ostia's mole or – bent to frame
The beaked Liburnian's triple bank –
　　Carry afar the Roman name;

But which, a tree, the season moves
　　Through gentler Gods than Wind or Tide,
Delightedly to harbour doves,
　　Or take some clasping vine for bride;

So this man – prescient to ensure
　　(Since even now his orders hold)
A little State might ride secure
　　At sea from foes her sloth made bold, –

Turned in his midmost harried round,
　　As Venus drove or Liber led,
And snatched from any shrine he found
　　The Stolen Draught, the Secret Bread.

Nor these alone. His life betrayed
　　No gust unslaked, no pleasure missed.
He called the obedient Nine to aid
　　The varied chase. And Clio kissed;

Bidding him write each sordid love,
　　Shame, panic, stratagem, and lie
In full, that sinners undiscov-
　　ered, like ourselves, might say: – ''Tis I!'

'When 'Omer Smote 'Is Bloomin' Lyre'

(Introduction to the 'Barrack-Room Ballads'
in *The Seven Seas*)

When 'Omer smote 'is bloomin' lyre,
    He'd 'eard men sing by land an' sea;
An' what he thought 'e might require,
    'E went an' took – the same as me!

The market-girls an' fishermen,
    The shepherds an' the sailors, too,
They 'eard old songs turn up again,
    But kep' it quiet – same as you!

They knew 'e stole; 'e knew they knowed.
    They didn't tell, nor make a fuss,
But winked at 'Omer down the road,
    An' 'e winked back – the same as us!

The Files

1903

(*The Sub-editor speaks*)

Files –
The Files –
Office Files!
Oblige me by referring to the Files.
Every question man can raise,
Every phrase of every phase
Of that question is on record in the Files –
(Threshed out threadbare – fought and finished in the Files).
Ere the Universe at large
Was our new-tipped arrows' targe –
Ere we rediscovered Mammon and his wiles –

Faenza, gentle reader, spent her – five-and-twentieth leader –
(You will find him, and some others, in the Files).
Warn all coming Robert Brownings and Carlyles,
It will interest them to hunt among the Files
Where unvisited, a-cold,
Lie the crowded years of old
In that Kensal-Green of greatness called the Files
(In our newspaPère-la-Chaise the Office Files),
Where the dead men lay them down,
Meekly sure of long renown,
And above them, sere and swift,
Packs the daily deepening drift
Of the all-recording, all-effacing Files –
The obliterating, automatic Files.
Count the mighty men who slung
Ink, Evangel, Sword, or Tongue
When Reform and you were young –
Made their boasts and spake according in the Files –
(Hear the ghosts that wake applauding in the Files!)
Trace each all-forgot career
From long primer through brevier
Unto Death, a para minion in the Files
(Para minion – solid – bottom of the Files) . . .
Some successful Kings and Queens adorn the Files.
They were great, their views were leaded,
And their deaths were triple-headed,
So they catch the eye in running through the Files
(Show as blazes in the mazes of the Files);
For their 'paramours and priests',
And their gross, jack-booted feasts,
And their 'epoch-marking actions' see the Files.
Was it Bomba fled the blue Sicilian isles?
Was it Saffi, a professor
Once of Oxford, brought redress or
Garibaldi? Who remembers
Forty-odd-year-old Septembers? –
Only sextons paid to dig among the Files
(Such as I am, born and bred among the Files).

You must hack through much deposit
Ere you know for sure who was it
Came to burial with such honour in the Files
(Only seven seasons back beneath the Files).
'Very great our loss and grievous –
'So our best and brightest leave us,
'And it ends the Age of Giants,' say the Files;
All the '60–'70–'80–'90 Files –
(The open-minded, opportunist files –
The easy 'O King, live for ever' Files).
It is good to read a little in the Files;
'Tis a sure and sovereign balm
Unto philosophic calm,
Yea, and philosophic doubt when Life beguiles.
When you know Success is Greatness,
When you marvel at your lateness
In apprehending facts so plain to Smiles
(Self-helpful, wholly strenuous Samuel Smiles).
When your Imp of Blind Desire
Bids you set the Thames afire,
You'll remember men have done so – in the Files.
You'll have seen those flames transpire – in the Files
(More than once that flood has run so – in the Files).
When the Conchimarian horns
Of the reboantic Norns
Usher gentlemen and ladies
With new lights on Heaven and Hades,
Guaranteeing to Eternity
All yesterday's modernity;
When Brocken-spectres made by
Some one's breath on ink parade by,
Very earnest and tremendous,
Let not shows of shows offend us.
When of everything we like we
Shout ecstatic: '*Quod ubique*,
'*Quod ab omnibus* means *semper*!'
Oh, my brother, keep your temper!
Light your pipe and take a look along the Files.

You've a better chance to guess
At the meaning of Success
(Which is Greatness – *vide* Press)
When you've seen it in perspective in the Files!

The Virginity

Try as he will, no man breaks wholly loose
    From his first love, no matter who she be.
Oh, was there ever sailor free to choose,
    That didn't settle somewhere near the sea?

Myself, it don't excite me nor amuse
    To watch a pack o' shipping on the sea;
But I can understand my neighbour's views
    From certain things which have occurred to me.

Men must keep touch with things they used to use
    To earn their living, even when they are free;
And so come back upon the least excuse –
    Same as the sailor settled near the sea.

He knows he's never going on no cruise –
    He knows he's done and finished with the sea;
And yet he likes to feel she's there to use –
    If he should ask her – as she used to be.

Even though she cost him all he had to lose,
    Even though she made him sick to hear or see,
Still, what she left of him will mostly choose
    Her skirts to sit by. How comes such to be?

Parsons in pulpits, tax-payers in pews,
    Kings on your thrones, you know as well as me,
We've only one virginity to lose,
    And where we lost it there our hearts will be!

Tomlinson

1891

Now Tomlinson gave up the ghost at his house in Berkeley Square,
And a Spirit came to his bedside and gripped him by the hair –
A Spirit gripped him by the hair and carried him far away,
Till he heard as the roar of a rain-fed ford the roar of the Milky Way:
Till he heard the roar of the Milky Way die down and drone and cease,
And they came to the Gate within the Wall where Peter holds the keys.
'Stand up, stand up now, Tomlinson, and answer loud and high
'The good that ye did for the sake of men or ever ye came to die –
'The good that ye did for the sake of men on little Earth so lone!'
And the naked soul of Tomlinson grew white as a rain-washed bone.

'Oh I have a friend on Earth,' he said, 'that was my priest and guide,
'And well would he answer all for me if he were at my side.'
– 'For that ye strove in neighbour-love it shall be written fair,
'But now ye wait at Heaven's Gate and not in Berkeley Square:
'Though we called your friend from his bed this night, he could not
        speak for you,
'For the race is run by one and one and never by two and two.'
Then Tomlinson looked up and down, and little gain was there,
For the naked stars grinned overhead, and he saw that his soul was
        bare.
The Wind that blows between the Worlds, it cut him like a knife,
And Tomlinson took up the tale and spoke of his good in life.
'O this I have read in a book,' he said, 'and that was told to me,
'And this I have thought that another man thought of a Prince in
        Muscovy.'
The good souls flocked like homing doves and bade him clear the
        path,
And Peter twirled the jangling Keys in weariness and wrath.
'Ye have read, ye have heard, ye have thought,' he said, 'and the tale
        is yet to run:
'By the worth of the body that once ye had, give answer – what ha' ye
        done?'

143

Then Tomlinson looked back and forth, and little good it bore,
For the darkness stayed at his shoulder-blade and Heaven's Gate
    before: –
'O this I have felt, and this I have guessed, and this I have heard men
    say,
'And this they wrote that another man wrote of a carl in Norroway.'
'Ye have read, ye have felt, ye have guessed, good lack! Ye have
    hampered Heaven's Gate;
'There's little room between the stars in idleness to prate!
'For none may reach by hired speech of neighbour, priest, and kin
'Through borrowed deed to God's good meed that lies so fair within;
'Get hence, get hence to the Lord of Wrong, for the doom has yet to
    run,
'And . . . the faith that ye share with Berkeley Square uphold you,
    Tomlinson!'

   .   .   .   .

The Spirit gripped him by the hair, and sun by sun they fell
Till they came to the belt of Naughty Stars that rim the mouth of Hell.
The first are red with pride and wrath, the next are white with pain,
But the third are black with clinkered sin that cannot burn again.
They may hold their path, they may leave their path, with never a soul
    to mark:
They may burn or freeze, but they must not cease in the Scorn of the
    Outer Dark.
The Wind that blows between the Worlds, it nipped him to the bone,
And he yearned to the flare of Hell-gate there as the light of his own
    hearth-stone.
The Devil he sat behind the bars, where the desperate legions drew,
But he caught the hasting Tomlinson and would not let him through.
'Wot ye the price of good pit-coal that I must pay?' said he,
'That ye rank yoursel' so fit for Hell and ask no leave of me?
'I am all o'er-sib to Adam's breed that ye should give me scorn,
'For I strove with God for your First Father the day that he was born.
'Sit down, sit down upon the slag, and answer loud and high
'The harm that ye did to the Sons of Men or ever you came to die.'
And Tomlinson looked up and up, and saw against the night
The belly of a tortured star blood-red in Hell-Mouth light;

And Tomlinson looked down and down, and saw beneath his feet
The frontlet of a tortured star milk-white in Hell-Mouth heat.
'O I had a love on earth,' said he, 'that kissed me to my fall;
'And if ye would call my love to me I know she would answer all.'
– 'All that ye did in love forbid it shall be written fair,
'But now ye wait at Hell-Mouth Gate and not in Berkeley Square:
'Though we whistled your love from her bed to-night, I trow she
        would not run,
'For the sin ye do by two and two ye must pay for one by one!'
The Wind that blows between the Worlds, it cut him like a knife,
And Tomlinson took up the tale and spoke of his sins in life: –
'Once I ha' laughed at the power of Love and twice at the grip of the
        Grave,
'And thrice I ha' patted my God on the head that men might call me
        brave.'
The Devil he blew on a brandered soul and set it aside to cool: –
'Do ye think I would waste my good pit-coal on the hide of a brain-
        sick fool?
'I see no worth in the hobnailed mirth or the jolthead jest ye did
'That I should waken my gentlemen that are sleeping three on a grid.'
Then Tomlinson looked back and forth, and there was little grace,
For Hell-Gate filled the houseless soul with the Fear of Naked Space.
'Nay, this I ha' heard,' quo' Tomlinson, 'and this was noised abroad,
'And this I ha' got from a Belgian book on the word of a dead French
        lord.'
– 'Ye ha' heard, ye ha' read, ye ha' got, good lack! and the tale begins
        afresh –
'Have ye sinned one sin for the pride o' the eye or the sinful lust of the
        flesh?'
Then Tomlinson he gripped the bars and yammered, 'Let me in –
'For I mind that I borrowed my neighbour's wife to sin the deadly
        sin.'
The Devil he grinned behind the bars, and banked the fires high:
'Did ye read of that sin in a book?' said he; and Tomlinson said, 'Ay!'
The Devil he blew upon his nails, and the little devils ran,
And he said: 'Go husk this whimpering thief that comes in the guise
        of a man:

'Winnow him out 'twixt star and star, and sieve his proper worth:
'There's sore decline in Adam's line if this be spawn of Earth.'
Empusa's crew, so naked-new they may not face the fire,
But weep that they bin too small to sin to the height of their desire,
Over the coal they chased the Soul, and racked it all abroad;
As children rifle a caddis-case or the raven's foolish hoard.
And back they came with the tattered Thing, as children after play,
And they said: 'The soul that he got from God he has bartered clean
    away.
'We have threshed a stook of print and book, and winnowed a chattering
    wind,
'And many a soul wherefrom he stole, but his we cannot find.
'We have handled him, we have dandled him, we have seared him to
    the bone,
'And, Sire, if tooth and nail show truth he has no soul of his own.'
The Devil he bowed his head on his breast and rumbled deep and
    low: —
'I'm all o'er-sib to Adam's breed that I should bid him go.
'Yet close we lie, and deep we lie, and if I gave him place,
'My gentlemen that are so proud would flout me to my face;
'They'd call my house a common stews and me a careless host,
'And — I would not anger my gentlemen for the sake of a shiftless
    ghost.'
The Devil he looked at the mangled Soul that prayed to feel the flame,
And he thought of Holy Charity, but he thought of his own good
    name: —
'Now ye could haste my coal to waste, and sit ye down to fry.
'Did ye think of that theft for yourself?' said he; and Tomlinson said,
    'Ay!'
The Devil he blew an outward breath, for his heart was free from
    care: —
'Ye have scarce the soul of a louse,' he said, 'but the roots of sin are
    there,
'And for that sin should ye come in were I the lord alone,
'But sinful pride has rule inside — ay, mightier than my own.
'Honour and Wit, for-damned they sit, to each his Priest and
    Whore;
'Nay, scarce I dare myself go there, and you they'd torture sore.

'Ye are neither spirit nor spirk,' he said; 'ye are neither book nor
      brute –
'Go, get ye back to the flesh again for the sake of Man's repute.
'I'm all o'er-sib to Adam's breed that I should mock your pain,
'But look that ye win to worthier sin ere ye come back again.
'Get hence, the hearse is at your door – the grim black stallions wait –
'They bear your clay to place to-day. Speed, lest ye come too late!
'Go back to Earth with a lip unsealed – go back with an open eye,
'And carry my word to the Sons of Men or ever ye come to die:
'That the sin they do by two and two they must pay for one by one,
'And . . . the God that you took from a printed book be with you,
      Tomlinson!'

En-dor

1914–19–?

'Behold there is a woman that hath a familiar spirit at En-dor.'
1 Samuel xxviii 7

The road to En-dor is easy to tread
      For Mother or yearning Wife.
There, it is sure, we shall meet our Dead
      As they were even in life.
Earth has not dreamed of the blessing in store
For desolate hearts on the road to En-dor.

Whispers shall comfort us out of the dark –
      Hands – ah, God! – that we knew!
Visions and voices – look and hark! –
      Shall prove that the tale is true,
And that those who have passed to the further shore
May be hailed – at a price – on the road to En-dor.

But they are so deep in their new eclipse
      Nothing they say can reach
Unless it be uttered by alien lips
      And framed in a stranger's speech.

The son must send word to the mother that bore,
Through an hireling's mouth. 'Tis the rule of En-dor.

And not for nothing these gifts are shown
    By such as delight our Dead.
They must twitch and stiffen and slaver and groan
    Ere the eyes are set in the head,
And the voice from the belly begins. Therefore,
We pay them a wage where they ply at En-dor.

Even so, we have need of faith
    And patience to follow the clue.
Often, at first, what the dear one saith
    Is babble, or jest, or untrue.
(Lying spirits perplex us sore
Till our loves – and their lives – are well known at En-dor) . . .

Oh, the road to En-dor is the oldest road
    And the craziest road of all!
Straight it runs to the Witch's abode,
    As it did in the days of Saul,
And nothing has changed of the sorrow in store
For such as go down on the road to En-dor!

The Female of the Species

1911

When the Himalayan peasant meets the he-bear in his pride,
He shouts to scare the monster, who will often turn aside.
But the she-bear thus accosted rends the peasant tooth and nail.
For the female of the species is more deadly than the male.

When Nag the basking cobra hears the careless foot of man,
He will sometimes wriggle sideways and avoid it if he can.
But his mate makes no such motion where she camps beside the trail.
For the female of the species is more deadly than the male.

When the early Jesuit fathers preached to Hurons and Choctaws,
They prayed to be delivered from the vengeance of the squaws.
'Twas the women, not the warriors, turned those stark enthusiasts
    pale.
For the female of the species is more deadly than the male.

Man's timid heart is bursting with the things he must not say,
For the Woman that God gave him isn't his to give away;
But when hunter meets with husband, each confirms the other's tale –
The female of the species is more deadly than the male.

Man, a bear in most relations – worm and savage otherwise, –
Man propounds negotiations, Man accepts the compromise.
Very rarely will he squarely push the logic of a fact
To its ultimate conclusion in unmitigated act.

Fear, or foolishness, impels him, ere he lay the wicked low,
To concede some form of trial even to his fiercest foe.
Mirth obscene diverts his anger – Doubt and Pity oft perplex
Him in dealing with an issue – to the scandal of The Sex!

But the Woman that God gave him, every fibre of her frame
Proves her launched for one sole issue, armed and engined for the
    same;
And to serve that single issue, lest the generations fail,
The female of the species must be deadlier than the male.

She who faces Death by torture for each life beneath her breast
May not deal in doubt or pity – must not swerve for fact or jest.
These be purely male diversions – not in these her honour dwells.
She the Other Law we live by, is that Law and nothing else.

She can bring no more to living than the powers that make her great
As the Mother of the Infant and the Mistress of the Mate.
And when Babe and Man are lacking and she strides unclaimed to
    claim
Her right as femme (and baron), her equipment is the same.

She is wedded to convictions – in default of grosser ties;
Her contentions are her children, Heaven help him who denies! –
He will meet no suave discussion, but the instant, white-hot, wild,
Wakened female of the species warring as for spouse and child.

Unprovoked and awful charges – even so the she-bear fights,
Speech that drips, corrodes, and poisons – even so the cobra bites,
Scientific vivisection of one nerve till it is raw
And the victim writhes in anguish – like the Jesuit with the squaw!

So it comes that Man, the coward, when he gathers to confer
With his fellow-braves in council, dare not leave a place for her
Where, at war with Life and Conscience, he uplifts his erring hands
To some God of Abstract Justice – which no woman understands.

And Man knows it! Knows, moreover, that the Woman that God gave
    him
Must command but may not govern – shall enthral but not enslave
    him.
And *She* knows, because She warns him, and Her instincts never fail,
That the Female of Her Species is more deadly than the Male.

The Explanation

1890

Love and Death once ceased their strife
At the Tavern of Man's Life.
Called for wine, and threw – alas! –
Each his quiver on the grass.
When the bout was o'er they found
Mingled arrows strewed the ground.
Hastily they gathered then
Each the loves and lives of men.
Ah, the fateful dawn deceived!
Mingled arrows each one sheaved.

Death's dread armoury was stored
With the shafts he most abhorred;
Love's light quiver groaned beneath
Venom-headed darts of Death.
Thus it was they wrought our woe
At the Tavern long ago.
Tell me, do our masters know,
Loosing blindly as they fly,
Old men love while young men die?

The Gift of the Sea

1890

The dead child lay in the shroud,
    And the widow watched beside;
And her mother slept, and the Channel swept
    The gale in the teeth of the tide.

But the mother laughed at all.
    'I have lost my man in the sea,
'And the child is dead. Be still,' she said,
    'What more can ye do to me?'

The widow watched the dead,
    And the candle guttered low,
And she tried to sing the Passing Song
    That bids the poor soul go.

And 'Mary take you now,' she sang,
    'That lay against my heart.'
And 'Mary smooth your crib to-night,'
    But she could not say 'Depart.'

Then came a cry from the sea,
    But the sea-rime blinded the glass,
And 'Heard ye nothing, mother?' she said,
    ''Tis the child that waits to pass.'

And the nodding mother sighed:
    ''Tis a lambing ewe in the whin,
'For why should the christened soul cry out
    'That never knew of sin?'

'Oh feet I have held in my hand,
    'O hands at my heart to catch,
'How should they know the road to go,
    'And how should they lift the latch?'

They laid a sheet to the door,
    With the little quilt atop,
That it might not hurt from the cold or the dirt,
    But the crying would not stop.

The widow lifted the latch
    And strained her eyes to see,
And opened the door on the bitter shore
    To let the soul go free.

There was neither glimmer nor ghost,
    There was neither spirit nor spark,
And 'Heard ye nothing, mother?' she said,
    ''Tis crying for me in the dark.'

And the nodding mother sighed:
    ''Tis sorrow makes ye dull;
'Have ye yet to learn the cry of the tern,
    'Or the wail of the wind-blown gull?'

'The terns are blown inland,
    'The grey gull follows the plough.
''Twas never a bird, the voice I heard,
    'Oh mother, I hear it now!'

'Lie still, dear lamb, lie still;
    'The child is passed from harm,
''Tis the ache in your breast that broke your rest,
    'And the feel of an empty arm.'

She put her mother aside,
  'In Mary's name let be!
'For the peace of my soul I must go,' she said,
  And she went to the calling sea.

In the heel of the wind-bit pier,
  Where the twisted weed was piled,
She came to the life she had missed by an hour,
  For she came to a little child.

She laid it into her breast,
  And back to her mother she came,
But it would not feed and it would not heed,
  Though she gave it her own child's name.

And the dead child dripped on her breast,
  And her own in the shroud lay stark;
And 'God forgive us, mother,' she said,
  'We let it die in the dark!'

The King
1894

'Farewell, Romance!' the Cave-men said;
  'With bone well carved He went away.
'Flint arms the ignoble arrowhead,
  'And jasper tips the spear to-day.
'Changed are the Gods of Hunt and Dance,
'And He with these. Farewell, Romance!'

'Farewell, Romance!' the Lake-folk sighed;
  'We lift the weight of flatling years;
'The caverns of the mountain-side
  'Hold Him who scorns our hutted piers.
'Lost hills whereby we dare not dwell,
'Guard ye His rest. Romance, Farewell!'

'Farewell, Romance!' the Soldier spoke;
    'By sleight of sword we may not win,
'But scuffle 'mid uncleanly smoke
    'Of arquebus and culverin.
'Honour is lost, and none may tell
'Who paid good blows. Romance, farewell!'

'Farewell, Romance!' the Traders cried;
    'Our keels have lain with every sea.
'The dull-returning wind and tide
    'Heave up the wharf where we would be;
'The known and noted breezes swell
'Our trudging sails. Romance, farewell!'

'Good-bye, Romance!' the Skipper said;
    'He vanished with the coal we burn.
'Our dial marks full-steam ahead,
    'Our speed is timed to half a turn.
'Sure as the ferried barge we ply
''Twixt port and port. Romance, good-bye!'

'Romance!' the season-tickets mourn,
    '*He* never ran to catch His train,
'But passed with coach and guard and horn –
    'And left the local – late again!
'Confound Romance!' . . . And all unseen
Romance brought up the nine-fifteen.

His hand was on the lever laid,
    His oil-can soothed the worrying cranks,
His whistle waked the snowbound grade,
    His fog-horn cut the reeking Banks;
By dock and deep and mind and mill
The Boy-god reckless laboured still!

Robed, crowned and throned, He wove His spell,
   Where heart-blood beat or hearth-smoke curled,
With unconsidered miracle,
   Hedged in a backward-gazing world:
Then taught His chosen bard to say:
'Our King was with us – yesterday!'

The Last Rhyme of True Thomas

1893

The King has called for priest and cup,
   The King has taken spur and blade
To dub True Thomas a belted knight,
   And all for the sake of the songs he made.

They have sought him high, they have sought him low,
   They have sought him over down and lea.
They have found him by the milk-white thorn
   That guards the Gates of Faerie.

'Twas bent beneath and blue above:
   Their eyes were held that they might not see
The kine that grazed beneath the knowes,
   Oh, they were the Queens of Faerie!

'Now cease your song,' the King he said,
   'Oh, cease your song and get you dight
'To vow your vow and watch your arms,
   'For I will dub you a belted knight.

'For I will give you a horse o' pride,
   'Wi' blazon and spur and page and squire;
'Wi' keep and tail and seizin and law,
   'And land to hold at your desire.'

True Thomas smiled above his harp,
  And turned his face to the naked sky,
Where, blown before the wastrel wind,
  The thistle-down she floated by.

'I ha' vowed my vow in another place,
  'And bitter oath it was on me.
'I ha' watched my arms the lee-long night,
  'Where five-score fighting men would flee.

'My lance is tipped o' the hammered flame,
  'My shield is beat o' the moonlight cold;
'And I won my spurs in the Middle World,
  'A thousand fathom beneath the mould.

'And what should I make wi' a horse o' pride,
  'And what should I make wi' a sword so brown,
'But spill the rings of the Gentle Folk
  'And flyte my kin in the Fairy Town?

'And what should I make wi' blazon and belt,
  'Wi' keep and tail and seizin and fee,
'And what should I do wi' page and squire
  'That am a king in my own countrie?

'For I send east and I send west,
  'And I send far as my will may flee,
'By dawn and dusk and the drinking rain,
  'And syne my Sendings return to me.

'They come wi' news of the groanin' earth,
  'They come wi' news of the roarin' sea.
'Wi' word of Spirit and Ghost and Flesh,
  'And man, that's mazed among the three.'

The King he bit his nether lip,
  And smote his hand upon his knee:
'By the faith of my soul, True Thomas,' he said,
  'Ye waste no wit in courtesie!

'As I desire, unto my pride,
  'Can I make Earls by three and three,
'To run before and ride behind
  'And serve the sons o' my body.'

'And what care I for your row-foot earls,
  'Or all the sons o' your body?
'Before they win to the Pride o' Name,
  'I trow they all ask leave o' me.

'For I make Honour wi' muckle mouth,
  'As I make Shame wi' mincing feet,
'To sing wi' the priests at the market-cross,
  'Or run wi' the dogs in the naked street.

'And some they give me the good red gold,
  'And some they give me the white money,
'And some they give me a clout o' meal,
  'For they be people of low degree.

'And the song I sing for the counted gold
  'The same I sing for the white money,
'But best I sing for the clout o' meal
  'That simple people give me.'

The King cast down a silver groat,
  A silver groat o' Scots money,
'If I come wi' a poor man's dole,' he said,
  'True Thomas, will ye harp to me?'

'Whenas I harp to the children small,
  'They press me close on either hand.
'And who are you,' True Thomas said,
  'That you should ride while they must stand?

'Light down, light down from your horse o' pride,
  'I trow ye talk too loud and hie,
'And I will make you a triple word,
  'And syne, if ye dare, ye shall 'noble me.'

He has lighted down from his horse o' pride,
    And set his back against a stone.
'Now guard you well,' True Thomas said,
    'Ere I rax your heart from your breast-bone!'

True Thomas played upon his harp,
    The fairy harp that couldna lee,
And the first least word the proud King heard,
    It harpit the salt tear out o' his e'e.

'Oh, I see the love that I lost long syne,
    'I touch the hope that I may not see,
'And all that I did of hidden shame,
    'Like little snakes they hiss at me.

'The sun is lost at noon – at noon!
    'The dread of doom has grippit me.
'True Thomas, hide me under your cloak,
    'God wot, I'm little fit to dee!'

'Twas bent beneath and blue above –
    'Twas open field and running flood –
Where, hot on heath and dyke and wall,
    The high sun warmed the adder's brood.

'Lie down, lie down,' True Thomas said.
    'The God shall judge when all is done,
'But I will bring you a better word
    'And lift the cloud that I laid on.'

True Thomas played upon his harp,
    That birled and brattled to his hand,
And the next least word True Thomas made,
    It garred the King take horse and brand.

'Oh, I hear the tread o' the fighting-men,
    'I see the sun on splent and spear.
'I mark the arrow outen the fern
    'That flies so low and sings so clear!

'Advance my standards to that war,
   'And bid my good knights prick and ride;
'The gled shall watch as fierce a fight
   'As e'er was fought on the Border-side!'

'Twas bent beneath and blue above,
   'Twas nodding grass and naked sky,
Where, ringing up the wastrel wind,
   The eyass stooped upon the pye.

True Thomas sighed above his harp,
   And turned the song on the midmost string;
And the last least word True Thomas made,
   He harpit his dead youth back to the King.

'Now I am prince, and I do well
   'To love my love withouten fear;
'To walk with man in fellowship,
   'And breathe my horse behind the deer.

'My hounds they bay unto the death,
   'The buck has couched beyond the burn,
'My love she waits at her window
   'To wash my hands when I return.

'For that I live am I content
   '(Oh! I have seen my true love's eyes)
'To stand with Adam in Eden-glade,
   'And run in the woods o' Paradise!'

'Twas naked sky and nodding grass,
   'Twas running flood and wastrel wind,
Where, checked against the open pass,
   The red deer turned to wait the hind.

True Thomas laid his harp away,
   And louted low at the saddle-side;
He has taken stirrup and hauden rein,
   And set the King on his horse o' pride.

'Sleep ye or wake,' True Thomas said,
  'That sit so still, that muse so long?
'Sleep ye or wake? – till the Latter Sleep
  'I trow ye'll not forget my song.

'I ha' harpit a Shadow out o' the sun
  'To stand before your face and cry;
'I ha' armed the earth beneath your heel,
  'And over your head I ha' dusked the sky.

'I ha' harpit ye up to the Throne o' God,
  'I ha' harpit your midmost soul in three.
'I ha' harpit ye down to the Hinges o' Hell,
  'And – ye – would – make – a Knight o' me!'

The Sons of Martha

1907

The Sons of Mary seldom bother, for they have inherited that good part;
But the Sons of Martha favour their Mother of the careful soul and the
    troubled heart.
And because she lost her temper once, and because she was rude to the
    Lord her Guest,
Her Sons must wait upon Mary's Sons, world without end, reprieve, or
    rest.

It is their care in all the ages to take the buffet and cushion the shock.
It is their care that the gear engages; it is their care that the switches lock.
It is their care that the wheels run truly; it is their care to embark and
    entrain,
Tally, transport, and deliver duly the Sons of Mary by land and main.

They say to mountains, 'Be ye removèd.' They say to the lesser floods,
    'Be dry.'
Under their rods are the rocks reprovèd – they are not afraid of that
    which is high.

Then do the hill-tops shake to the summit – then is the bed of the
    deep laid bare,
That the Sons of Mary may overcome it, pleasantly sleeping and
    unaware.

They finger death at their gloves' end where they piece and repiece the
    living wires.
He rears against the gates they tend: they feed him hungry behind
    their fires.
Early at dawn, ere men see clear, they stumble into his terrible
    stall,
And hale him forth like a haltered steer, and goad and turn him till
    evenfall.

To these from birth is Belief forbidden; from these till death is Relief
    afar.
They are concerned with matters hidden – under the earth-line their
    altars are –
The secret fountains to follow up, waters withdrawn to restore to the
    mouth,
And gather the floods as in a cup, and pour them again at a city's
    drouth.

They do not preach that their God will rouse them a little before the
    nuts work loose.
They do not teach that His Pity allows them to drop their job when
    they dam'-well choose.
As in the thronged and the lighted ways, so in the dark and the desert
    they stand,
Wary and watchful all their days that their brethren's days may be long
    in the land.

Raise ye the stone or cleave the wood to make a path more fair or flat –
Lo, it is black already with blood some Son of Martha spilled for that!
Not as a ladder from earth to Heaven, not as a witness to any creed,
But simple service simply given to his own kind in their common need.

And the Sons of Mary smile and are blessèd – they know the Angels
are on their side.
They know in them is the Grace confessed, and for them are the
Mercies multiplied.
They sit at the Feet – they hear the Word – they see how truly the
Promise runs.
They have cast their burden upon the Lord, and – the Lord He lays it
on Martha's Sons!

Epitaphs of the War

1914–18

'EQUALITY OF SACRIFICE'

A. 'I was a Have.' B. 'I was a "have–not".'
(*Together*.) 'What hast thou given which I gave not?'

A SERVANT

We were together since the War began.
He was my servant – and the better man.

A SON

My son was killed while laughing at some jest. I would I knew
What it was, and it might serve me in a time when jests are few.

AN ONLY SON

I have slain none except my Mother. She
(Blessing her slayer) died of grief for me.

EX-CLERK

Pity not! The Army gave
Freedom to a timid slave:

In which Freedom did he find
Strength of body, will, and mind:
By which strength he came to prove
Mirth, Companionship, and Love:
For which Love to Death he went:
In which Death he lies content.

THE WONDER

Body and Spirit I surrendered whole
To harsh Instructors – and received a soul . . .
If mortal man could change me through and through
From all I was – what may The God not do?

HINDU SEPOY IN FRANCE

This man in his own country prayed we know not to what Powers.
We pray Them to reward him for his bravery in ours.

THE COWARD

I could not look on Death, which being known,
Men led me to him, blindfold and alone.

SHOCK

My name, my speech, my self I had forgot.
My wife and children came – I knew them not.
I died. My Mother followed. At her call
And on her bosom I remembered all.

A GRAVE NEAR CAIRO

Gods of the Nile, should this stout fellow here
Get out – get out! He knows not shame nor fear.

PELICANS IN THE WILDERNESS
A Grave near Halfa

The blown sand heaps on me, that none may learn
    Where I am laid for whom my children grieve . . .
O wings that beat at dawning, ye return
    Out of the desert to your young at eve!

TWO CANADIAN MEMORIALS
I

We giving all gained all.
    Neither lament us nor praise.
Only in all things recall,
    It is Fear, not Death that slays.

II

From little towns in a far land we came,
    To save our honour and a world aflame.
By little towns in a far land we sleep;
    And trust that world we won for you to keep!

THE FAVOUR

Death favoured me from the first, well knowing I could not endure
    To wait on him day by day. He quitted my betters and came
Whistling over the fields, and, when he had made all sure,
    'Thy line is at end,' he said, 'but at least I have saved its name.'

THE BEGINNER

On the first hour of my first day
    In the front trench I fell.
(Children in boxes at a play
    Stand up to watch it well.)

R.A.F. (AGED EIGHTEEN)

Laughing through clouds, his milk-teeth still unshed,
Cities and men he smote from overhead.
His deaths delivered, he returned to play
Childlike, with childish things now put away.

THE REFINED MAN

I was of delicate mind. I stepped aside for my needs,
  Disdaining the common office. I was seen from afar and killed . . .
How is this matter for mirth? Let each man be judged by his deeds.
  I have paid my price to live with myself on the terms that I willed.

NATIVE WATER-CARRIER (M.E.F.)

Prometheus brought down fire to men.
  This brought up water.
The Gods are jealous – now, as then,
  Giving no quarter.

BOMBED IN LONDON

On land and sea I strove with anxious care
To escape conscription. It was in the air!

THE SLEEPY SENTINEL

Faithless the watch that I kept: now I have none to keep.
I was slain because I slept: now I am slain I sleep.
Let no man reproach me again, whatever watch is unkept –
I sleep because I am slain. They slew me because I slept.

BATTERIES OUT OF AMMUNITION

If any mourn us in the workshop, say
We died because the shift kept holiday.

COMMON FORM

If any question why we died,
Tell them, because our fathers lied.

A DEAD STATESMAN

I could not dig: I dared not rob:
Therefore I lied to please the mob.
Now all my lies are proved untrue
And I must face the men I slew.
What tale shall serve me here among
Mine angry and defrauded young?

THE REBEL

If I had clamoured at Thy Gate
  For gift of Life on Earth,
And, thrusting through the souls that wait,
  Flung headlong into birth –
Even then, even then, for gin and snare
  About my pathway spread,
Lord, I had mocked Thy thoughtful care
  Before I joined the Dead!
But now? . . . I was beneath Thy Hand
  Ere yet the Planets came.
And now – though Planets pass, I stand
  The witness to Thy shame!

THE OBEDIENT

Daily, though no ears attended,
  Did my prayers arise.
Daily, though no fire descended,
  Did I sacrifice.
Though my darkness did not lift,
  Though I faced no lighter odds,
Though the Gods bestowed no gift,

None the less,
None the less, I served the Gods!

A DRIFTER OFF TARENTUM

He from the wind-bitten North with ship and companions descended,
    Searching for eggs of death spawned by invisible hulls.
Many he found and drew forth. Of a sudden the fishery ended
    In flame and a clamorous breath known to the eye-pecking gulls.

DESTROYERS IN COLLISION

For Fog and Fate no charm is found
    To lighten or amend.
I, hurrying to my bride, was drowned –
    Cut down by my best friend.

CONVOY ESCORT

I was a shepherd to fools
    Causelessly bold or afraid.
They would not abide by my rules.
    Yet they escaped. For I stayed.

UNKNOWN FEMALE CORPSE

Headless, lacking foot and hand,
Horrible I come to land.
I beseech all women's sons
Know I was a mother once.

RAPED AND REVENGED

One used and butchered me: another spied
Me broken – for which thing an hundred died.
So it was learned among the heathen hosts
How much a freeborn woman's favour costs.

SALONIKAN GRAVE

I have watched a thousand days
Push out and crawl into night
Slowly as tortoises.
Now I, too, follow these.
It is fever, and not the fight –
Time, not battle, – that slays.

THE BRIDEGROOM

Call me not false, beloved,
    If, from thy scarce-known breast
So little time removed,
    In other arms I rest.

For this more ancient bride,
    Whom coldly I embrace,
Was constant at my side
    Before I saw thy face.

Our marriage, often set –
    By miracle delayed –
At last is consummate,
    And cannot be unmade.

Live, then, whom Life shall cure,
    Almost, of Memory,
And leave us to endure
    Its immortality.

V.A.D. (MEDITERRANEAN)

Ah, would swift ships had never been, for then we ne'er had found,
These harsh Ægean rocks between, this little virgin drowned,
Whom neither spouse nor child shall mourn, but men she nursed
    through pain
And – certain keels for whose return the heathen look in vain.

ACTORS

On a Memorial Tablet in Holy Trinity Church,
Stratford-on-Avon

We counterfeited once for your disport
    Men's joy and sorrow: but our day has passed.
We pray you pardon all where we fell short –
    Seeing we were your servants to this last.

JOURNALISTS

On a Panel in the Hall of the Institute of Journalists
We have served our day.

Danny Deever

'What are the bugles blowin' for?' said Files-on-Parade.
'To turn you out, to turn you out,' the Colour-Sergeant said.
'What makes you look so white, so white?' said Files-on-Parade.
'I'm dreadin' what I've got to watch,' the Colour-Sergeant said.
    For they're hangin' Danny Deever, you can hear the Dead March
        play,
    The Regiment's in 'ollow square – they're hangin' him to-day;
    They've taken of his buttons off an' cut his stripes away,
    An' they're hangin' Danny Deever in the mornin'.

'What makes the rear-rank breathe so 'ard?' said Files-on-Parade.
'It's bitter cold, it's bitter cold,' the Colour-Sergeant said.
'What makes that front-rank man fall down?' said Files-on-Parade.
'A touch o' sun, a touch o' sun,' the Colour-Sergeant said.
    They are hangin' Danny Deever, they are marchin' of 'im round,
    They 'ave 'alted Danny Deever by 'is coffin on the ground;
    An' 'e'll swing in 'arf a minute for a sneakin' shootin' hound –
    O they're hangin' Danny Deever in the mornin'!

DANNY DEEVER

''Is cot was right-'and cot to mine,' said Files-on-Parade.
''E's sleepin' out an' far to-night,' the Colour-Sergeant said.
'I've drunk 'is beer a score o' times,' said Files-on-Parade.
''E's drinkin' bitter beer alone,' the Colour-Sergeant said.
   They are hangin' Danny Deever, you must mark 'im to 'is place,
   For 'e shot a comrade sleepin' – you must look 'im in the face;
   Nine 'undred of 'is county an' the Regiment's disgrace,
   While they're hangin' Danny Deever in the mornin'.

'What's that so black agin the sun?' said Files-on-Parade.
'It's Danny fightin' 'ard for life,' the Colour-Sergeant said.
'What's that that whimpers over'ead?' said Files-on-Parade.
'It's Danny's soul that's passin' now,' the Colour-Sergeant said.
   For they're done with Danny Deever, you can 'ear the quickstep
      play,
   The Regiment's in column, an' they're marchin' us away;
   Ho! the young recruits are shakin', an' they'll want their beer to-day,
   After hangin' Danny Deever in the mornin'!

Tommy

I went into a public-'ouse to get a pint o' beer,
The publican 'e up an' sez, 'We serve no red-coats here.'
The girls be'ind the bar they laughed an' giggled fit to die,
I outs into the street again an' to myself sez I:
   O it's Tommy this, an' Tommy that, an' 'Tommy, go away';
   But it's 'Thank you, Mister Atkins,' when the band begins to play –
   The band begins to play, my boys, the band begins to play,
   O it's 'Thank you, Mister Atkins,' when the band begins to play.

I went into a theatre as sober as could be,
They gave a drunk civilian room, but 'adn't none for me;
They sent me to the gallery or round the music-'alls,
But when it comes to fightin', Lord! they'll shove me in the stalls!

For it's Tommy this, an' Tommy that, an' 'Tommy, wait outside';
But it's 'Special train for Atkins' when the trooper's on the tide –
The troopship's on the tide, my boys, the troopship's on the tide,
O it's 'Special train for Atkins' when the trooper's on the tide.

Yes, makin' mock o' uniforms that guard you while you sleep
Is cheaper than them uniforms, an' they're starvation cheap;
An' hustlin' drunken soldiers when they're goin' large a bit
Is five times better business than paradin' in full kit.
    Then it's Tommy this, an' Tommy that, an' 'Tommy, 'ow's yer
        soul?'
    But it's 'Thin red line of 'eroes' when the drums begin to roll –
    The drums begin to roll, my boys, the drums begin to roll,
    O it's 'Thin red line of 'eroes' when the drums begin to roll.

We aren't no thin red 'eroes, nor we aren't no blackguards too,
But single men in barricks, most remarkable like you;
An' if sometimes our conduck isn't all your fancy paints,
Why, single men in barricks don't grow into plaster saints;
    While it's Tommy this, an' Tommy that, an' 'Tommy, fall be'ind,'
    But it's 'Please to walk in front, sir,' when there's trouble in the
        wind –
    O it's 'Please to walk in front, sir,' when there's trouble in the wind.

You talk o' better food for us, an' schools, an' fires, an' all:
We'll wait for extry rations if you treat us rational.
Don't mess about the cook-room slops, but prove it to our face
The Widow's Uniform is not the soldier-man's disgrace.
    For it's Tommy this, an' Tommy that, an' 'Chuck him out, the
        brute!'
    But it's 'Saviour of 'is country' when the guns begin to shoot;
    An' it's Tommy this, an' Tommy that, an' anything you please;
    An' Tommy ain't a bloomin' fool – you bet that Tommy sees!

'Fuzzy-Wuzzy'

(*Soudan Expeditionary Force. Early Campaigns*)

We've fought with many men acrost the seas,
    An' some of 'em was brave an' some was not:
The Paythan an' the Zulu an' Burmese;
    But the Fuzzy was the finest o' the lot.
We never got a ha'porth's change of 'im:
    'E squatted in the scrub an' 'ocked our 'orses,
'E cut our sentries up at Sua*kim*,
    An' 'e played the cat an' banjo with our forces.
        So 'ere's *to* you, Fuzzy-Wuzzy, at your 'ome in the Soudan;
        You're a pore benighted 'eathen but a first-class fightin' man;
        We gives you your certificate, an' if you want it signed
        We'll come an' 'ave a romp with you whenever you're inclined.

We took our chanst among the Kyber 'ills,
    The Boers knocked us silly at a mile,
The Burman give us Irriwaddy chills,
    An' a Zulu *impi* dished us up in style:
But all we ever got from such as they
    Was pop to what the Fuzzy made us swaller;
We 'eld our bloomin' own, the papers say,
    But man for man the Fuzzy knocked us 'oller.
        Then 'ere's *to* you, Fuzzy-Wuzzy, an' the missis and the kid;
        Our orders was to break you, an' of course we went an' did.
        We sloshed you with Martinis, an' it wasn't 'ardly fair;
        But for all the odds agin' you, Fuzzy-Wuz, you broke the square.

'E 'asn't got no papers of 'is own.
    'E 'asn't got no medals nor rewards,
So *we* must certify the skill 'e's shown
    In usin' of 'is long two-'anded swords:
When 'e's 'oppin' in an' out among the bush
    With 'is coffin-'eaded shield an' shovel-spear,
An 'appy day with Fuzzy on the rush
    Will last an 'ealthy Tommy for a year.

So 'ere's *to* you, Fuzzy-Wuzzy, an' your friends which are no more,
If we 'adn't lost some messmates we would 'elp you to deplore.
But give an' take's the gospel, an' we'll call the bargain fair,
For if you 'ave lost more than us, you crumpled up the square!

'E rushes at the smoke when we let drive,
  An', before we know, 'e's 'ackin' at our 'ead;
'E's all 'ot sand an' ginger when alive,
  An' 'e's generally shammin' when 'e's dead.
'E's a daisy, 'e's a ducky, 'e's a lamb!
  'E's a injia-rubber idiot on the spree,
'E's the on'y thing that doesn't give a damn
  For a Regiment o' British Infantree!
    So 'ere's *to* you, Fuzzy-Wuzzy, at your 'ome in the Soudan;
    You're a pore benighted 'eathen but a first-class fightin' man;
    An' 'ere's *to* you, Fuzzy-Wuzzy, with your 'ayrick 'ead of 'air –
    You big black boundin' beggar – for you broke a British square!

Soldier, Soldier

'Soldier, soldier come from the wars,
'Why don't you march with my true love?'
'We're fresh from off the ship an' 'e's, maybe, give the slip,
'An' you'd best go look for a new love.'

    New love! True love!
    Best go look for a new love,
    The dead they cannot rise, an' you'd better dry your eyes,
    An' you'd best go look for a new love.

'Soldier, soldier come from the wars,
'What did you see o' my true love?'
'I seen 'im serve the Queen in a suit o' rifle-green,
'An' you'd best go look for a new love.'

173

'Soldier, soldier come from the wars,
'Did ye see no more o' my true love?'
'I seen 'im runnin' by when the shots begun to fly –
'But you'd best go look for a new love.'

'Soldier, soldier come from the wars,
'Did aught take 'arm to my true love?'
'I couldn't see the fight, for the smoke it lay so white –
'And you'd best go look for a new love.'

'Soldier, soldier come from the wars,
'I'll up an' tend to my true love!'
''E's lying on the dead with a bullet through 'is 'ead,
'An' you'd best go look for a new love.'

'Soldier, soldier come from the wars,
'I'll down an' die with my true love!'
'The pit we dug'll 'ide 'im an' the twenty more beside 'im –
'An' you'd best go look for a new love.'

'Soldier, soldier come from the wars,
'Do you bring no sign from my true love?'
'I bring a lock of 'air that 'e allus used to wear,
'An' you'd best go look for a new love.'

'Soldier, soldier come from the wars,
'O then I know it's true I've lost my true love!'
'An' I tell you truth again – when you've lost the feel o' pain
'You'd best take me for your new love.'

       True love! New love!
       Best take 'im for a new love,
       The dead they cannot rise, an' you'd better dry your eyes
       An' you'd best take 'im for your new love.

Screw-Guns

Smokin' my pipe on the mountings, sniffin' the mornin'-cool,
I walks in my old brown gaiters along o' my old brown mule,
With seventy gunners be'ind me, an' never a beggar forgets
It's only the pick of the Army that handles the dear little pets –
　　　'Tss! 'Tss!
　　　For you all love the screw-guns – the screw-guns they all love
　　　　　you!
　　　So when we call round with a few guns, o' course you will know
　　　　　what to do – hoo! hoo!
　　　Jest send in your Chief an' surrender – it's worse if you fights or
　　　　　you runs:
　　　You can go where you please, you can skid up the trees, but you
　　　　　don't get away from the guns!

They sends us along where the roads are, but mostly we goes where
　　　they ain't.
We'd climb up the side of a sign-board an' trust to the stick o' the
　　　paint:
We've chivied the Naga an' Looshai; we've give the Afreedeeman fits;
For we fancies ourselves at two thousand, we guns that are built in two
　　　bits – 'Tss! 'Tss!
　　　For you all love the screw-guns . . .

If a man doesn't work, why, we drills 'im an' teaches 'im 'ow to
　　　behave.
If a beggar can't march, why, we kills 'im an' rattles 'im into 'is grave.
You've got to stand up to our business an' spring without snatchin' or
　　　fuss.
D'you say that you sweat with the field-guns? By God, you must lather
　　　with us – 'Tss! 'Tss!
　　　For you all love the screw-guns . . .

The eagles is screamin' around us, the river's a-moanin' below,
We're clear o' the pine an' the oak-scrub, we're out on the rocks an'
　　　the snow,

175

An' the wind is as thin as a whip-lash what carries away to the plains
The rattle an' stamp o' the lead-mules – the jinglety-jink o' the chains
      – 'Tss! 'Tss!
    For you all love the screw-guns . . .

There's a wheel on the Horns o' the Mornin', an' a wheel on the edge
        o' the Pit,
An' a drop into nothin' beneath you as straight as a beggar can spit:
With the sweat runnin' out o' your shirt-sleeves, an' the sun off the
        snow in your face,
An' 'arf o' the men on the drag-ropes to hold the old gun in 'er place –
      'Tss! 'Tss!
    For you all love the screw-guns . . .

Smokin' my pipe on the mountings, sniffin' the mornin'-cool,
I climbs in my old brown gaiters along o' my old brown mule.
The monkey can say what our road was – the wild-goat 'e knows where
        we passed.
Stand easy, you long-eared old darlin's! Out drag-ropes! With shrapnel!
        Hold fast – 'Tss! 'Tss!
    For you all love the screw-guns – the screw-guns they all love you!
    So when we take tea with a few guns, o' course you will know what to
        do – hoo! hoo!
    Jest send in your Chief an' surrender – it's worse if you fights or
        you runs:
    You may hide in the caves, they'll be only your graves, but you
        can't get away from the guns!

Gunga Din

You may talk o' gin and beer
When you're quartered safe out 'ere,
An' you're sent to penny-fights an' Aldershot it;
But when it comes to slaughter
You will do your work on water,
An' you'll lick the bloomin' boots of 'im that's got it.

Now in Injia's sunny clime,
Where I used to spend my time
A-servin' of 'Er Majesty the Queen,
Of all them blackfaced crew
The finest man I knew
Was our regimental bhisti, Gunga Din.
        He was 'Din! Din! Din!
  'You limpin' lump o' brick-dust, Gunga Din!
      'Hi! Slippy *hitherao!*
      'Water, get it! *Panee lao,*[1]
  'You squidgy-nosed old idol, Gunga Din.'

The uniform 'e wore
Was nothin' much before,
An' rather less than 'arf o' that be'ind,
For a piece o' twisty rag
An' a goatskin water-bag
Was all the field-equipment 'e could find.
When the sweatin' troop-train lay
In a sidin' through the day,
Where the 'eat would make your bloomin' eyebrows crawl,
We shouted 'Harry By!'[2]
Till our throats were bricky-dry,
Then we wopped 'im 'cause 'e couldn't serve us all.
        It was 'Din! Din! Din!
  'You 'eathen, where the mischief 'ave you been?
      'You put some *juldee*[3] in it
      'Or I'll *marrow*[4] you this minute
  'If you don't fill up my helmet, Gunga Din!'

'E would dot an' carry one
Till the longest day was done;
An' 'e didn't seem to know the use o' fear.
If we charged or broke or cut,
You could bet your bloomin' nut,
'E'd be waitin' fifty paces right flank rear.

    1. Bring water swiftly.   2. O brother   3. Be quick.   4. Hit you.

With 'is mussick[1] on 'is back,
'E would skip with our attack,
An' watch us till the bugles made 'Retire',
An' for all 'is dirty 'ide
'E was white, clear white, inside
When 'e went to tend the wounded under fire!
      It was 'Din! Din! Din!'
  With the bullets kickin' dust-spots on the green.
     When the cartridges ran out,
     You could hear the front-ranks shout,
  'Hi! ammunition-mules an' Gunga Din!'

I shan't forgit the night
When I dropped be'ind the fight
With a bullet where my belt-plate should 'a' been.
I was chokin' mad with thirst,
An' the man that spied me first
Was our good old grinnin', gruntin' Gunga Din.
'E lifted up my 'ead,
An' he plugged me where I bled,
An' 'e guv me 'arf-a-pint o' water green.
It was crawlin' and it stunk,
But of all the drinks I've drunk,
I'm gratefullest to one from Gunga Din.
      It was 'Din! Din! Din!
  ''Ere's a beggar with a bullet through 'is spleen;
     ''E's chawin' up the ground.
     'An' 'e's kickin' all around:
  'For Gawd's sake git the water, Gunga Din!'

'E carried me away
To where a dooli lay,
An' a bullet come an' drilled the beggar clean.
'E put me safe inside,
An' just before 'e died,
'I 'ope you liked your drink,' sez Gunga Din.

1. Water-skin.

178

So I'll meet 'im later on
At the place where 'e is gone –
Where it's always double drill and no canteen.
'E'll be squattin' on the coals
Givin' drink to poor damned souls,
An' I'll get a swig in hell from Gunga Din!
   Yes, Din! Din! Din!
  You Lazarushian-leather Gunga Din!
   Though I've belted you and flayed you,
   By the livin' Gawd that made you,
  You're a better man than I am, Gunga Din!

'Snarleyow'

This 'appened in a battle to a batt'ry of the corps
Which is first among the women an' amazin' first in war;
An' what the bloomin' battle was I don't remember now,
But Two's off-lead[1] 'e answered to the name o' *Snarleyow*.
  Down in the Infantry, nobody cares;
  Down in the Cavalry, Colonel 'e swears;
  But down in the lead with the wheel at the flog
  Turns the bold Bombardier to a little whipped dog!

They was movin' into action, they was needed very sore,
To learn a little schoolin' to a native army-core,
They 'ad nipped against an uphill, they was tuckin' down the brow,
When a tricky trundlin' roundshot give the knock to *Snarleyow*.

They cut 'im loose an' left 'im – 'e was almost tore in two –
But he tried to follow after as a well-trained 'orse should do;
'E went an' fouled the limber, an' the Driver's Brother squeals:
'Pull up, pull up for *Snarleyow* – 'is head's between 'is 'eels!'

The Driver 'umped 'is shoulder, for the wheels was goin' round,
An' there ain't no 'Stop, conductor!' when a batt'ry's changin' ground;

---

1. The leading right-hand horse of No. 2 gun.

179

Sez 'e: 'I broke the beggar in, an' very sad I feels,
'But I couldn't pull up, not for *you* – your 'ead between your 'eels!'

'E 'adn't 'ardly spoke the word, before a droppin' shell
A little right the batt'ry an' between the sections fell;
An' when the smoke 'ad cleared away, before the limber-wheels,
There lay the Driver's Brother with 'is 'ead between 'is 'eels.

Then sez the Driver's Brother, an' 'is words was very plain,
'For Gawd's own sake get over me, an' put me out o' pain.'
They saw 'is wounds was mortial, an' they judged that it was best,
So they took an' drove the limber straight across 'is back 'an chest.

The Driver 'e give nothin' 'cept a little coughin' grunt,
But 'e swung 'is 'orses 'andsome when it came to 'Action Front!'
An' if one wheel was juicy, you may lay your Monday head
'Twas juicier for the niggers when the case begun to spread.

The moril of this story, it is plainly to be seen:
You 'aven't got no families when servin' of the Queen –
You 'aven't got no brothers, fathers, sisters, wives, or sons –
If you want to win your battles take an' work your bloomin' guns!
      Down in the Infantry, nobody cares;
      Down in the Cavalry, Colonel 'e swears;
      But down in the lead with the wheel at the flog
      Turns the bold Bombardier to a little whipped dog!

Belts

There was a row in Silver Street that's near to Dublin Quay,
Between an Irish regiment an' English cavalree;
It started at Revelly an' it lasted on till dark:
The first man dropped at Harrison's, the last forninst the Park.
      For it was: – 'Belts, belts, belts, an' that's one for you!'
      An' it was 'Belts, belts, belts, an' that's done for you!'
      O buckle an' tongue
      Was the song that we sung
      From Harrison's down to the Park!

There was a row in Silver Street – the regiments was out,
They called us 'Delhi Rebels', an' we answered 'Threes about!'
That drew them like a hornets' nest – we met them good an' large,
The English at the double an' the Irish at the charge.
        Then it was: – 'Belts, &c.'

There was a row in Silver Street – an' I was in it too;
We passed the time o' day, an' then the belts went whirraru!
I misremember what occurred, but, subsequint the storm,
A *Freeman's Journal Supplemint* was all *my* uniform.
        O it was: – 'Belts, &c.'

There was a row in Silver Street – they sent the Polis there,
The English were too drunk to know, the Irish didn't care;
But when they grew impertinint we simultaneous rose,
Till half o' them was Liffey mud an' half was tatthered clo'es.
        For it was: – 'Belts, &c.'

There was a row in Silver Street – it might ha' raged till now,
But some one drew his side-arm clear, an' nobody knew how;
'Twas Hogan took the point an' dropped; we saw the red blood run:
An' so we all was murderers that started out in fun.
        While it was: 'Belts, &c.'

There was a row in Silver Street – but that put down the shine,
Wid each man whisperin' to his next: – ''Twas never work o' mine!'
We went away like beaten dogs, an' down the street we bore him,
The poor dumb corpse that couldn't tell the bhoys were sorry for him.
        When it was: – 'Belts, &c.'

There was a row in Silver Street – it isn't over yet,
For half of us are under guard wid punishments to get;
'Tis all a mericle to me as in the Clink I lie:
There was a row in Silver Street – begod, I wonder why!
        But it was: – 'Belts, belts, belts, an' that's one for you!'
        An' it was 'Belts, belts, belts, an' that's done for you!'
        O buckle an' tongue
        Was the song that we sung
        From Harrison's down to the Park!

Mandalay

By the old Moulmein Pagoda, lookin' lazy at the sea,
There's a Burma girl a-settin', and I know she thinks o' me;
For the wind is in the palm-trees, and the temple-bells they say:
'Come you back, you British soldier; come you back to Mandalay!'
 Come you back to Mandalay,
 Where the old Flotilla lay:
 Can't you 'ear their paddles chunkin' from Rangoon to Mandalay?
 On the road to Mandalay,
 Where the flyin'-fishes play,
 An' the dawn comes up like thunder outer China 'crost the Bay!

'Er petticoat was yaller an' 'er little cap was green,
An' 'er name was Supi-yaw-lat – jes' the same as Theebaw's Queen,
An' I seed her first a-smokin' of a whackin' white cheroot,
An' a-wastin' Christian kisses on an 'eathen idol's foot:
 Bloomin' idol made o' mud –
 Wot they called the Great Gawd Budd –
 Plucky lot she cared for idols when I kissed 'er where she stud!
 On the road to Mandalay . . .

When the mist was on the rice-fields an' the sun was droppin' slow,
She'd git 'er little banjo an' she'd sing '*Kulla-lo-lo!*'
With 'er arm upon my shoulder an' 'er cheek agin my cheek
We useter watch the steamers an' the *hathis* pilin' teak.
 Elephints a-pilin' teak
 In the sludgy, squdgy creek,
 Where the silence 'ung that 'eavy you was 'arf afraid to speak!
 On the road to Mandalay . . .

But that's all shove be'ind me – long ago an' fur away,
An' there ain't no 'buses runnin' from the Bank to Mandalay;
An' I'm learnin' 'ere in London what the ten-year soldier tells:
'If you've 'eard the East a-callin', you won't never 'eed naught else.'

No! you won't 'eed nothin' else
But them spicy garlic smells,
An' the sunshine an' the palm-trees an' the tinkly temple-bells;
On the road to Mandalay . . .

I am sick o' wastin' leather on these gritty pavin'-stones,
An' the blasted English drizzle wakes the fever in my bones;
Tho' I walks with fifty 'ousemaids outer Chelsea to the Strand,
An' they talks a lot o' lovin', but wot do they understand?
  Beefy face an' grubby 'and –
  Law! wot do they understand?
  I've a neater, sweeter maiden in a cleaner, greener land!
  On the road to Mandalay . . .

Ship me somewheres east of Suez, where the best is like the worst,
Where there aren't no Ten Commandments an' a man can raise a
      thirst;
For the temple-bells are callin', an' it's there that I would be –
By the old Moulmein Pagoda, looking lazy at the sea;
  On the road to Mandalay,
  Where the old Flotilla lay,
  With our sick beneath the awnings when we went to Mandalay!
  O the road to Mandalay,
  Where the flyin'-fishes play,
  An' the dawn comes up like thunder outer China 'crost the Bay!

Troopin'

(*Old English Army in the East*)

Troopin', troopin', troopin' to the sea:
'Ere's September come again – the six-year men are free.
O leave the dead be'ind us, for they cannot come away
To where the ship's a-coalin' up that takes us 'ome to-day.

We're goin' 'ome, we're goin' 'ome,
  Our ship is *at* the shore,
An' you must pack your 'aversack,
  For we won't come back no more.
Ho, don't you grieve for me,
  My lovely Mary-Ann!
For I'll marry you yit on a fourp'ny bit
  As a time-expired man.

The *Malabar*'s in 'arbour with the *Jumner* at 'er tail,
An' the time-expired's waitin' of 'is orders for to sail.
Ho! the weary waitin' when on Khyber 'ills we lay,
But the time-expired's waitin' of 'is orders 'ome to-day.

They'll turn us out at Portsmouth wharf in cold an' wet an' rain,
All wearin' Injian cotton kit, but we will not complain.
They'll kill us of pneumonia – for that's their little way –
But damn the chills and fever, men, we're goin' 'ome to-day!

Troopin', troopin', winter's round again!
See the new draft's pourin' in for the old campaign;
Ho, you poor recruities, but you've got to earn your pay –
What's the last from Lunnon, lads? We're goin' there to-day.

Troopin', troopin', give another cheer –
'Ere's to English women an' a quart of English beer.
The Colonel an' the Regiment an' all who've got to stay,
Gawd's Mercy strike 'em gentle! Whoop! we're goin' 'ome to-day.
  We're goin' 'ome, we're goin' 'ome,
    Our ship is *at* the shore,
  An' you must pack your 'aversack,
    For we won't come back no more.
  Ho, don't you grieve for me,
    My lovely Mary-Ann!
  For I'll marry you yit on a fourp'ny bit
    As a time-expired man.

The Widow's Party

'Where have you been this while away,
                Johnnie, Johnnie?'
Out with the rest on a picnic lay.
                Johnnie, my Johnnie, aha!
They called us out of the barrack-yard
To Gawd knows where from Gosport Hard,
And you can't refuse when you get the card,
                And the Widow gives the party.
                (*Bugle*: Ta–rara–ra-ra-rara!)

'What did you get to eat and drink,
                Johnnie, Johnnie?'
Standing water as thick as ink,
                Johnnie, my Johnnie, aha!
A bit o' beef that were three year stored,
A bit o' mutton as tough as a board,
And a fowl we killed with a sergeant's sword,
                When the Widow give the party.

'What did you for knives and forks,
                Johnnie, Johnnie?'
We carries 'em with us wherever we walks,
                Johnnie, my Johnnie, aha!
And some was sliced and some was halved,
And some was crimped and some was carved,
And some was gutted and some was starved,
                When the Widow give the party.

'What ha' you done with half your mess,
                Johnnie, Johnnie?'
They couldn't do more and they wouldn't do less.
                Johnnie, my Johnnie, aha!
They ate their whack and they drank their fill,
And I think the rations has made them ill,
For half my comp'ny's lying still
                Where the Widow give the party.

'How did you get away – away,
                    Johnnie, Johnnie?'
On the broad o' my back at the end o' the day,
                    Johnnie, my Johnnie, aha!
I comed away like a bleedin' toff,
For I got four niggers to carry me off,
As I lay in the bight of a canvas trough,
                    When the Widow give the party.

'What was the end of all the show,
                    Johnnie, Johnnie?'
Ask my Colonel, for I don't know,
                    Johnnie, my Johnnie, aha!
We broke a King and we built a road –
A court-house stands where the Reg'ment goed.
And the river's clean where the raw blood flowed
                    When the Widow give the party.
                    (*Bugle*: Ta–rara–ra-ra-rara!)

Gentlemen-Rankers

To the legion of the lost ones, to the cohort of the damned,
    To my brethren in their sorrow overseas,
Sings a gentleman of England cleanly bred, machinely crammed,
    And a trooper of the Empress, if you please.
Yes, a trooper of the forces who has run his own six horses,
    And faith he went the pace and went it blind,
And the world was more than kin while he held the ready tin,
    But to-day the Sergeant's something less than kind.
                    We're poor little lambs who've lost our way,
                        Baa! Baa! Baa!
                    We're little black sheep who've gone astray,
                        Baa–aa–aa!
                    Gentlemen-rankers out on the spree,
                    Damned from here to Eternity,
                    God ha' mercy on such as we,
                        Baa! Yah! Bah!

Oh, it's sweet to sweat through stables, sweet to empty kitchen slops,
    And it's sweet to hear the tales the troopers tell,
To dance with blowzy housemaids at the regimental hops
    And thrash the cad who says you waltz too well.
Yes, it makes you cock-a-hoop to be 'Rider' to your troop,
    And branded with a blasted worsted spur,
When you envy, O how keenly, one poor Tommy living cleanly
    Who blacks your boots and sometimes calls you 'Sir'.

If the home we never write to, and the oaths we never keep,
    And all we know most distant and most dear,
Across the snoring barrack-room return to break our sleep,
    Can you blame us if we soak ourselves in beer?
When the drunken comrade mutters and the great guard-lantern
        gutters
    And the horror of our fall is written plain,
Every secret, self-revealing on the aching whitewashed ceiling,
    Do you wonder that we drug ourselves from pain?

We have done with Hope and Honour, we are lost to Love and Truth,
    We are dropping down the ladder rung by rung,
And the measure of our torment is the measure of our youth.
    God help us, for we knew the worst too young!
Our shame is clean repentance for the crime that brought the sentence,
    Our pride it is to know no spur of pride,
And the Curse of Reuben holds us till an alien turf enfolds us
    And we die, and none can tell Them where we died.
        We're poor little lambs who've lost our way,
            Baa! Baa! Baa!
        We're little black sheep who've gone astray,
            Baa–aa–aa!
        Gentlemen-rankers out on the spree,
        Damned from here to Eternity,
        God ha' mercy on such as we,
            Baa! Yah! Bah!

Route Marchin'

We're marchin' on relief over Injia's sunny plains,
A little front o' Christmas-time an' just be'ind the Rains;
Ho! get away, you bullock-man, you've 'eard the bugle blowed,
There's a regiment a-comin' down the Grand Trunk Road;
      With its best foot first
      And the road a-sliding past,
      An' every bloomin' campin'-ground exactly like the last;
      While the Big Drum says,
      With 'is *'rowdy-dowdy-dow!'* –
      'Kiko kissywarsti don't you *hamsher argy jow?'* [1]

Oh, there's them Injian temples to admire when you see.
There's the peacock round the corner an' the monkey up the tree,
An' there's that rummy silver-grass a-wavin' in the wind,
An' the old Grand Trunk a-trailin' like a rifle-sling be'ind.
      While it's best foot first, . . .

At half-past five's Revelly, an' our tents they down must come,
Like a lot of button-mushrooms when you pick 'em up at 'ome.
But it's over in a minute, an' at six the column starts,
While the women and kiddies sit an' shiver in the carts.
      An' it's best foot first, . . .

Oh, then it's open order, an' we lights our pipes an' sings,
An' we talks about our rations an' a lot of other things,
An' we thinks o' friends in England, an' we wonders what they're at,
An' 'ow they would admire for to hear us sling the *bat*.[2]
      An' it's best foot first, . . .

---

1. Why don't you get on?
2. Language. Thomas's first and firmest conviction is that he is a profound Orientalist and a fluent speaker of Hindustani. As a matter of fact, he depends largely on the sign-language.

It's none so bad o' Sundays, when you're lyin' at your ease,
To watch the kites a-wheelin' round them feather-'eaded trees,
For although there ain't no women, yet there ain't no barrick-yards,
So the orficers goes shootin' an' the men they plays at cards.
  Till it's best foot first, . . .

So 'ark an' 'eed, you rookies, which is always grumblin' sore,
There's worser things than marchin' from Umballa to Cawnpore;
An' if your 'eels are blistered an' they feels to 'urt like 'ell,
You drop some tallow in your socks an' that will make 'em well.
  For it's best foot first, . . .

We're marchin' on relief over Injia's coral strand,
Eight 'undred fightin' Englishmen, the Colonel, and the Band;
Ho! get away, you bullock-man, you've 'eard the bugle blowed,
There's a regiment a-comin' down the Grand Trunk Road;
  With its best foot first
  And the road a-sliding past,
  An' every bloomin' campin'-ground exactly like the last;
  While the Big Drum says,
  With 'is *rowdy-dowdy-dow!* –
'*Kiko kissywarsti* don't you *hamsher argy jow?*'

'*Back to the Army Again*'

I'm 'ere in a ticky ulster an' a broken billycock 'at,
A-layin' on to the sergeant I don't know a gun from a bat;
My shirt's doin' duty for jacket, my sock's stickin' out o' my boots,
An' I'm learnin' the damned old goose-step along o' the new recruits!

  Back to the Army again, sergeant,
   Back to the Army again,
  Don't look so 'ard, for I 'aven't no card,
   I'm back to the Army again!

I done my six years' service. 'Er Majesty sez: 'Good day –
You'll please to come when you're rung for, an' 'ere's your 'ole back-pay;
An' fourpence a day for baccy – an' bloomin' gen'rous, too;
An' now you can make your fortune – the same as your orf'cers do.'

> Back to the Army again, sergeant,
>   Back to the Army again.
> 'Ow did I learn to do right-about-turn?
>   I'm back to the Army again!

A man o' four-an'-twenty that 'asn't learned of a trade –
Beside 'Reserve' agin' him – 'e'd better be never made.
I tried my luck for a quarter, an' that was enough for me,
An' I thought of 'Er Majesty's barricks, an' I thought I'd go an' see.

> Back to the Army again, sergeant,
>   Back to the Army again.
> 'Tisn't my fault if I dress when I 'alt –
>   I'm back to the Army again!

The sergeant arst no questions, but 'e winked the other eye,
'E sez to me, "'Shun!" an' I shunted, the same as in days gone by;
For 'e saw the set o' my shoulders, an' I couldn't 'elp 'oldin' straight
When me an' the other rookies come under the barrick-gate.

> Back to the Army again, sergeant,
>   Back to the Army again.
> 'Oo would ha' thought I could carry an' port?[1]
>   I'm back to the Army again!

I took my bath, an' I wallered – for, Gawd, I needed it so!
I smelt the smell o' the barricks, I 'eard the bugles go.
I 'eard the feet on the gravel – the feet o' the men what drill –
An' I sez to my flutterin' 'eart-strings, I sez to 'em, 'Peace, be still!'

1. Carry and port his rifle.

Back to the Army again, sergeant,
    Back to the Army again.
'Oo said I knew when the troopship was due?
    I'm back to the Army again!

I carried my slops to the tailor; I sez to 'im, 'None o' your lip!
You tight 'em over the shoulders, an' loose 'em over the 'ip,
For the set o' the tunic's 'orrid.' An' 'e sez to me, 'Strike me dead,
But I thought you was used to the business!' an' so 'e done what I said.

Back to the Army again, sergeant,
    Back to the Army again.
Rather too free with my fancies? Wot – me?
    I'm back to the Army again!

Next week I'll 'ave 'em fitted; I'll buy me a swagger-cane;
They'll let me free o' the barricks to walk on the Hoe again,
In the name o' William Parsons, that used to be Edward Clay,
An' – any pore beggar that wants it can draw my fourpence a day!

Back to the Army again, sergeant,
    Back to the Army again.
Out o' the cold an' the rain, sergeant,
    Out o' the cold an' the rain.
            'Oo's there?
    A man that's too good to be lost to you,
    A man that is 'andled an' made –
A man that will pay what 'e cost you
    In learnin' the others their trade – parade!
You're droppin' the pick o' the Army
    Because you don't 'elp 'em remain,
But drives 'em to cheat to get out o' the street
    An' back to the Army again!

Sappers

(*Royal Engineers*)

When the Waters were dried an' the Earth did appear,
  ('It's all one,' says the Sapper),
The Lord He created the Engineer,
  Her Majesty's Royal Engineer,
  With the rank and pay of a Sapper!

When the Flood come along for an extra monsoon,
'Twas Noah constructed the first pontoon
  To the plans of Her Majesty's, etc.

But after fatigue in the wet an' the sun,
Old Noah got drunk, which he wouldn't ha' done
  If he'd trained with, etc.

When the Tower o' Babel had mixed up men's *bat*,[1]
Some clever civilian was managing that,
  An' none of, etc.

When the Jews had a fight at the foot of a hill,
Young Joshua ordered the sun to stand still,
  For he was a Captain of Engineers, etc.

When the Children of Israel made bricks without straw,
They were learnin' the regular work of our Corps,
  The work of, etc.

For ever since then, if a war they would wage,
Behold us a-shinin' on history's page –
  First page for, etc.

1. Talk.

We lay down their sidings an' help 'em entrain,
An' we sweep up their mess through the bloomin' campaign
   In the style of, etc.

They send us in front with a fuse an' a mine
To blow up the gates that are rushed by the Line,
   But bent by, etc.

They send us behind with a pick an' a spade,
To dig for the guns of a bullock-brigade
   Which has asked for, etc.

We work under escort in trousers and shirt,
An' the heathen they plug us tail-up in the dirt,
   Annoying, etc.

We blast out the rock an' we shovel the mud,
We make em' good roads an' – they roll down the *khud*,[1]
   Reporting, etc.

We make 'em their bridges, their wells, an' their huts,
An' the telegraph-wire the enemy cuts,
   An' it's blamed on, etc.

An' when we return, an from war we would cease,
They grudge us adornin' the billets of peace,
   Which are kept for, etc.

We build 'em nice barracks – they swear they are bad,
That our Colonels are Methodist, married or mad,
   Insultin', etc.

They haven't no manners nor gratitude too,
For the more that we help 'em, the less will they do,
   But mock at, etc.

1. Hillside.

Now the Line's but a man with a gun in his hand,
An' Cavalry's only what horses can stand,
  When helped by, etc.

Artillery moves by the leave o' the ground,
But *we* are the men that do something all round,
  For *we* are, etc.

I have stated it plain, an' my argument's thus
    ('It's all one,' says the Sapper)
There's only one Corps which is perfect – that's us;
    An' they call us Her Majesty's Engineers,
    Her Majesty's Royal Engineers,
    With the rank and pay of a Sapper!

That Day

It got beyond all orders an' it got beyond all 'ope;
  It got to shammin' wounded an' retirin' from the 'alt.
'Ole companies was lookin' for the nearest road to slope;
  It were just a bloomin' knock-out – an' our fault!

> *Now there ain't no chorus 'ere to give,*
>   *Nor there ain't no band to play;*
> *An' I wish I was dead 'fore I done what I did,*
>   *Or seen what I seed that day!*

We was sick o' bein' punished, an' we let 'em know it, too;
  An' a company-commander up an' 'it us with a sword,
An' some one shouted ''Ook it!' an' it come to *sove-ki-poo*,
  An' we chucked our rifles from us – O my Gawd!

There was thirty dead an' wounded on the ground we wouldn't keep –
  No, there wasn't more than twenty when the front begun to go –
But, Christ! along the line o' flight they cut us up like sheep,
  An' that was all we gained by doin' so!

I 'eard the knives be'ind me, but I dursn't face my man,
  Nor I don't know where I went to, 'cause I didn't 'alt to see,
Till I 'eard a beggar squealin' out for quarter as 'e ran,
  An' I thought I knew the voice an' – it was me!

We was 'idin' under bedsteads more than 'arf a march away:
  We was lyin' up like rabbits all about the country-side;
An' the Major cursed 'is Maker 'cause 'e'd lived to see that day,
  An' the Colonel broke 'is sword acrost, an' cried.

We were rotten 'fore we started – we was never disci*plined*;
  We made it out a favour if an order was obeyed.
Yes, every little drummer 'ad 'is rights an' wrongs to mind,
  So we had to pay for teachin' – an' we paid!

The papers 'id it 'andsome, but you know the Army knows;
  We was put to groomin' camels till the regiments withdrew,
An' they gave us each a medal for subduin' England's foes,
  An' I 'ope you like my song – because it's true!

> *An' there ain't no chorus 'ere to give,*
>   *Nor there ain't no band to play;*
> *But I wish I was dead 'fore I done what I did,*
>   *Or seen what I seed that day!*

Cholera Camp

(*Infantry in India*)

We've got the cholerer in camp – it's worse than forty fights;
We're dyin' in the wilderness the same as Isrulites.
It's before us, an' be'ind us, an' we cannot get away,
An' the doctor's just reported we've ten more to-day!

> *Oh, strike your camp an' go, the bugle's callin',*
>   *The Rains are fallin' –*

The dead are bushed an' stoned to keep 'em safe below.
The Band's a-doin' all she knows to cheer us;
The Chaplain's gone and prayed to Gawd to 'ear us –
    To 'ear us –
O Lord, for it's a-killin' of us so!

Since August, when it started, it's been stickin' to our tail,
Though they've 'ad us out by marches an' they've 'ad us back by rail;
But it runs as fast as troop trains, and we cannot get away,
An' the sick-list to the Colonel makes ten more to-day.

There ain't no fun in women nor there ain't no bite to drink;
It's much too wet for shootin'; we can only march and think;
An' at evenin', down the *nullahs*, we can 'ear the jackals say,
'Get up, you rotten beggars, you've ten more to-day!'

'Twould make a monkey cough to see our way o' doin' things –
Lieutenants takin' companies an' Captains takin' wings,
An' Lances actin' Sergeants – eight file to obey –
For we've lots o' quick promotion on ten deaths a day!

Our Colonel's white an' twitterly – 'e gets no sleep nor food,
But mucks about in 'orspital where nothing does no good.
'E sends up 'eaps o' comforts, all bought from 'is pay –
But there aren't much comfort 'andy on ten deaths a day.

Our Chaplain's got a banjo, an' a skinny mule e' rides,
An' the stuff he says an' sings us, Lord, it makes us split our sides!
With 'is black coat-tails a-bobbin' to *Ta-ra-ra Boom-der-ay*!
'E's the proper kind o' *padre* for ten deaths a day.

An' Father Victor 'elps 'im with our Roman Catholicks –
He knows an 'eap of Irish songs an' rummy conjurin'-tricks;
An' the two they works together when it comes to play or pray.
So we keep the ball a-rollin' on ten deaths a day.

We've got the cholerer in camp – we've got it 'ot an' sweet.
It ain't no Christmas dinner, but it's 'elped an' we must eat.

We've gone beyond the funkin', 'cause we've found it doesn't pay,
An' we're rockin' round the Districk on ten deaths a day!

> Then strike your camp an' go, the Rains are fallin',
>   The Bugle's callin'!
> The dead are bushed an' stoned to keep 'em safe below!
> An' them that do not like it they can lump it,
> An' them that cannot stand it they can jump it;
> We've got to die somewhere – some way – some 'ow –
> We might as well begin to do it now!
> Then, Number One, let down the tent-pole slow,
> Knock out the pegs an' 'old the corners – so!
> Fold in the flies, furl up the ropes, an' stow!
> Oh, strike – oh, strike your camp an' go!
>   (Gawd 'elp us!)

'Follow Me 'Ome'

> There was no one like 'im, 'Orse or Foot,
>   Nor any o' the Guns I knew;
> An' because it was so, why, o' course 'e went an' died,
>   Which is just what the best men do.

> So it's knock out your pipes an' follow me!
> An' it's finish up your swipes an' follow me!
>   Oh, 'ark to the big drum callin',
>   Follow me – follow me 'ome!

> 'Is mare she neighs the 'ole day long,
>   She paws the 'ole night through,
> An' she won't take 'er feed 'cause o' waitin' for 'is step,
>   Which is just what a beast would do.

> 'Is girl she goes with a bombardier
>   Before 'er month is through;
> An' the banns are up in church, for she's got the beggar hooked,
>   Which is just what a girl would do.

197

We fought 'bout a dog – last week it were –
    No more than a round or two;
But I strook 'im cruel 'ard, an' I wish I 'adn't now,
    Which is just what a man can't do.

'E was all that I 'ad in the way of a friend,
    An' I've 'ad to find one new;
But I'd give my pay an' stripe for to get the beggar back,
    Which it's just too late to do!

So it's knock out your pipes an' follow me!
An' it's finish up your swipes an' follow me!
    Oh, 'ark to the fifes a-crawlin'!
      Follow me – follow me 'ome!

Take 'im away! 'E's gone where the best men go.
Take 'im away! An' the gun-wheels turnin' slow.
Take 'im away! There's more from the place 'e come.
Take 'im away, with the limber an' the drum.

For it's 'Three rounds blank' an' follow me,
An' it's 'Thirteen rank' an' follow me;
    Oh, passin' the love o' women,
      Follow me – follow me 'ome!

The Sergeant's Weddin'

'E was warned agin' 'er –
    That's what made 'im look:
She was warned agin' 'im –
    That is why she took.
'Wouldn't 'ear no reason,
    'Went an' done it blind;
We know all about 'em,
    They've got all to find!

Cheer for the Sergeant's weddin' –
  Give 'em one cheer more!
Grey gun-'orses in the lando,
  An' a rogue is married to, etc.

What's the use o' tellin'
  'Arf the lot she's been?
'E's a bloomin' robber,
  An' 'e keeps canteen.
'Ow did 'e get 'is buggy?
  Gawd, you needn't ask!
'Made 'is forty gallon
  Out of every cask!

Watch 'im, with 'is 'air cut,
  Count us filin' by –
Won't the Colonel praise 'is
  Pop–u–lar–i–ty!
We 'ave scores to settle –
  Scores for more than beer;
She's the girl to pay 'em –
  That is why we're 'ere!

See the Chaplain thinkin'?
  See the women smile?
Twig the married winkin'
  As they take the aisle?
Keep your side-arms quiet,
  Dressin' by the Band.
Ho! You 'oly beggars,
  Cough be'ind your 'and!

Now it's done an' over,
  'Ear the organ squeak,
  'Voice that breathed o'er Eden' –
  Ain't she got the cheek!

White an' laylock ribbons,
    'Think yourself so fine!
I'd pray Gawd to take yer
    'Fore I made yer mine!

Escort to the kerridge,
    Wish 'im luck, the brute!
Chuck the slippers after –
    (Pity 'tain't a boot!)
Bowin' like a lady,
    Blushin' like a lad –
'Oo would say to see 'em
    Both is rotten bad?

Cheer for the Sergeant's weddin' –
    Give 'em one cheer more!
Grey gun-'orses in the lando,
    An' a rogue is married to, etc.

The 'Eathen

The 'eathen in 'is blindness bows down to wood an' stone;
'E don't obey no orders unless they is 'is own;
'E keeps 'is side-arms awful: 'e leaves 'em all about,
An' then comes up the Regiment an' pokes the 'eathen out.

All along o' dirtiness, all along o' mess,
All along o' doin' things rather-more-or-less,
All along of abby-nay,[1] kul,[2] an' hazar-ho,[3]
Mind you keep your rifle an' yourself jus' so!

The young recruit is 'aughty – 'e draf's from Gawd knows where;
They bid 'im show 'is stockin's an' lay 'is mattress square;
'E calls it bloomin' nonsense – 'e doesn't know, no more –
An' then up comes 'is Company an' kicks 'im round the floor!

1. Not now.   2. To-morrow.   3. Wait a bit.

The young recruit is 'ammered – 'e takes it very hard;
'E 'angs 'is 'ead an' mutters – 'e sulks about the yard;
'E talks o' 'cruel tyrants' which 'e'll swing for by-an'-by,
An' the others 'ears an' mocks 'im, an' the boy goes orf to cry.

The young recruit is silly – 'e thinks o' suicide.
'E's lost 'is gutter-devil; 'e 'asn't got 'is pride;
But day by day they kicks 'im, which 'elps 'im on a bit,
Till 'e finds 'isself one mornin' with a full an' proper kit.

Gettin' clear o' dirtiness, gettin' done with mess,
Gettin' shut o' doin' things rather-more-or-less;
Not so fond of abby-nay, kul, nor hazar-ho,
Learns to keep 'is rifle an' 'isself jus' so!

The young recruit is 'appy – 'e throws a chest to suit;
You see 'im grow mustaches; you 'ear 'im slap 'is boot.
'E learns to drop the 'bloodies' from every word 'e slings,
An' 'e shows an 'ealthy brisket when 'e strips for bars an' rings.

The cruel-tyrant-sergeants they watch 'im 'arf a year;
They watch 'im with 'is comrades, they watch 'im with 'is beer;
They watch 'im with the women at the regimental dance,
And the cruel-tyrant-sergeants send 'is name along for 'Lance'.

An' now 'e's 'arf o' nothin', an' all a private yet,
'Is room they up an' rags 'im to see what they will get.
They rags 'im low an' cunnin', each dirty trick they can,
But 'e learns to sweat 'is temper an' 'e learns to sweat 'is man.

An', last, a Colour-Sergeant, as such to be obeyed,
'E schools 'is men at cricket, 'e tells 'em on parade;
They sees 'im quick an' 'andy, uncommon set an' smart,
An' so 'e talks to orficers which 'ave the Core at 'eart.

'E learns to do 'is watchin' without it showin' plain;
'E learns to save a dummy, an' shove 'im straight again;
'E learns to check a ranker that's buyin' leave to shirk;
An' 'e learns to make men like 'im so they'll learn to like their work.

An' when it comes to marchin' he'll see their socks are right,
An' when it comes to action 'e shows 'em how to sight.
'E knows their ways of thinkin' and just what's in their mind;
'E knows when they are takin' on an' when they've fell be'ind.

'E knows each talkin' corp'ral that leads a squad astray;
'E feels 'is innards 'eavin', 'is bowels givin' way;
'E sees the blue-white faces all tryin' 'ard to grin,
An' 'e stands an' waits an' suffers till it's time to cap 'em in.

An' now the hugly bullets come peckin' through the dust,
An' no one wants to face 'em, but every beggar must;
So, like a man in irons, which isn't glad to go,
They moves 'em off by companies uncommon stiff an' slow.

Of all 'is five years' schoolin' they don't remember much
Excep' the not retreatin', the step an' keepin' touch.
It looks like teachin' wasted when they duck an' spread an' 'op –
But if 'e 'adn't learned 'em they'd be all about the shop.

An' now it's ''Oo goes backward?' an' now it's ''Oo comes on?'
And now it's 'Get the doolies,' an' now the Captain's gone;
An' now it's bloody murder, but all the while they 'ear
'Is voice, the same as barrick-drill, a-shepherdin' the rear.

'E's just as sick as they are, 'is 'eart is like to split,
But 'e works 'em, works 'em, works 'em till he feels 'em take the bit;
The rest is 'oldin' steady till the watchful bugles play,
An' 'e lifts 'em, lifts 'em, lifts 'em through the charge that wins the
    day!

The 'eathen in 'is blindness bows down to wood an' stone;
'E don't obey no orders unless they is 'is own.
The 'eathen in 'is blindness must end where 'e began,
But the backbone of the Army is the Non-commissioned Man!

Keep away from dirtiness – keep away from mess,
Don't get into doin' things rather-more-or-less!
Let's ha' done with abby-nay, kul, and hazar-ho;
Mind you keep your rifle an' yourself jus' so!

'Mary, Pity Women!'

You call yourself a man,
    For all you used to swear,
An' leave me, as you can,
    My certain shame to bear?
    I 'ear! You do not care –
You done the worst you know.
    I 'ate you, grinnin' there . . .
Ah, Gawd, I love you so!

Nice while it lasted, an' now it is over –
Tear out your 'eart an' good-bye to your lover!
What's the use o' grievin', when the mother that bore you
(Mary, pity women!) knew it all before you?

It aren't no false alarm,
    The finish to your fun;
You – you 'ave brung the 'arm,
    An' I'm the ruined one!
    An' now you'll off an' run
With some new fool in tow.
    Your 'eart? You 'aven't none . . .
Ah, Gawd, I love you so!

When a man is tired there is naught will bind 'im;
All 'e solemn promised 'e will shove be'ind 'im.
What's the good o' prayin' for The Wrath to strike 'im
(Mary, pity women!), when the rest are like 'im?

What 'ope for me or – it?
    What's left for us to do?
I've walked with men a bit,
    But this – but this is you.
    So 'elp me, Christ, it's true!
Where can I 'ide or go?
    You coward through and through! . . .
Ah, Gawd, I love you so!

All the more you give 'em the less are they for givin' –
Love lies dead, an' you cannot kiss 'im livin'.
Down the road 'e led you there is no returnin'
(Mary, pity women!), but you're late in learnin'!

You'd like to treat me fair?
    You can't, because we're pore?
We'd starve? What do I care!
    We might, but *this* is shore!
    I want the name – no more –
The name, an' lines to show,
    An' not to be an 'ore . . .
Ah, Gawd, I love you so!

What's the good o' pleadin', when the mother that bore you
(Mary, pity women!) knew it all before you?
Sleep on 'is promises an' wake to your sorrow
(Mary, pity women!), for we sail to-morrow!

'For to Admire'

The Injian Ocean sets an' smiles
    So sof', so bright, so bloomin' blue;
There aren't a wave for miles an' miles
    Excep' the jiggle from the screw.

The ship is swep', the day is done,
    The bugle's gone for smoke and play;
An' black ag'in in the settin' sun
    The Lascar sings, '*Hum deckty hai!*' [1]

For to admire an' for to see,
    For to be'old this world so wide –
It never done no good to me,
    But I can't drop it if I tried!

I see the sergeants pitchin' quoits,
    I 'ear the women laugh an' talk,
I spy upon the quarter-deck
    The orficers an' lydies walk.
I thinks about the things that was,
    An' leans an' looks acrost the sea,
Till, spite of all the crowded ship,
    There's no one lef' alive but me.

The things that was which I 'ave seen,
    In barrick, camp, an' action too,
I tells them over by myself,
    An' sometimes wonders if they're true;
For they was odd – most awful odd –
    But all the same, now they are o'er,
There must be 'eaps o' plenty such,
    An' if I wait I'll see some more.

Oh, I 'ave come upon the books,
    An' frequent broke a barrick-rule,
An' stood beside an' watched myself
    Be'avin' like a bloomin' fool.
I paid my price for findin' out,
    Nor never grutched the price I paid,
But sat in Clink without my boots,
    Admirin' 'ow the world was made.

1. I'm looking out.

Be'old a cloud upon the beam,
    An' 'umped above the sea appears
Old Aden, like a barrick-stove
    That no one's lit for years an' years.
I passed by that when I began,
    An' I go 'ome the road I came,
A time-expired soldier-man
    With six years' service to 'is name.

My girl she said, 'Oh, stay with me!'
    My mother 'eld me to 'er breast.
They've never written none, an' so
    They must 'ave gone with all the rest –
With all the rest which I 'ave seen
    An' found an' known an' met along.
I cannot say the things I feel,
    And so I sing my evenin' song:

For to admire an' for to see,
    For to be'old this world so wide –
It never done no good to me,
    But I can't drop it if I tried!

The Absent-Minded Beggar

When you've shouted 'Rule Britannia', when you've sung 'God save
    the Queen',
    When you've finished killing Kruger with your mouth,
Will you kindly drop a shilling in my little tambourine
    For a gentleman in khaki ordered South?
He's an absent-minded beggar, and his weaknesses are great –
    But we and Paul must take him as we find him –
He is out on active service, wiping something off a slate –
    And he's left a lot of little things behind him!

Duke's son – cook's son – son of a hundred kings –
    (Fifty thousand horse and foot going to Table Bay!)
Each of 'em doing his country work
    (and who's to look after their things?)
Pass the hat for your credit's sake,
              and pay – pay – pay!

There are girls he married secret, asking no permission to,
    For he knew he wouldn't get it if he did.
There is gas and coals and vittles, and the house-rent falling due,
    And it's more than rather likely there's a kid.
There are girls he walked with casual. They'll be sorry now he's gone,
    For an absent-minded beggar they will find him,
But it ain't the time for sermons with the winter coming on.
    We must help the girl that Tommy's left behind him!
Cook's son – Duke's son – son of a belted Earl –
    Son of a Lambeth publican – it's all the same to-day!
Each of 'em doing his country's work
    (and who's to look after the girl?)
Pass the hat for your credit's sake,
              and pay – pay – pay!

There are families by thousands, far too proud to beg or speak,
    And they'll put their sticks and bedding up the spout,
And they'll live on half o' nothing, paid 'em punctual once a week,
    'Cause the man that earns the wage is ordered out.
He's an absent-minded beggar, but he heard his country call,
    And his reg'ment didn't need to send to find him!
He chucked his job and joined it – so the job before us all
    Is to help the home that Tommy's left behind him!
Duke's job – cook's job – gardener, baronet, groom,
    Mews or palace or paper-shop, there's someone gone away!
Each of 'em doing his country's work
    (and who's to look after the room?)
Pass the hat for your credit's sake,
              and pay – pay – pay!

Let us manage so as, later, we can look him in the face,
    And tell him – what he'd very much prefer –
That, while he saved the Empire, his employer saved his place,
    And his mates (that's you and me) looked out for *her*.
He's an absent-minded beggar and he may forget it all,
    But we do not want his kiddies to remind him
That we sent 'em to the workhouse while their daddy hammered Paul,
    So we'll help the homes that Tommy left behind him!
Cook's home – Duke's home – home of a millionaire,
    (Fifty thousand horse and foot going to Table Bay!)
Each of 'em doing his country's work
    (and what have you got to spare?)
Pass the hat for your credit's sake,
            and pay – pay – pay!

Chant-Pagan

(*English Irregular, discharged*)

Me that 'ave been what I've been –
Me that 'ave gone where I've gone –
Me that 'ave seen what I've seen –
    'Ow can I ever take on
With awful old English again,
An' 'ouses both sides of the street,
And 'edges two sides of the lane,
And the parson an' gentry between,
An' touchin' my 'at when we meet –
    Me that 'ave been what I've been?

Me that 'ave watched 'arf a world
'Eave up all shiny with dew,
Kopje on kop to the sun,
An' as soon as the mist let 'em through
Our 'elios winkin' like fun –
Three sides of a ninety-mile square,

Over valleys as big as a shire –
'*Are ye there? Are ye there? Are ye there?*'
An' then the blind drum of our fire . . .
An' I'm rollin' 'is lawns for the Squire,

> Me!

Me that 'ave rode through the dark
Forty mile, often, on end,
Along the Ma'ollisberg Range,
With only the stars for my mark
An' only the night for my friend,
An' things runnin' off as you pass,
An' things jumpin' up in the grass,
An' the silence, the shine an' the size
Of the 'igh, unexpressible skies –
I am takin' some letters almost
As much as a mile to the post,
An' 'mind you come back with the change'!

> Me!

Me that saw Barberton took
When we dropped through the clouds on their 'ead,
An' they 'ove the guns over and fled –
Me that was through Di'mond 'Ill,
An' Pieters an' Springs an' Belfast –
From Dundee to Vereeniging all –
Me that stuck out to the last
(An' five bloomin' bars on my chest) –
I am doin' my Sunday-school best,
By the 'elp of the Squire an' 'is wife
(Not to mention the 'ousemaid an' cook),
To come in an' 'ands up an' be still,
An' honestly work for my bread,
My livin' in that state of life
To which it shall please God to call

> Me!

Me that 'ave followed my trade
In the place where the Lightnin's are made;
'Twixt the Rains and the Sun and the Moon –
Me that lay down an' got up
Three years with sky for my roof –
That 'ave ridden my 'unger an' thirst
Six thousand raw mile on the hoof,
With the Vaal and the Orange for cup,
An' the Brandwater Basin for dish, –
Oh! it's 'ard to be'ave as they wish
(Too 'ard, an' a little too soon),
I'll 'ave to think over it first –

                                Me!

I will arise an' get 'ence –
I will trek South and make sure
If it's only my fancy or not
That the sunshine of England is pale,
And the breezes of England are stale,
An' there's somethin' gone small with the lot.
For *I* know of a sun an' a wind,
An' some plains and a mountain be'ind,
An' some graves by a barb-wire fence,
An' a Dutchman I've fought 'oo might give
Me a job were I ever inclined
To look in an' offsaddle an' live
Where there's neither a road nor a tree –
But only my Maker an' me,
And I think it will kill me or cure,
So I think I will go there an' see.

                                Me!

Boots

(*Infantry Columns*)

We're foot – slog – slog – slog – sloggin' over Africa –
Foot – foot – foot – foot – sloggin' over Africa –
(Boots – boots – boots – boots – movin' up and down again!)
    There's no discharge in the war!

Seven – six – eleven – five – nine-an'-twenty mile to-day –
Four – eleven – seventeen – thirty-two the day before –
(Boots – boots – boots – boots – movin' up an' down again!)
    There's no discharge in the war!

Don't – don't – don't – don't – look at what's in front of you.
(Boots – boots – boots – boots – movin' up an' down again);
Men – men – men – men – men go mad with watchin' 'em,
    An' there's no discharge in the war!

Try – try – try – try – to think o' something different –
Oh – my – God – keep – me from goin' lunatic!
(Boots – boots – boots – boots – movin' up an' down again!)
    There's no discharge in the war!

Count – count – count – count – the bullets in the bandoliers.
If – your – eyes – drop – they will get atop o' you!
(Boots – boots – boots – boots – movin' up and down again) –
    There's no discharge in the war!

We – can – stick – out – 'unger, thirst, an' weariness,
But – not – not – not – not the chronic sight of 'em –
Boots – boots – boots – boots – movin' up an' down again,
    An' there's no discharge in the war!

'Tain't – so – bad – by – day because o' company,
But night – brings – long – strings – o' forty thousand million
Boots – boots – boots – boots – movin' up an' down again.
    There's no discharge in the war!

I – 'ave – marched – six – weeks in 'Ell an' certify
It – is – not – fire – devils, dark, or anything,
But boots – boots – boots – boots – movin' up an' down again,
    An' there's no discharge in the war!

The Married Man

(Reservist of the Line)

The bachelor 'e fights for one
   As joyful as can be;
But the married man don't call it fun,
   Because 'e fights for three –
For 'Im an' 'Er an' It
   (An' Two an' One make Three)
'E wants to finish 'is little bit,
   An' 'e wants to go 'ome to 'is tea!

The bachelor pokes up 'is 'ead
   To see if you are gone;
But the married man lies down instead,
   An' waits till the sights come on,
For 'Im an' 'Er an' a hit
   (Direct or ricochee)
'E wants to finish 'is little bit,
   An' 'e wants to go 'ome to 'is tea.

The bachelor will miss you clear
   To fight another day;
But the married man, 'e says 'No fear!'
   'E wants you out of the way
Of 'Im an' 'Er an' It
   (An' 'is road to 'is farm or the sea),
'E wants to finish 'is little bit,
   An' 'e wants to go 'ome to 'is tea.

The bachelor 'e fights 'is fight
   An' stretches out an' snores;
But the married man sits up all night –
   For 'e don't like out-o'-doors.
'E'll strain an' listen an' peer
   An' give the first alarm –
For the sake o' the breathin' 'e's used to 'ear,
   An' the 'ead on the thick of 'is arm.

The bachelor may risk 'is 'ide
   To 'elp you when you're downed;
But the married man will wait beside
   Till the ambulance comes round.
'E'll take your 'ome address
   An' all you've time to say,
Or if 'e sees there's 'ope, 'e'll press
   Your art'ry 'alf the day –

For 'Im an' 'Er an' It
   (An' One from Three leaves Two),
For 'e knows you wanted to finish your bit,
   An' 'e knows 'oo's wantin' you.
Yes, 'Im an' 'Er an' It
   (Our 'oly One in Three),
We're all of us anxious to finish our bit,
   An' we want to get 'ome to our tea!

Yes, It an' 'Er an' 'Im,
   Which often makes me think
The married man must sink or swim
   An' – 'e can't afford to sink!
Oh, 'Im an' It an' 'Er
   Since Adam an' Eve began!
So I'd rather fight with the bacheler
   An' be nursed by the married man!

Lichtenberg

(*New South Wales Contingent*)

Smells are surer than sounds or sights
    To make your heart-strings crack –
They start those awful voices o' nights
    That whisper, 'Old man, come back!'
That must be why the big things pass
    And the little things remain,
Like the smell of the wattle by Lichtenberg,
    Riding in, in the rain.

There was some silly fire on the flank
    And the small wet drizzling down –
There were the sold-out shops and the bank
    And the wet, wide-open town;
And we were doing escort-duty
    To somebody's baggage-train,
And I smelt wattle by Lichtenberg –
    Riding in, in the rain.

It was all Australia to me –
    All I had found or missed:
Every face I was crazy to see,
    And every woman I'd kissed:
All that I shouldn't ha' done, God knows!
    (As He knows I'll do it again),
That smell of the wattle round Lichtenberg,
    Riding in, in the rain!

And I saw Sydney the same as ever,
    The picnics and brass-bands;
And my little homestead on Hunter River
    And my new vines joining hands.

It all came over me in one act
   Quick as a shot through the brain –
With the smell of the wattle round Lichtenberg,
   Riding in, in the rain.

I have forgotten a hundred fights,
   But one I shall not forget –
With the raindrops bunging up my sights
   And my eyes bunged up with wet;
And through the crack and the stink of the cordite,
   (Ah, Christ! My country again!)
The smell of the wattle by Lichtenberg,
   Riding in, in the rain!

Piet

(*Regular of the Line*)

I do not love my Empire's foes,
   Nor call 'em angels; still,
What *is* the sense of 'atin' those
   'Oom you are paid to kill?
So, barrin' all that foreign lot
   Which only joined for spite,
Myself, I'd just as soon as not
   Respect the man I fight.
     Ah, there, Piet – 'is trousies to 'is knees,
     'Is coat-tails lyin' level in the bullet-sprinkled breeze;
     'E does not lose 'is rifle an' 'e does not lose 'is seat.
     I've known a lot o' people ride a dam' sight worse than Piet.

I've 'eard 'im cryin' from the ground
   Like Abel's blood of old,
An' skirmished out to look, an' found
   The beggar nearly cold.

I've waited on till 'e was dead
  (Which couldn't 'elp 'im much),
But many grateful things 'e's said
  To me for doin' such.
    Ah, there, Piet! whose time 'as come to die,
    'Is carcase past rebellion, but 'is eyes inquirin' why.
    Though dressed in stolen uniform with badge o' rank complete,
    I've known a lot o' fellers go a dam' sight worse than Piet.

An' when there wasn't aught to do
  But camp and cattle-guards,
I've fought with 'im the 'ole day through
  At fifteen 'undred yards;
Long afternoons o' lyin' still,
  An' 'earin as you lay
The bullets swish from 'ill to 'ill
  Like scythes among the 'ay.
    Ah, there, Piet! – be'ind 'is stony kop –
    With 'is Boer bread an' biltong,[1] an' 'is flask of awful Dop;[2]
    'Is Mauser for amusement an' 'is pony for retreat,
    I've known a lot o' fellers shoot a dam' sight worse than Piet.

He's shoved 'is rifle 'neath my nose
  Before I'd time to think,
An' borrowed all my Sunday clo'es
  An' sent me 'ome in pink;
An' I 'ave crept (Lord, 'ow I've crept!)
  On 'ands an' knees I've gone,
And spoored and floored and caught and kept
  An' sent him to Ceylon![3]
    Ah, there, Piet! – you've sold me many a pup,
    When week on week alternate it was you an' me ''ands up!'
    But though I never made *you* walk man-naked in the 'eat,
    I've known a lot of fellows stalk a dam' sight worse than Piet.

1. Dried meat. 2. Cape brandy.
3. One of the camps for prisoners of this war was in Ceylon.

From Plewman's to Marabastad,
   From Ookiep to De Aar,
Me an' my trusty friend 'ave ad,
   As you might say, a war;
But seein' what both parties done
   Before 'e owned defeat,
I ain't more proud of 'avin' won
   Than I am pleased with Piet.
      Ah, there, Piet! – picked up be'ind the drive!
      The wonder wasn't 'ow 'e fought, but 'ow 'e kep' alive,
      With nothin' in 'is belly, on 'is back, or to 'is feet –
      I've known a lot o' men behave a dam' sight worse than Piet.

No more I'll 'ear 'is rifle crack
   Along the block'ouse fence –
The beggar's on the peaceful tack,
   Regardless of expense;
For countin' what 'e eats an' draws,
   An' gifts an' loans as well,
'E's gettin' 'alf the Earth, because
   'E didn't give us 'Ell!
      Ah, there, Piet! with your brand-new English plough,
      Your gratis tents an' cattle, an' your most ungrateful frow,
      You've made the British taxpayer rebuild your country-seat –
      I've known some pet battalions charge a dam' sight less than Piet.

'Wilful-Missing'

(Deserters of the Boer War)

There is a world outside the one you know,
   To which for curiousness 'Ell can't compare –
It is the place where 'wilful-missings' go,
   As we can testify, for we are there.

You may 'ave read a bullet laid us low,
    That we was gathered in 'with reverent care'
And buried proper. But it was not so,
    As we can testify, – for we are there!

They can't be certain – faces alter so
    After the old aasvogel's[1] 'ad 'is share.
The uniform's the mark by which they go –
    And – ain't it odd? – the one we best can spare.

We might 'ave seen our chance to cut the show –
    Name, number, record, an' begin elsewhere –
Leavin' some not too late-lamented foe
    One funeral – private – British – for 'is share.

We may 'ave took it yonder in the low
    Bush-veldt that sends men stragglin' unaware
Among the Kaffirs, till their columns go,
    An' they are left past call or count or care.

We might 'ave been your lovers long ago,
    'Usbands or children – comfort or despair.
Our death (*an'* burial) settles all we owe,
    An' why we done it is our own affair.

Marry again, and we will not say no,
    Nor come to barstardize the kids you bear.
Wait on in 'ope – you've all your life below
    Before you'll ever 'ear us on the stair.

There is no need to give our reasons, though
    Gawd knows we all 'ad reasons which were fair;
But other people might not judge 'em so –
    And now it doesn't matter what they were.

1. Vulture.

What man can weigh or size another's woe?
    There are some things too bitter 'ard to bear.
Suffice it we 'ave finished – Domino!
    As we can testify, for we are there,
In the side-world where 'wilful-missings' go.

Ubique

(*Royal Artillery*)

There is a word you often see, pronounce it as you may –
'You bike', 'you bykwee', 'ubbikwe' – alludin' to R.A.
It serves 'Orse, Field, an' Garrison as motto for a crest;
An' when you've found out all it means I'll tell you 'alf the rest.

Ubique means the long-range Krupp be'ind the low-range 'ill –
Ubique means you'll pick it up an', while you do, stand still.
Ubique means you've caught the flash an' timed it by the sound.
Ubique means five gunners' 'ash before you've loosed a round.

Ubique means Blue Fuse,[1] an' make the 'ole to sink the trail.
Ubique means stand up an' take the Mauser's 'alf-mile 'ail.
Ubique means the crazy team not God nor man can 'old.
Ubique means the 'orse's scream which turns your innards cold!

Ubique means 'Bank, 'Olborn, Bank – a penny all the way' –
The soothin', jingle-bump-an'-clank from day to peaceful day.
Ubique means 'They've caught De Wet, an' now we shan't be long.'
Ubique means 'I much regret, the beggar's goin' strong!'

Ubique means the tearin' drift where, breech-blocks jammed with
    mud,
The khaki muzzles duck an' lift across the khaki flood.
Ubique means the dancing plain that changes rocks to Boers.
Ubique means mirage again an' shellin' all outdoors.

---

1. Extreme range.

219

Ubique means 'Entrain at once for Grootdefeatfontein.'
Ubique means 'Off-load your guns' – at midnight in the rain!
Ubique means 'More mounted men. Return all guns to store.'
Ubique means the R.A.M.R. Infantillery Corps.[1]

Ubique means that warnin' grunt the perished linesman knows,
When o'er 'is strung an' sufferin' front the shrapnel sprays 'is foes;
An' as their firin' dies away the 'usky whisper runs
From lips that 'aven't drunk all day: 'The Guns! Thank Gawd, the
    Guns!'

Extreme, depressed, point-blank or short, end-first or any'ow,
From Colesberg Kop to Quagga's Poort – from Ninety-Nine till now –
By what I've 'eard the others tell an' I in spots 'ave seen,
There's nothin' this side 'Eaven or 'Ell Ubique doesn't mean!

The Return

(All Arms)

    Peace is declared, an' I return
      To 'Ackneystadt, but not the same;
    Things 'ave transpired which made me learn
      The size and meanin' of the game.
    I did no more than others did,
      I don't know where the change began.
    I started as a average kid,
      I finished as a thinkin' man.

      If England was what England seems,
        An' not the England of our dreams,
      But only putty, brass, an' paint,
        'Ow quick we'd drop 'er! But she ain't!

1. The Royal Artillery Mounted Rifles – when mounted infantry were badly needed.

Before my gappin' mouth could speak
   I 'eard it in my comrade's tone.
I saw it on my neighbour's cheek
   Before I felt it flush my own.
An' last it come to me – not pride,
   Nor yet conceit, but on the 'ole
(If such a term may be applied),
   The makin's of a bloomin' soul.

Rivers at night that cluck an' jeer,
   Plains which the moonshine turns to sea,
Mountains which never let you near,
   An' stars to all eternity;
An' the quick-breathin' dark that fills
   The 'ollows of the wilderness,
When the wind worries through the 'ills –
   These may 'ave taught me more or less.

Towns without people, ten times took,
   An' ten times left an' burned at last;
An' starvin' dogs that come to look
   For owners when a column passed;
An' quiet, 'omesick talks between
   Men, met by night, you never knew
Until – 'is face – by shellfire seen –
   Once – an' struck off. *They* taught me too.

The day's lay-out – the mornin' sun
   Beneath your 'at-brim as you sight;
The dinner-'ush from noon till one,
   An' the full roar that lasts till night;
An' the pore dead that look so old
   An' was so young an hour ago,
An' legs tied down before they're cold –
   These are the things which make you know.

Also Time runnin' into years –
   A thousand Places left be'ind –

An' Men from both two 'emispheres
 Discussin' things of every kind;
So much more near than I 'ad known,
 So much more great than I 'ad guessed –
An' me, like all the rest, alone –
 But reachin' out to all the rest!

So 'ath it come to me – not pride,
 Nor yet conceit, but on the 'ole
(If such a term may be applied),
 The makin's of a bloomin' soul.
But now, discharged, I fall away
 To do with little things again . . .
Gawd, 'oo knows all I cannot say,
 Look after me in Thamesfontein![1]

> *If England was what England seems,*
> *An' not the England of our dreams,*
> *But only putty, brass, an' paint,*
> *'Ow quick we'd chuck 'er! But she ain't!*

Puck's Song

(Enlarged from 'Puck of Pook's Hill')

See you the ferny ride that steals
Into the oak-woods far?
O that was whence they hewed the keels
That rolled to Trafalgar.

And mark you where the ivy clings
To Bayham's mouldering walls?
O there we cast the stout railings
That stand around St Paul's.

1. London.

See you the dimpled track that runs
All hollow through the wheat?
O that was where they hauled the guns
That smote King Philip's fleet.

(Out of the Weald, the secret Weald,
Men sent in ancient years
The horse-shoes red at Flodden Field,
The arrows at Poitiers!)

See you our little mill that clacks,
So busy by the brook?
She has ground her corn and paid her tax
Ever since Domesday Book.

See you our stilly woods of oak,
And the dread ditch beside?
O that was where the Saxons broke
On the day that Harold died.

See you the windy levels spread
About the gates of Rye?
O that was where the Northmen fled,
When Alfred's ships came by.

See you our pastures wide and lone,
Where the red oxen browse?
O there was a City thronged and known,
Ere London boasted a house.

And see you, after rain, the trace
Of mound and ditch and wall?
O that was a Legion's camping-place,
When Cæsar sailed from Gaul.

And see you marks that show and fade,
Like shadows on the Downs?
O they are the lines the Flint Men made,
To guard their wondrous towns.

Trackway and Camp and City lost,
Salt Marsh where now is corn –
Old Wars, old Peace, old Arts that cease,
And so was England born!

She is not any common Earth,
Water or wood or air,
But Merlin's Isle of Gramarye,
Where you and I will fare!

The Way through the Woods

('Marklake Witches' – *Rewards and Fairies*)

They shut the road through the woods
Seventy years ago.
Weather and rain have undone it again,
And now you would never know
There was once a road through the woods
Before they planted the trees.
It is underneath the coppice and heath
And the thin anemones.
Only the keeper sees
That, where the ring-dove broods,
And the badgers roll at ease,
There was once a road through the woods.

Yet, if you enter the woods
Of a summer evening late,
When the night-air cools on the trout-ringed pools
Where the otter whistles his mate,
(They fear not men in the woods,
Because they see so few)
You will hear the beat of a horse's feet,
And the swish of a skirt in the dew,

Steadily cantering through
The misty solitudes,
As though they perfectly knew
The old lost road through the woods . . .
But there is no road through the woods.

The Kingdom

(Enlarged from *The Naulahka*)

Now we are come to our Kingdom,
And the State is thus and thus;
Our legions wait at the Palace gate –
Little it profits us.
Now we are come to our Kingdom!

Now we are come to our Kingdom,
And the Crown is ours to take –
With a naked sword at the Council board,
And under the throne the snake.
Now we are come to our Kingdom!

Now we are come to our Kingdom,
And the Realm is ours by right,
With shame and fear for our daily cheer,
And heaviness at night.
Now we are come to our Kingdom!

Now we are come to our Kingdom,
But my love's eyelids fall.
All that I wrought for, all that I fought for,
Delight her nothing at all.
My crown is of withered leaves,
For she sits in the dust and grieves.
Now we are come to our Kingdom!

225

Tarrant Moss

(Enlarged from *Plain Tales from the Hills*)

I closed and drew for my love's sake
That now is false to me,
And I slew the Reiver of Tarrant Moss
And set Dumeny free.

They have gone down, they have gone down,
They are standing all arow –
Twenty knights in the peat-water,
That never struck a blow!

Their armour shall not dull nor rust,
Their flesh shall not decay,
For Tarrant Moss holds them in trust
Until the Judgment Day.

Their soul went from them in their youth,
Ah, God, that mine had gone,
Whenas I leaned on my love's truth
And not on my sword alone!

Whenas I leaned on lad's belief
And not on my naked blade –
And I slew a thief, and an honest thief,
For the sake of a worthless maid.

They have laid the Reiver low in his place,
They have set me up on high.
But the twenty knights in the peat-water
Are luckier than I!

And ever they give me gold and praise
And ever I mourn my loss –
For I struck the blow for my false love's sake
And not for the Men of the Moss!

A Charm

(Introduction to *Rewards and Fairies*)

Take of English earth as much
As either hand may rightly clutch.
In the taking of it breathe
Prayer for all who lie beneath.
Not the great nor well-bespoke,
But the mere uncounted folk
Of whose life and death is none
Report or lamentation.
 Lay that earth upon thy heart,
 And thy sickness shall depart!

It shall sweeten and make whole
Fevered breath and festered soul.
It shall mightily restrain
Over-busied hand and brain.
It shall ease thy mortal strife
'Gainst the immortal woe of life,
Till thyself, restored, shall prove
By what grace the Heavens do move.

Take of English flowers these –
Spring's full-facèd primroses,
Summer's wild wide-hearted rose,
Autumn's wall-flower of the close,
And, thy darkness to illume,
Winter's bee-thronged ivy-bloom.
Seek and serve them where they bide
From Candlemas to Christmas-tide,
 For these simples, used aright,
 Can restore a failing sight.

These shall cleanse and purify
Webbed and inward-turning eye;

These shall show thee treasure hid
Thy familiar fields amid;
And reveal (which is thy need)
Every man a King indeed!

Jobson's Amen

('In the Presence' – *A Diversity of Creatures*)

'Blessèd be the English and all their ways and works.
Cursèd be the Infidels, Hereticks, and Turks!'
'Amen,' quo' Jobson, 'but where I used to lie
Was neither Candle, Bell nor Book to curse my brethren by,

'But a palm-tree in full bearing, bowing down, bowing down,
To a surf that drove unsparing at the brown, walled town –
Conches in a temple, oil-lamps in a dome –
And a low moon out of Africa said: "This way home!"'

'Blessèd be the English and all that they profess.
Cursèd be the Savages that prance in nakedness!'
'Amen,' quo' Jobson, 'but where I used to lie
Was neither shirt nor pantaloons to catch my brethren by:

'But a well-wheel slowly creaking, going round, going round,
By a water-channel leaking over drowned, warm ground –
Parrots very busy in the trellised pepper-vine –
And a high sun over Asia shouting: "Rise and shine!"'

'Blessèd be the English and everything they own.
Cursèd be the Infidels that bow to wood and stone!'
'Amen,' quo' Jobson, 'but where I used to lie
Was neither pew nor Gospelleer to save my brethren by:

'But a desert stretched and stricken, left and right, left and right,
Where the piled mirages thicken under white-hot light –

A skull beneath a sand-hill and a viper coiled inside –
And a red wind out of Libya roaring: "Run and hide!"'

'Blessèd be the English and all they make or do.
Cursèd be the Hereticks who doubt that this is true!'
'Amen,' quo' Jobson, 'but where I mean to die
Is neither rule nor calliper to judge the matter by:

'But Himalaya heavenward-heading, sheer and vast, sheer and vast,
In a million summits bedding on the last world's past –
A certain sacred mountain where the scented cedars climb,
And – the feet of my Belovèd hurrying back through Time!'

Chapter Headings

Plain Tales from the Hills

Look, you have cast out Love! What Gods are these
You bid me please?
The Three in One, the One in Three? Not so!
To my own Gods I go.
It may be they shall give me greater ease
Than your cold Christ and tangled Trinities.

Lispeth

When the earth was sick and the skies were grey,
And the woods were rotten with rain,
The Dead Man rode through the autumn day
To visit his love again.

His love she neither saw nor heard,
So heavy was her shame;
And tho' the babe within her stirred
She knew not that he came.

The Other Man

Ride with an idle whip, ride with an unused heel,
But, once in a way, there will come a day
When the colt must be taught to feel
The lash that falls, and the curb that galls, and the
    sting of the rowelled steel.
           The Conversion of Aurelian McGoggin

It was not in the open fight
We threw away the sword,
But in the lonely watching
In the darkness by the ford.
The waters lapped, the night-wind blew,
Full-armed the Fear was born and grew,
And we were flying ere we knew
From panic in the night.
           The Rout of the White Hussars

Cold Iron

('Cold Iron' – *Rewards and Fairies*)

'Gold is for the mistress – silver for the maid –
Copper for the craftsman cunning in his trade.'
'Good!' said the Baron, sitting in his hall,
'But Iron – Cold Iron – is master of them all.'

So he made rebellion 'gainst the King his liege,
Camped before his citadel and summoned it to siege.
'Nay!' said the cannoneer on the castle wall,
'But Iron – Cold Iron – shall be master of you all!'

Woe for the Baron and his knights so strong,
When the cruel cannon-balls laid 'em all along;
He was taken prisoner, he was cast in thrall,
And Iron – Cold Iron – was master of it all!

Yet his King spake kindly (ah, how kind a Lord!)
'What if I release thee now and give thee back thy sword?'
'Nay!' said the Baron, 'mock not at my fall,
For Iron – Cold Iron – is master of men all.'

'Tears are for the craven, prayers are for the clown –
Halters for the silly neck that cannot keep a crown.'
'As my loss is grievous, so my hope is small,
For Iron – Cold Iron – must be master of men all!'

Yet his King made answer (few such Kings there be!)
'Here is Bread and here is Wine – sit and sup with me.
Eat and drink in Mary's Name, the whiles I do recall
How Iron – Cold Iron – can be master of men all!'

He took the Wine and blessed it. He blessed and brake the Bread.
With His own Hands He served Them, and presently He said:
'See! These Hands they pierced with nails, outside My city wall,
Show Iron – Cold Iron – to be master of men all.

'Wounds are for the desperate, blows are for the strong.
Balm and oil for weary hearts all cut and bruised with wrong.
I forgive thy treason – I redeem thy fall –
For Iron – Cold Iron – must be master of men all!'

'Crowns are for the valiant – sceptres for the bold!
Thrones and powers for mighty men who dare to take and hold!'
'Nay!' said the Baron, kneeling in his hall,
'But Iron – Cold Iron – is master of men all!
Iron out of Calvary is master of men all!'

The Quest

The Knight came home from the quest,
    Muddied and sore he came.
Battered of shield and crest,
    Bannerless, bruised and lame.
    Fighting we take no shame,
    Better is man for a fall.
Merrily borne, the bugle-horn
    Answered the warder's call: –
'Here is my lance to mend (Haro!),
    'Here is my horse to be shot!
Ay, they were strong, and the fight was long;
    But I paid as good as I got!'

'Oh, dark and deep their van,
    That mocked my battle-cry.
I could not miss my man,
    But I could not carry by:
    Utterly whelmed was I,
    Flung under, horse and all.'
Merrily borne, the bugle-horn
    Answered the warder's call!

'My wounds are noised abroad;
    But theirs my foemen cloaked.
Ye see my broken sword –
    But never the blades she broke;
    Paying them stroke for stroke,
    Good handsel over all.'
Merrily borne, the bugle-horn
    Answered the warder's call!

'My shame ye count and know.
    Ye say the quest is vain.
Ye have not seen my foe.
    Ye have not told his slain.

Surely he fights again, again;
    But when ye prove his line,
There shall come to your aid my broken blade
    In the last, lost fight of mine!
And here is my lance to mend (Haro!),
    And here is my horse to be shot!
Ay, they were strong, and the fight was long;
    But I paid as good as I got!'

The Children

1914–18

('The Honours of War' – *A Diversity of Creatures*)

These were our children who died for our lands: they were dear in our
    sight.
  We have only the memory left of their home-treasured sayings and
    laughter.
  The price of our loss shall be paid to our hands, not another's
    hereafter.
Neither the Alien nor Priest shall decide on it. That is our right.
    But who shall return us the children?

At the hour the Barbarian chose to disclose his pretences,
  And raged against Man, they engaged, on the breasts that they bared
    for us,
  The first felon-stroke of the sword he had long-time prepared for
    us –
Their bodies were all our defence while we wrought our defences.

They bought us anew with their blood, forbearing to blame us,
Those hours which we had not made good when the Judgment o'ercame
    us.
They believed us and perished for it. Our statecraft, our learning
Delivered them bound to the Pit and alive to the burning

Whither they mirthfully hastened as jostling for honour –
Not since her birth has our Earth seen such worth loosed upon her.

Nor was their agony brief, or once only imposed on them.
   The wounded, the war-spent, the sick received no exemption:
   Being cured they returned and endured and achieved our
       redemption,
Hopeless themselves of relief, till Death, marvelling, closed on them.

That flesh we had nursed from the first in all cleanness was given
To corruption unveiled and assailed by the malice of Heaven –
By the heart-shaking jests of Decay where it lolled on the wires –
To be blanched or gay-painted by fumes – to be cindered by fires –
To be senselessly tossed and retossed in stale mutilation
From crater to crater. For this we shall take expiation.
       But who shall return us our children?

A Song to Mithras

Hymn of the XXX Legion: circa A.D. 350

('On the Great Wall' – *Puck of Pook's Hill*)

Mithras, God of the Morning, our trumpets waken the Wall!
'Rome is above the Nations, but Thou art over all!'
Now as the names are answered, and the guards are marched away,
Mithras, also a soldier, give us strength for the day!

Mithras, God of the Noontide, the heather swims in the heat.
Our helmets scorch our foreheads, our sandals burn our feet.
Now in the ungirt hour – now lest we blink and drowse,
Mithras, also a soldier, keep us true to our vows!

Mithras, God of the Sunset, low on the Western main –
Thou descending immortal, immortal to rise again!
Now when the watch is ended, now when the wine is drawn,
Mithras, also a soldier, keep us pure till the dawn!

Mithras, God of the Midnight, here where the great Bull dies,
Look on Thy children in darkness. Oh, take our sacrifice!
Many roads Thou hast fashioned – all of them lead to the Light!
Mithras, also a soldier, teach us to die aright!

The New Knighthood

('A Deal in Cotton' – *Actions and Reactions*)

Who gives him the Bath?
'I,' said the wet,
Rank Jungle-sweat,
'I'll give him the Bath!'

Who'll sing the psalms?
'We,' said the Palms.
'As the hot wind becalms,
'We'll sing the psalms.'

Who lays on the sword?
'I,' said the Sun,
'Before he has done,
'I'll lay on the sword.'

Who fastens his belt?
'I,' said Short-Rations,
'I know all the fashions
'Of tightening a belt!'

Who gives him his spur?
'I,' said his Chief,
Exacting and brief,
'I'll give him the spur.'

Who'll shake his hand?
'I,' said the Fever,
'And I'm no deceiver,
'I'll shake his hand.'

Who brings him the wine?
'I,' said Quinine,
'It's a habit of mine.
'*I'*ll come with his wine.'

Who'll put him to proof?
'I,' said All Earth.
'Whatever he's worth,
'I'll put to the proof.'

Who'll choose him for Knight?
'I,' said his Mother,
'Before any other,
'My very own Knight.'

And after this fashion, adventure to seek,
Was Sir Galahad made – as it might be last week!

Harp Song of the Dane Women

('The Knights of the Joyous Venture' – *Puck of Pook's Hill*)

What is a woman that you forsake her,
And the hearth-fire and the home-acre,
To go with the old grey Widow-maker?

She has no house to lay a guest in –
But one chill bed for all to rest in,
That the pale suns and the stray bergs nest in.

She has no strong white arms to fold you,
But the ten-times-fingering weed to hold you –
Out on the rocks where the tide has rolled you.

Yet, when the signs of summer thicken,
And the ice breaks, and the birch-buds quicken,
Yearly you turn from our side, and sicken –

Sicken again for the shouts and the slaughters.
You steal away to the lapping waters,
And look at your ship in her winter-quarters.

You forget our mirth, and talk at the tables,
The kine in the shed and the horse in the stables –
To pitch her sides and go over her cables.

Then you drive out where the storm-clouds swallow,
And the sound of your oar-blades, falling hollow,
Is all we have left through the months to follow.

Ah, what is Woman that you forsake her,
And the hearth-fire and the home-acre,
To go with the old grey Widow-maker?

The Winners

(The Story of the Gadsbys)

What is the moral? Who rides may read.
When the night is thick and the tracks are blind
A friend at a pinch is a friend indeed,
But a fool to wait for the laggard behind.
Down to Gehenna or up to the Throne,
He travels the fastest who travels alone.

White hands cling to the tightened rein,
Slipping the spur from the booted heel,
Tenderest voices cry 'Turn again!'
Red lips tarnish the scabbarded steel.
High hopes faint on a warm hearth-stone –
He travels the fastest who travels alone.

One may fall but he falls by himself –
Falls by himself with himself to blame.

One may attain and to him is pelf –
Loot of the city in Gold or Fame.
Plunder of earth shall be all his own
Who travels the fastest and travels alone.

Wherefore the more ye be holpen and stayed,
Stayed by a friend in the hour of toil,
Sing the heretical song I have made –
His be the labour and yours be the spoil.
Win by his aid and the aid disown –
He travels the fastest who travels alone!

from *Chapter Headings*

The Naulahka

There is pleasure in the wet, wet clay,
When the artist's hand is potting it.
There is pleasure in the wet, wet lay,
When the poet's pad is blotting it.
There is pleasure in the shine of your picture on the line
At the Royal Acade-my;
But the pleasure felt in these is as chalk to Cheddar cheese
When it comes to a well-made Lie. –
To a quite unwreckable Lie,
To a most impeccable Lie!
To a water-tight, fire-proof, angle-iron, sunk-hinge, time-lock, steel-
    faced Lie!
Not a private hansom Lie,
But a pair-and-brougham Lie,
Not a little-place-at-Tooting, but a country-house-with-shooting
And a ring-fence-deer-park Lie.

Road-Song of the Bandar-Log

('Kaa's Hunting' – *The Jungle Book*)

Here we go in a flung festoon,
Half-way up to the jealous moon!
Don't you envy our pranceful bands?
Don't you wish you had extra hands?
Wouldn't you like if your tails were – *so* –
Curved in the shape of a Cupid's bow?
   Now you're angry, but – never mind,
   Brother, thy tail hangs down behind!

Here we sit in a branchy row,
Thinking of beautiful things we know;
Dreaming of deeds that we mean to do,
All complete, in a minute or two –
Something noble and grand and good,
Won by merely wishing we could.
   Now we're going to – never mind,
   Brother, thy tail hangs down behind!

All the talk we ever have heard
Uttered by bat or beast or bird –
Hide or fin or scale or feather –
Jabber it quickly and all together!
Excellent! Wonderful! Once again!
Now we are talking just like men.
   Let's pretend we are . . . Never mind!
   Brother, thy tail hangs down behind!
   This is the way of the Monkey-kind!

Then join our leaping lines that scumfish through the pines,
That rocket by where, light and high, the wild-grape swings.
By the rubbish in our wake, and the noble noise we make,
Be sure – be sure, we're going to do some splendid things!

The Fabulists

1914–18

('The Vortex' – *A Diversity of Creatures*)

When all the world would keep a matter hid,
   Since Truth is seldom friend to any crowd,
Men write in fable, as old Æsop did,
   Jesting at that which none will name aloud.
And this they needs must do, or it will fall
Unless they please they are not heard at all.

When desperate Folly daily laboureth
   To work confusion upon all we have,
When diligent Sloth demandeth Freedom's death,
   And banded Fear commandeth Honour's grave –
Even in that certain hour before the fall,
Unless men please they are not heard at all.

Needs must all please, yet some not all for need,
   Needs must all toil, yet some not all for gain,
But that men taking pleasure may take heed,
   Whom present toil shall snatch from later pain.
Thus some have toiled, but their reward was small
Since, though they pleased, they were not heard at all.

This was the lock that lay upon our lips,
   This was the yoke that we have undergone,
Denying us all pleasant fellowships
   As in our time and generation.
Our pleasures unpursued age past recall,
And for our pains – we are not heard at all.

What man hears aught except the groaning guns?
   What man heeds aught save what each instant brings?

When each man's life all imaged life outruns,
   What man shall pleasure in imaginings?
So it hath fallen, as it was bound to fall,
We are not, nor we were not, heard at all.

'Our Fathers Also'

('Below the Mill Dam' – *Traffics and Discoveries*)

Thrones, Powers, Dominions, Peoples, Kings,
Are changing 'neath our hand.
Our fathers also see these things
But they do not understand.

By – they are by with mirth and tears,
Wit or the works of Desire –
Cushioned about on the kindly years
Between the wall and the fire.

The grapes are pressed, the corn is shocked –
Standeth no more to glean;
For the Gates of Love and Learning locked
When they went out between.

All lore our Lady Venus bares,
Signalled it was or told
By the dear lips long given to theirs
And longer to the mould.

All Profit, all Device, all Truth,
Written it was or said
By the mighty men of their mighty youth,
Which is mighty being dead.

The film that floats before their eyes
The Temple's Veil they call;
And the dust that on the Shewbread lies
Is holy over all.

Warn them of seas that slip our yoke,
Of slow-conspiring stars –
The ancient Front of Things unbroke
But heavy with new wars?

By – they are by with mirth and tears,
Wit or the waste of Desire –
Cushioned about on the kindly years
Between the wall and the fire!

Jubal and Tubal Cain

(*Canadian*)

Jubal sang of the Wrath of God
   And the curse of thistle and thorn –
But Tubal got him a pointed rod,
   And scrabbled the earth for corn.
  Old – old as that early mould,
     Young as the sprouting grain –
  Yearly green is the strife between
    Jubal and Tubal Cain!

Jubal sang of the new-found sea,
   And the love that its waves divide –
But Tubal hollowed a fallen tree
   And passed to the further side.
  Black – black as the hurricane-wrack,
     Salt as the under-main –
  Bitter and cold is the hate they hold –
    Jubal and Tubal Cain!

Jubal sang of the golden years
   When wars and wounds shall cease –
But Tubal fashioned the hand-flung spears
   And showèd his neighbours peace.
   New – new as the Nine-point-Two,
     Older than Lamech's slain –
   Roaring and loud is the feud avowed
     Twix' Jubal and Tubal Cain!

Jubal sang of the cliffs that bar
   And the peaks that none may crown –
But Tubal clambered by jut and scar
   And there he builded a town.
   High – high as the snowsheds lie,
     Low as the culverts drain –
   Wherever they be they can never agree –
     Jubal and Tubal Cain!

If –

('Brother Square-Toes' – *Rewards and Fairies*)

If you can keep your head when all about you
   Are losing theirs and blaming it on you,
If you can trust yourself when all men doubt you,
   But make allowance for their doubting too;
If you can wait and not be tired by waiting,
   Or being lied about, don't deal in lies,
Or being hated, don't give way to hating,
   And yet don't look too good, nor talk too wise:

If you can dream – and not make dreams your master;
   If you can think – and not make thoughts your aim;
If you can meet with Triumph and Disaster
   And treat those two impostors just the same;

If you can bear to hear the truth you've spoken
   Twisted by knaves to make a trap for fools,
Or watch the things you gave your life to, broken,
   And stoop and build 'em up with worn-out tools:

If you can make one heap of all your winnings
   And risk it on one turn of pitch-and-toss,
And lose, and start again at your beginnings
   And never breathe a word about your loss;
If you can force your heart and nerve and sinew
   To serve your turn long after they are gone,
And so hold on when there is nothing in you
   Except the Will which says to them: 'Hold on!'

If you can talk with crowds and keep your virtue,
   Or walk with Kings – nor lose the common touch,
If neither foes nor loving friends can hurt you,
   If all men count with you, but none too much;
If you can fill the unforgiving minute
   With sixty seconds' worth of distance run,
Yours is the Earth and everything that's in it,
   And – which is more – you'll be a Man, my son!

The Rabbi's Song

('The House Surgeon' – *Actions and Reactions*)

2 Samuel xiv 14

If thought can reach to Heaven,
   On Heaven let it dwell,
For fear thy Thought be given
   Like power to reach to Hell.
For fear the desolation
   And darkness of thy mind
Perplex an habitation
   Which thou hast left behind.

Let nothing linger after –
  No whimpering ghost remain,
In wall, or beam, or rafter,
  Of any hate or pain.
Cleanse and call home thy spirit,
  Deny her leave to cast,
On aught thy heirs inherit,
  The shadow of her past.

For think, in all thy sadness,
  What road our griefs may take;
Whose brain reflect our madness,
  Or whom our terrors shake:
For think, lest any languish
  By cause of thy distress –
The arrows of our anguish
  Fly farther than we guess.

Our lives, our tears, as water,
  Are spilled upon the ground;
God giveth no man quarter,
  Yet God a means hath found,
Though Faith and Hope have vanished,
  And even Love grows dim –
A means whereby His banished
  Be not expelled from Him!

The Return of the Children

('They' – *Traffics and Discoveries*)

Neither the harps nor the crowns amused, nor the cherubs' dove-
    winged races –
Holding hands forlornly the Children wandered beneath the Dome,
Plucking the splendid robes of the passers-by, and with pitiful faces
Begging what Princes and Powers refused: – 'Ah, please will you let
    us go home?'

245

Over the jewelled floor, nigh weeping, ran to them Mary the Mother,
Kneeled and caressed and made promise with kisses, and drew them
    along to the gateway –
Yea, the all-iron unbribeable Door which Peter must guard and none
    other.
Straightway She took the Keys from his keeping, and opened and freed
    them straightway.

Then, to Her Son, Who had seen and smiled, She said: 'On the night
    that I bore Thee,
What didst Thou care for a love beyond mine or a heaven that was not
    my arm?
Didst Thou push from the nipple, O Child, to hear the angels adore
    Thee
When we two lay in the breath of the kine?' And He said: – 'Thou hast
    done no harm.'

So through the Void the Children ran homeward merrily hand in hand,
Looking neither to left nor right where the breathless Heavens stood
    still.
And the Guards of the Void resheathed their swords, for they heard
    the Command:
'Shall I that have suffered the Children to come to Me hold them
    against their will?'

The Land

('Friendly Brook' – *A Diversity of Creatures*)

When Julius Fabricius, Sub-Prefect of the Weald,
In the days of Diocletian owned our Lower River-field,
He called to him Hobdenius – a Briton of the Clay,
Saying: 'What about that River-piece for layin' in to hay?'

And the aged Hobden answered: 'I remember as a lad
My father told your father that she wanted dreenin' bad.

An' the more that you neeglect her the less you'll get her clean.
Have it jest *as* you've a mind to, but, if I was you, I'd dreen.'

So they drained it long and crossways in the lavish Roman style –
Still we find among the river-drift their flakes of ancient tile,
And in drouthy middle August, when the bones of meadows show,
We can trace the lines they followed sixteen hundred years ago.

Then Julius Fabricius died as even Prefects do,
And after certain centuries, Imperial Rome died too.
Then did robbers enter Britain from across the Northern main
And our Lower River-field was won by Ogier the Dane.

Well could Ogier work his war-boat – well could Ogier wield his
        brand –
Much he knew of foaming waters – not so much of farming land.
So he called to him a Hobden of the old unaltered blood,
Saying: 'What about that River-piece; she doesn't look no good?'

And the aged Hobden answered: ''Tain't for *me* to interfere,
But I've known that bit o' meadow now for five and fifty year.
Have it *jest* as you've a mind to, but I've proved it time on time,
If you want to change her nature you have *got* to give her lime!'

Ogier sent his wains to Lewes, twenty hours' solemn walk,
And drew back great abundance of the cool, grey, healing chalk.
And old Hobden spread it broadcast, never heeding what was in 't. –
Which is why in cleaning ditches, now and then we find a flint.

Ogier died. His sons grew English – Anglo-Saxon was their name –
Till out of blossomed Normandy another pirate came;
For Duke William conquered England and divided with his men,
And our Lower River-field he gave to William of Warenne.

But the Brook (you know her habit) rose one rainy autumn night
And tore down sodden flitches of the bank to left and right.
So, said William to his Bailiff as they rode their dripping rounds:
'Hob, what about that River-bit – the Brook's got up no bounds?'

And that aged Hobden answered: ''Tain't my business to advise,
But ye might ha' known 'twould happen from the way the valley lies.
Where ye can't hold back the water you must try and save the sile.
Hev it jest as you've a *mind* to, but, if I was you, I'd spile!'

They spiled along the water-course with trunks of willow-trees,
And planks of elms behind 'em and immortal oaken knees.
And when the spates of Autumn whirl the gravel-beds away
You can see their faithful fragments, iron-hard in iron clay.

.   .   .   .

Georgii Quinti Anno Sexto, I, who own the River-field,
Am fortified with title-deeds, attested, signed and sealed,
Guaranteeing me, my assigns, my executors and heirs
All sorts of powers and profits which – are neither mine nor theirs.

I have rights of chase and warren, as my dignity requires.
I can fish – but Hobden tickles. I can shoot – but Hobden wires.
I repair, but he reopens, certain gaps which, men allege,
Have been used by every Hobden since a Hobden swapped a hedge.

Shall I dog his morning progress o'er the track-betraying dew?
Demand his dinner-basket into which my pheasant flew?
Confiscate his evening faggot under which my conies ran,
And summons him to judgment? I would sooner summons Pan.

His dead are in the churchyard – thirty generations laid.
Their names were old in history when Domesday Book was made;
And the passion and the piety and prowess of his line
Have seeded, rooted, fruited in some land the Law calls mine.

Not for any beast that burrows, not for any bird that flies,
Would I lose his large sound counsel, miss his keen amending eyes.
He is bailiff, woodman, wheelwright, field-surveyor, engineer,
And if flagrantly a poacher – 'tain't for me to interfere.

'Hob, what about the River-bit?' I turn to him again,
With Fabricius and Ogier and William of Warenne.
'Hev it jest as you've a mind to, *but*' – and here he takes command.
For whoever pays the taxes old Mus' Hobden owns the land.

Just So Verses

When the cabin port-holes are dark and green
   Because of the seas outside;
When the ship goes *wop* (with a wiggle between)
And the steward falls into the soup-tureen,
   And the trunks begin to slide;
When Nursey lies on the floor in a heap,
And Mummy tells you to let her sleep,
And you aren't waked or washed or dressed,
Why, then you will know (if you haven't guessed)
You're 'Fifty North and Forty West'!

                          How the Whale Got his Throat

    The Camel's hump is an ugly lump
       Which well you may see at the Zoo;
    But uglier yet is the hump we get
       From having too little to do.

    Kiddies and grown-ups too-oo-oo,
    If we haven't enough to do-oo-oo,
                We get the hump –
                Cameelious hump –
    The hump that is black and blue!

We climb out of bed with a frouzly head,
    And a snarly-yarly voice.
We shiver and scowl and we grunt and we growl
    At our bath and our boots and our toys;

And there ought to be a corner for me
(And I know there is one for you)
                When we get the hump –
                Cameelious hump –
The hump that is black and blue!

The cure for this ill is not to sit still,
 Or frowst with a book by the fire;
But to take a large hoe and a shovel also,
 And dig till you gently perspire;

And then you will find that the sun and the wind,
And the Djinn of the Garden too,
 Have lifted the hump –
 The horrible hump –
The hump that is black and blue!

I get it as well as you-oo-oo –
If I haven't enough to do-oo-oo!
 We all get hump –
 Cameelious hump –
Kiddies and grown-ups too!

How the Camel Got his Hump

The Looking-Glass

A Country Dance

(Enlarged from *Rewards and Fairies*)

Queen Bess was Harry's daughter. Stand forward partners all!
 In ruff and stomacher and gown
She danced King Philip down-a-down,
And left her shoe to show 'twas true –
 (The very tune I'm playing you)
In Norgem at Brickwall! [1]

The Queen was in her chamber, and she was middling old.
Her petticoat was satin, and her stomacher was gold.
Backwards and forwards and sideways did she pass,
Making up her mind to face the cruel looking-glass.

1. A pair of Queen Elizabeth's shoes are still at Brickwall House, Northiam, Sussex.

The cruel looking-glass that will never show a lass
As comely or as kindly or as young as what she was!

Queen Bess was Harry's daughter. Now hand your partners all!

The Queen was in her chamber, a-combing of her hair.
There came Queen Mary's spirit and It stood behind her chair,
Singing 'Backwards and forwards and sideways may you pass,
But I will stand behind you till you face the looking-glass.
The cruel looking-glass that will never show a lass
As lovely or unlucky or as lonely as I was!'

Queen Bess was Harry's daughter. Now turn your partners all!

The Queen was in her chamber, a-weeping very sore,
There came Lord Leicester's spirit and It scratched upon the door,
Singing 'Backwards and forwards and sideways may you pass,
But I will walk beside you till you face the looking-glass.
The cruel looking-glass that will never show a lass,
As hard and unforgiving or as wicked as you was!'

Queen Bess was Harry's daughter. Now kiss your partners all!

The Queen was in her chamber, her sins were on her head.
She looked the spirits up and down and statelily she said: –
'Backwards and forwards and sideways though I've been,
Yet I am Harry's daughter and I am England's Queen!'
And she faced the looking-glass (and whatever else there was)
And she saw her day was over and she saw her beauty pass
In the cruel looking-glass, that can always hurt a lass
More hard than any ghost there is or any man there was!

The Widower

For a season there must be pain –
For a little, little space
I shall lose the sight of her face,
Take back the old life again
While She is at rest in her place.

For a season this pain must endure,
For a little, little while
I shall sigh more often than smile
Till Time shall work me a cure,
And the pitiful days beguile.

For that season we must be apart,
For a little length of years,
Till my life's last hour nears,
And, above the beat of my heart,
I hear Her voice in my ears.

But I shall not understand –
Being set on some later love,
Shall not know her for whom I strove,
Till she reach me forth her hand,
Saying, 'Who but I have the right?'
And out of a troubled night
Shall draw me safe to the land.

The Song of the Little Hunter

('The King's Ankus' – *The Second Jungle Book*)

Ere Mor the Peacock flutters, ere the Monkey People cry,
  Ere Chil the Kite swoops down a furlong sheer,
Through the Jungle very softly flits a shadow and a sigh –
  He is Fear, O Little Hunter, he is Fear!

Very softly down the glade runs a waiting, watching shade,
  And the whisper spreads and widens far and near.
And the sweat is on thy brow, for he passes even now –
  He is Fear, O Little Hunter, he is Fear!

Ere the moon has climbed the mountain, ere the rocks are ribbed with
      light,
  When the downward-dipping trails are dank and drear,
Comes a breathing hard behind thee – *snuffle-snuffle* through the night –
  It is Fear, O Little Hunter, it is Fear!
On thy knees and draw the bow; bid the shrilling arrow go;
  In the empty, mocking thicket plunge the spear!
But thy hands are loosed and weak, and the blood has left thy cheek –
  It is Fear, O Little Hunter, it is Fear!

When the heat-cloud sucks the tempest, when the slivered pine-trees
      fall,
  When the blinding, blaring rain-squalls lash and veer,
Through the war-gongs of the thunder rings a voice more loud than all –
  It is Fear, O Little Hunter, it is Fear!
Now the spates are banked and deep; now the footless boulders leap –
  Now the lightning shows each littlest leaf-rib clear –
But thy throat is shut and dried, and thy heart against thy side
  Hammers: Fear, O Little Hunter – this is Fear!

Mine Sweepers

1914–18

(Sea Warfare)

Dawn off the Foreland – the young flood making
  Jumbled and short and steep –
Black in the hollows and bright where it's breaking –
  Awkward water to sweep.
  'Mines reported in the fairway,
  'Warn all traffic and detain.
"Sent up *Unity, Claribel, Assyrian, Stormcock,* and *Golden Gain.*'

Noon off the Foreland – the first ebb making
  Lumpy and strong in the bight.
Boom after boom, and the golf-hut shaking
  And the jackdaws wild with fright!
    'Mines located in the fairway,
    'Boats now working up the chain,
'Sweepers – *Unity*, *Claribel*, *Assyrian*, *Stormcock*, and *Golden Gain*.'

Dusk off the Foreland – the last light going
  And the traffic crowding through,
And five damned trawlers with their syreens blowing
  Heading the whole review!
    'Sweep completed in the fairway.
    'No more mines remain.
'Sent back *Unity*, *Claribel*, *Assyrian*, *Stormcock*, and *Golden Gain*.'

Mother o' Mine

(Dedication to *The Light that Failed*)

If I were hanged on the highest hill,
Mother o' mine, O mother o' mine!
I know whose love would follow me still,
Mother o' mine, O mother o' mine!

If I were drowned in the deepest sea,
Mother o' mine, O mother o' mine!
I know whose tears would come down to me,
Mother o' mine, O mother o' mine!

If I were damned of body and soul,
I know whose prayers would make me whole,
Mother o' mine, O mother o' mine!

The Only Son

(Enlarged from *Many Inventions*)

She dropped the bar, she shot the bolt, she fed the fire anew,
For she heard a whimper under the sill and a great grey paw came
    through.
The fresh flame comforted the hut and shone on the roof-beam,
And the Only Son lay down again and dreamed that he dreamed a
    dream.
The last ash fell from the withered log with the click of a falling spark,
And the Only Son woke up again, and called across the dark: —
'Now was I born of womankind and laid in a mother's breast?
For I have dreamed of a shaggy hide whereon I went to rest.
And was I born of womankind and laid on a father's arm?
For I have dreamed of clashing teeth that guarded me from harm.

And was I born an Only Son and did I play alone?
For I have dreamed of comrades twain that bit me to the bone.
And did I break the barley-cake and steep it in the tyre?
For I have dreamed of a youngling kid new-riven from the byre:
For I have dreamed of a midnight sky and a midnight call to blood
And red-mouthed shadows racing by, that thrust me from my food.
'Tis an hour yet and an hour yet to the rising of the moon,
But I can see the black roof-tree as plain as it were noon.
'Tis a league and a league to the Lena Falls where the trooping
    blackbuck go;
But I can hear the little fawn that bleats behind the doe.
'Tis a league and a league to the Lena Falls where the crop and the
    upland meet,
But I can smell the wet dawn-wind that wakes the sprouting wheat.
Unbar the door. I may not bide, but I must out and see
If those are wolves that wait outside or my own kin to me!'

    .   .   .   .

She loosed the bar, she slid the bolt, she opened the door anon,
And a grey bitch-wolf came out of the dark and fawned on the Only
    Son!

Mowgli's Song against People

('Letting in the Jungle' – *The Second Jungle Book*)

I will let loose against you the fleet-footed vines –
I will call in the Jungle to stamp out your lines!
    The roofs shall fade before it,
      The house-beams shall fall;
    And the *Karela*,[1] the bitter *Karela*,
      Shall cover it all!

In the gates of these your councils my people shall sing.
In the doors of these your garners the Bat-folk shall cling;
    And the snake shall be your watchman,
      By a hearthstone unswept;
    For the *Karela*, the bitter *Karela*,
      Shall fruit where ye slept!

Ye shall not see my strikers; ye shall hear them and guess.
By night, before the moon-rise, I will send for my cess,
    And the wolf shall be your herdsman
      By a landmark removed;
    For the *Karela*, the bitter *Karela*,
      Shall seed where ye loved!

I will reap your fields before you at the hands of a host.
Ye shall glean behind my reapers for the bread that is lost;
    And the deer shall be your oxen
      On a headland untilled:
    For the *Karela*, the bitter *Karela*,
      Shall leaf where ye build!

I have untied against you the club-footed vines –
I have sent in the Jungle to swamp out your lines!
    The trees – the trees are on you!
      The house-beams shall fall;
    And the *Karela*, the bitter *Karela*,
      Shall cover you all!

1. A wild melon.

Chapter Headings

The Jungle Books

Veil them, cover them, wall them round –
    Blossom, and creeper, and weed –
Let us forget the sight and the sound,
    The smell and the touch of the breed!
Fat black ash by the altar-stone,
    Here is the white-foot rain,
And the does bring forth in the fields unsown,
    And none shall affright them again;
And the blind walls crumble, unknown, o'erthrown,
    And none shall inhabit again!

Letting in the Jungle

The People of the Eastern Ice, they are melting like the snow –
They beg for coffee and sugar; they go where the white men go.
The People of the Western Ice, they learn to steal and fight;
They sell their furs to the trading post; they sell their souls to the white.
The People of the Southern Ice, they trade with the whaler's crew;
Their women have many ribbons, but their tents are torn and few.
But the People of the Elder Ice, beyond the white man's ken –
Their spears are made of the narwhal-horn, and they are the last of the
    Men!

Quiquern

'The Trade'

1914–18

(*Sea Warfare*)

They bear, in place of classic names,
    Letters and numbers on their skin.
They play their grisly blindfold games
    In little boxes made of tin.

Sometimes they stalk the Zeppelin,
Sometimes they learn where mines are laid,
   Or where the Baltic ice is thin.
That is the custom of 'The Trade'.

Few prize-courts sit upon their claims.
   They seldom tow their targets in.
They follow certain secret aims
   Down under, far from strife or din.
   Where they are ready to begin
No flag is flown, no fuss is made
   More than the shearing of a pin.
That is the custom of 'The Trade'.

The Scout's quadruple funnel flames
   A mark from Sweden to the Swin,
The Cruiser's thund'rous screw proclaims
   Her comings out and goings in:
   But only whiffs of paraffin
Or creamy rings that fizz and fade
   Show where the one-eyed Death has been.
That is the custom of 'The Trade'.

Their feats, their fortunes and their fames
   Are hidden from their nearest kin;
No eager public backs or blames,
   No journal prints the yarn they spin
   (The Censor would not let it in!)
When they return from run or raid.
   Unheard they work, unseen they win.
That is the custom of 'The Trade'.

The King's Task

1902

(Enlarged from *Traffics and Discoveries*)

After the sack of the City, when Rome was sunk to a name,
In the years that the lights were darkened, or ever St Wilfrid came,
Low on the borders of Britain (the ancient poets sing)
Between the Cliff and the Forest there ruled a Saxon King.
Stubborn all were his people from cottar to overlord –
Not to be cowed by the cudgel, scarce to be schooled by the sword;
Quick to turn at their pleasure, cruel to cross in their mood,
And set on paths of their choosing as the hogs of Andred's Wood.
Laws they made in the Witan – the laws of flaying and fine –
Common, loppage and pannage, the theft and the track of kine –
Statutes of tun and of market for the fish and the malt and the meal –
The tax on the Bramber packhorse and the tax on the Hastings keel.
Over the graves of the Druids and under the wreck of Rome,
Rudely but surely they bedded the plinth of the days to come.
Behind the feet of the Legions and before the Norseman's ire
Rudely but greatly begat they the framing of State and Shire.
Rudely but deeply they laboured, and their labour stands till now,
If we trace on our ancient headlands the twist of their eight-ox
    plough . . .
There came a king from Hamtun, by Bosenham he came,
He filled Use with slaughter, and Lewes he gave to flame.
He smote while they sat in the Witan – sudden he smote and sore,
That his fleet was gathered at Selsea ere they mustered at Cymen's
    Ore.
Blithe went the Saxons to battle, by down and wood and mere,
But thrice the acorns ripened ere the western mark was clear.
Thrice was the beechmast gathered, and the Beltane fires burned
Thrice, and the beeves were salted thrice ere the host returned.
They drove that king from Hamtun, by Bosenham o'erthrown,
Out of Rugnor to Wilton they made his land their own.
Camps they builded at Gilling, at Basing and Alresford,
But wrath abode in the Saxons from cottar to overlord.

Wrath at the weary war-game, at the foe that snapped and ran,
Wolf-wise feigning and flying, and wolf-wise snatching his man.
Wrath for their spears unready, their levies new to the blade –
Shame for the helpless sieges and the scornful ambuscade.
At hearth and tavern and market, wherever the tale was told,
Shame and wrath had the Saxons because of their boasts of old.
And some would drink and deny it, and some would pray and atone;
But the most part, after their anger, avouched that the sin was their
    own.
Wherefore, girding together, up to the Witan they came,
And as they had shouldered their bucklers so did they shoulder their
    blame;
(For that was the wont of the Saxons, the ancient poets sing),
And first they spoke in the Witan and then they spoke to the King:
'Edward King of the Saxons, thou knowest from sire to son,
'One is the King and his People – in gain and ungain one.
'Count we the gain together. With doubtings and spread dismays
'We have broken a foolish people – but after many days.
'Count we the loss together. Warlocks hampered our arms.
'We were tricked as by magic, we were turned as by charms.
'We went down to the battle and the road was plain to keep,
'But our angry eyes were holden, and we struck as they strike in
    sleep –
'Men new shaken from slumber, sweating, with eyes a-stare,
'Little blows uncertain, dealt on the useless air.
'Also a vision betrayed us and a lying tale made bold,
'That we looked to hold what we had not and to have what we did
    not hold:
'That a shield should give us shelter – that a sword should give us
    power –
'A shield snatched up a venture and a hilt scarce handled an hour:
'That being rich in the open, we should be strong in the close –
'And the Gods would sell us a cunning for the day that we met our
    foes.
'This was the work of wizards, but not with our foe they bide,
'In our own camp we took them, and their names are Sloth and Pride.
'Our pride was before the battle, our sloth ere we lifted spear,
'But hid in the heart of the people, as the fever hides in the mere,

'Waiting only the war-game, the heat of the strife to rise
'As the ague fumes round Oxeney when the rotting reed-bed dries.
'But now we are purged of that fever – cleansed by the letting of
    blood,
'Something leaner of body – something keener of mood.
'And the men new-freed from the levies return to the fields again,
'Matching a hundred battles, cottar and lord and thane;
'And they talk loud in the temples where the ancient war-gods are;
'They thumb and mock and belittle the holy harness of war.
'They jest at the sacred chariots, the robes and the gilded staff.
'These things fill them with laughter, they lean on their spears and
    laugh.
'The men grown old in the war-game, hither and thither they range –
'And scorn and laughter together are sire and dam of change;
'And change may be good or evil – but we know not what it will bring;
'Therefore our King must teach us. That is thy task, O King!'

King Henry VII and the Shipwrights

(A.D. *1487*)

('The Wrong Thing' – *Rewards and Fairies*)

Harry, our King in England, from London town is gone,
And comen to Hamull on the Hoke in the Countie of Suthampton.
For there lay the *Mary of the Tower*, his ship of war so strong,
And he would discover, certaynely, if his shipwrights did him wrong.

He told none of his setting forth, nor yet where he would go,
(But only my Lord of Arundel) and meanly did he show,
In an old jerkin and patched hose that no man might him mark.
With his frieze hood and cloak above, he looked like any clerk.

He was at Hamull on the Hoke about the hour of the tide,
And saw the *Mary* haled into dock, the winter to abide,
With all her tackle and habiliments which are the King his own;
But then ran on his false shipwrights and stripped her to the bone.

They heaved the main-mast overboard, that was of a trusty tree,
And they wrote down it was spent and lost by force of weather at sea.
But they sawen it into planks and strakes as far as it might go,
To maken beds for their own wives and little children also.

There was a knave called Slingawai, he crope beneath the deck,
Crying: 'Good felawes, come and see! The ship is nigh a wreck!
For the storm that took our tall main-mast, it blew so fierce and fell,
Alack! it hath taken the kettles and pans, and this brass pott as well!'

With that he set the pott on his head and hied him up the hatch,
While all the shipwrights ran below to find what they might snatch;
All except Bob Brygandyne and he was a yeoman good.
He caught Slingawai round the waist and threw him on to the mud.

'I have taken plank and rope and nail, without the King his leave,
After the custom of Portesmouth, but I will not suffer a thief.
Nay, never lift up thy hand at me – there's no clean hands in the trade.
Steal in measure,' quo' Brygandyne. 'There's measure in all things
     made!'

'Gramercy, yeoman!' said our King. 'Thy counsel liketh me.'
And he pulled a whistle out of his neck and whistled whistles three.
Then came my Lord of Arundel pricking across the down,
And behind him the Mayor and Burgesses of merry Suthampton town.

They drew the naughty shipwrights up, with the kettles in their hands,
And bound them round the forecastle to wait the King's commands.
But 'Sith ye have made your beds,' said the King, 'ye needs must lie
     thereon.
For the sake of your wives and little ones – felawes, get you gone!'

When they had beaten Slingawai, out of his own lips
Our King appointed Brygandyne to be Clerk of all his ships.
'Nay, never lift up thy hands to me – there's no clean hands in the
     trade.
But steal in measure,' said Harry our King. 'There's measure in all
     things made!'

God speed the Mary of the Tower, the Sovereign, and Grace Dieu,
The Sweepstakes and the Mary Fortune, and the Henry of Bristol too!
All tall ships that sail on the sea, or in our harbours stand,
That they may keep measure with Harry our King and peace in Engeland!

The Wet Litany

('Their Lawful Occasions' – *Traffics and Discoveries*)

When the waters' countenance
Blurs 'twixt glance and second glance;
When our tattered smokes forerun
Ashen 'neath a silvered sun;
When the curtain of the haze
Shuts upon our helpless ways –
    Hear the Channel Fleet at sea:
    Libera nos Domine!

When the engines' bated pulse
Scarcely thrills the nosing hulls;
When the wash along the side
Sounds, a-sudden, magnified;
When the intolerable blast
Marks each blindfold minute passed;

When the fog-buoy's squattering flight
Guides us through the haggard night;
When the warning bugle blows;
When the lettered doorways close;
When our brittle townships press,
Impotent, on emptiness;

When the unseen leadsmen lean
Questioning a deep unseen;
When their lessened count they tell
To a bridge invisible;

When the hid and perilous
Cliffs return our cry to us;

When the treble thickness spread
Swallows up our next-ahead;
When her siren's frightened whine
Shows her sheering out of line;
When – her passage undiscerned –
We must turn where she has turned,
    Hear the Channel Fleet at sea:
    Libera nos Domine!

Thorkild's Song

('The Knights of the Joyous Venture' – *Puck of Pook's Hill*)

There's no wind along these seas,
Out oars for Stavanger!
Forward all for Stavanger!
So we must wake the white-ash breeze,
Let fall for Stavanger!
A long pull for Stavanger!

Oh, hear the benches creak and strain!
(A long pull for Stavanger!)
She thinks she smells the Northland rain!
(A long pull for Stavanger!)

She thinks she smells the Northland snow,
And she's as glad as we to go.

She thinks she smells the Northland rime,
And the dear dark nights of winter-time.

She wants to be at her own home pier,
To shift her sails and standing gear.

She wants to be in her winter-shed,
To strip herself and go to bed.

Her very bolts are sick for shore,
And we – we want it ten times more!

So all you Gods that love brave men,
Send us a three-reef gale again!

Send us a gale, and watch us come,
With close-cropped canvas slashing home!

But – there's no wind on all these seas,
A long pull for Stavanger!
So we must wake the white-ash breeze.
A long pull for Stavanger!

'Angutivaun Taina'

Song of the Returning Hunter (Esquimaux)

('Quiquern' – *The Second Jungle Book*)

Our gloves are stiff with the frozen blood,
    Our furs with the drifted snow,
As we come in with the seal – the seal!
    In from the edge of the floe.

Au jana! Aua! Oha! Haq!
    And the yelping dog-teams go;
And the long whips crack, and the men come back,
    Back from the edge of the floe!

We tracked our seal to his secret place,
    We heard him scratch below,
We made our mark, and we watched beside,
    Out on the edge of the floe.

We raised our lance when he rose to breathe,
    We drove it downward – so!
And we played him thus, and we killed him thus,
    Out on the edge of the floe.

Our gloves are glued with the frozen blood,
    Our eyes with the drifting snow;
But we come back to our wives again,
    Back from the edge of the floe!

Au jana! Aua! Oha! Haq!
    And the loaded dog-teams go;
And the wives can hear their men come back,
    Back from the edge of the floe!

The Runes on Weland's Sword

1906

('Old Men at Pevensey' – *Puck of Pook's Hill*)

A Smith makes me
To betray my Man
In my first fight.

To gather Gold
At the world's end
I am sent.

The Gold I gather
Comes into England
Out of deep Water.

Like a shining Fish
Then it descends
Into deep Water.

266

It is not given
For goods or gear,
But for The Thing.

The Gold I gather
A king covets
For an ill use.

The Gold I gather
Is drawn up
Out of deep Water.

Like a shining Fish
Then it descends
Into deep Water.

It is not given
For goods or gear,
But for The Thing.

Song of the Galley-Slaves

('The Finest Story in the World' – *Many Inventions*)

We pulled for you when the wind was against us and the sails were low.
   Will you never let us go?
We ate bread and onions when you took towns, or ran aboard quickly
   when you were beaten back by the foe.
The Captains walked up and down the deck in fair weather singing
   songs, but we were below.
We fainted with our chins on the oars and you did not see that we
   were idle, for we still swung to and fro.
   Will you never let us go?
The salt made the oar-handles like shark-skin; our knees were cut to
   the bone with salt-cracks; our hair was stuck to our foreheads; and
   our lips were cut to the gums, and you whipped us because we
   could not row.
   Will you never let us go?

But, in a little time, we shall run out of the port-holes as the water
    runs along the oar-blade, and though you tell the others to row
    after us you will never catch us till you catch the oar-thresh and
    tie up the winds in the belly of the sail. Aho!
        Will you never let us go?

The Prayer

(*Kim*)

My brother kneels, so saith Kabir,
To stone and brass in heathen wise,
But in my brother's voice I hear
My own unanswered agonies.
His God is as his fates assign,
His prayer is all the world's – and mine.

THREE POEMS FROM
THE MUSE AMONG THE MOTORS

Arterial

(*Early Chinese*)

I

Frost upon small rain – the ebony-lacquered avenue
    Reflecting lamps as a pool shows goldfish.
The sight suddenly emptied out of the young man's eyes
    Entering upon it sideways.

II

In youth, by hazard, I killed an old man.
    In age I maimed a little child.
Dead leaves under foot reproach not:
But the lop-sided cherry-branch – whenever the sun rises,
    How black a shadow!

The Idiot Boy

(*Wordsworth*)

He wandered down the mountain grade
   Beyond the speed assigned –
A youth whom Justice often stayed
   And generally fined.

He went alone, that none might know
   If he could drive or steer.
Now he is in the ditch, and Oh!
   The differential gear!

The Bother

(*Clough*)

Hastily Adam our driver swallowed a curse in the darkness –
Petrol nigh at end and something wrong with a sprocket
Made him speer for the nearest town, when lo! at the cross-ways
Four blank letterless arms the virginal signpost extended.
'Look!' thundered Hugh the Radical. 'This is the England we boast
   of –
Bland, white-bellied, obese, but utterly useless for business.
They are repainting the signs and have left the job in the middle.
They are repainting the signs and traffic may stop till they've done it,
Which is to say till the son-of-a-gun of a local contractor,
Having laboriously wiped out every name for
Probably thirty miles round, be minded to finish his labour!
Had not the fool the sense to paint out and paint in together?'

Thus, not seeing his speech belied his Radical Gospel
(Which is to paint out the earth and then write 'Damn' on the shutter),
Hugh embroidered the theme imperially and stretched it
Making himself, reformer-wise, a bit of a nuisance
Till, with the help of Adam, we cast him out on the landscape.

The Roman Centurion's Song

(*Roman occupation of Britain*, AD 300)

Legate, I had the news last night – my cohort ordered home
By ship to Portus Itius and thence by road to Rome.
I've marched the companies aboard, the arms are stowed below:
Now let another take my sword. Command me not to go!

I've served in Britain forty years, from Vectis to the Wall.
I have none other home than this, nor any life at all.
Last night I did not understand, but, now the hour draws near
That calls me to my native land, I feel that land is here.

Here where men say my name was made, here where my work was
     done;
Here where my dearest dead are laid – my wife – my wife and son;
Here where time, custom, grief and toil, age, memory, service, love,
Have rooted me in British soil. Ah, how can I remove?

For me this land, that sea, these airs, those folk and fields suffice.
What purple Southern pomp can match our changeful Northern skies,
Black with December snows unshed or pearled with August haze –
The clanging arch of steel-grey March, or June's long-lighted days?

You'll follow widening Rhodanus till vine and olive lean
Aslant before the sunny breeze that sweeps Nemausus clean
To Arelate's triple gate; but let me linger on,
Here where our stiff-necked British oaks confront Euroclydon!

You'll take the old Aurelian Road through shore-descending pines
Where, blue as any peacock's neck, the Tyrrhene Ocean shines.
You'll go where laurel crowns are won, but – will you e'er forget
The scent of hawthorn in the sun, or bracken in the wet?

Let me work here for Britain's sake – at any task you will –
A marsh to drain, a road to make or native troops to drill.

Some Western camp (I know the Pict) or granite Border keep,
Mid seas of heather derelict, where our old messmates sleep.

Legate, I come to you in tears – My cohort ordered home!
I've served in Britain forty years. What should I do in Rome?
Here is my heart, my soul, my mind – the only life I know.
I cannot leave it all behind. Command me not to go!

Edgehill Fight

(*Civil Wars, 1642*)

Naked and grey the Cotswolds stand
    Beneath the autumn sun,
And the stubble-fields on either hand
    Where Stour and Avon run.
There is no change in the patient land
    That has bred us every one.

She should have passed in cloud and fire
    And saved us from this sin
Of war – red war – 'twixt child and sire,
    Household and kith and kin,
In the heart of a sleepy Midland shire,
    With the harvest scarcely in.

But there is no change as we meet at last
    On the brow-head or the plain,
And the raw astonished ranks stand fast
    To slay or to be slain
By the men they knew in the kindly past
    That shall never come again –

By the men they met at dance or chase,
    In the tavern or the hall,

At the justice-bench and the market-place,
    At the cudgel-play or brawl –
Of their own blood and speech and race,
    Comrades or neighbours all!

More bitter than death this day must prove
    Whichever way it go,
For the brothers of the maids we love
    Make ready to lay low
Their sisters' sweethearts, as we move
    Against our dearest foe.

Thank Heaven! At last the trumpets peal
    Before our strength gives way.
For King or for the Commonweal –
    No matter which they say,
The first dry rattle of new-drawn steel
    Changes the world to-day!

The Secret of the Machines

(Modern Machinery)

We were taken from the ore-bed and the mine,
    We were melted in the furnace and the pit –
We were cast and wrought and hammered to design,
    We were cut and filed and tooled and gauged to fit.
Some water, coal, and oil is all we ask,
    And a thousandth of an inch to give us play:
And now, if you will set us to our task,
    We will serve you four and twenty hours a day!

    We can pull and haul and push and lift and drive,
    We can print and plough and weave and heat and light,
    We can run and race and swim and fly and dive,
    We can see and hear and count and read and write!

Would you call a friend from half across the world?
  If you'll let us have his name and town and state,
You shall see and hear your crackling question hurled
  Across the arch of heaven while you wait.
Has he answered? Does he need you at his side?
  You can start this very evening if you choose,
And take the Western Ocean in the stride
  Of seventy thousand horses and some screws!

  The boat express is waiting your command!
  You will find the *Mauretania* at the quay,
  Till her captain turns the lever 'neath his hand,
  And the monstrous nine-decked city goes to sea.

Do you wish to make the mountains bare their head
  And lay their new-cut forests at your feet?
Do you want to turn a river in its bed,
  Or plant a barren wilderness with wheat?
Shall we pipe aloft and bring you water down
  From the never-failing cisterns of the snows,
To work the mills and tramways in your town,
  And irrigate your orchards as it flows?

  It is easy! Give us dynamite and drills!
  Watch the iron-shouldered rocks lie down and quake,
  As the thirsty desert-level floods and fills,
  And the valley we have dammed becomes a lake.

But remember, please, the Law by which we live,
  We are not built to comprehend a lie,
We can neither love nor pity nor forgive.
  If you make a slip in handling us you die!
We are greater than the Peoples or the Kings –
  Be humble, as you crawl beneath our rods! –
Our touch can alter all created things,
  We are everything on earth – except The Gods!

Though our smoke may hide the Heavens from your eyes,
It will vanish and the stars will shine again,
Because, for all our power and weight and size,
We are nothing more than children of your brain!

The Glory of the Garden

Our England is a garden that is full of stately views,
Of borders, beds and shrubberies and lawns and avenues,
With statues on the terraces and peacocks strutting by;
But the Glory of the Garden lies in more than meets the eye.

For where the old thick laurels grow, along the thin red wall,
You find the tool- and potting-sheds which are the heart of all;
The cold-frames and the hot-houses, the dungpits and the tanks,
The rollers, carts and drain-pipes, with the barrows and the planks.

And there you'll see the gardeners, the men and 'prentice boys
Told off to do as they are bid and do it without noise;
For, except when seeds are planted and we shout to scare the birds,
The Glory of the Garden it abideth not in words.

And some can pot begonias and some can bud a rose,
And some are hardly fit to trust with anything that grows;
But they can roll and trim the lawns and sift the sand and loam,
For the Glory of the Garden occupieth all who come.

Our England is a garden, and such gardens are not made
By singing: – 'Oh, how beautiful!' and sitting in the shade,
While better men than we go out and start their working lives
At grubbing weeds from gravel-paths with broken dinner-knives.

There's not a pair of legs so thin, there's not a head so thick,
There's not a hand so weak and white, nor yet a heart so sick,
But it can find some needful job that's crying to be done,
For the Glory of the Garden glorifieth every one.

Then seek your job with thankfulness and work till further orders,
If it's only netting strawberries or killing slugs on borders;
And when your back stops aching and your hands begin to harden,
You will find yourself a partner in the Glory of the Garden.

Oh, Adam was a gardener, and God who made him sees
That half a proper gardener's work is done upon his knees,
So when your work is finished, you can wash your hands and pray
For the Glory of the Garden, that it may not pass away!
And the Glory of the Garden it shall never pass away!

The Last Lap

('*The Burning of the* Sarah Sands')

How do we know, by the bank-high river,
    Where the mired and sulky oxen wait,
And it looks as though we might wait for ever,
    How do we know that the floods abate?
There is no change in the current's brawling –
    Louder and harsher the freshet scolds;
Yet we can feel she is falling, falling,
    And the more she threatens the less she holds.
Down to the drift, with no word spoken,
    The wheel-chained wagons slither and slue . . .
Achtung! The back of the worst is broken!
    And – lash your leaders! – we're through – we're through!

How do we know, when the port-fog holds us
    Moored and helpless, a mile from the pier,
And the week-long summer smother enfolds us –
    How do we know it is going to clear?
There is no break in the blindfold weather,
    But, one and another, about the bay,
The unseen capstans clink together,
    Getting ready to go up and away.

A pennon whimpers – the breeze has found us –
    A headsail jumps through the thinning haze.
The whole hull follows, till – broad around us –
    The clean-swept ocean says: 'Go your ways!'

How do we know, when the long fight rages,
    On the old, stale front that we cannot shake,
And it looks as though we were locked for ages,
    How do we know they are going to break?
There is no lull in the level firing,
    Nothing has shifted except the sun.
Yet we can feel they are tiring, tiring –
    Yet we can tell they are ripe to run.
Something wavers, and, while we wonder,
    Their centre-trenches are emptying out,
And, before their useless flanks go under,
    Our guns have pounded retreat to rout!

A Departure

('*The Parable of Boy Jones*')

Since first the White Horse Banner blew free,
    By Hengist's horde unfurled,
Nothing has changed on land or sea
    Of the things that steer the world.
(As it was when the long-ships scudded through the gale
    So it is where the Liners go.)
Time and Tide, they are both in a tale –
    'Woe to the weaker – woe!'

No charm can bridle the hard-mouthed wind
    Or smooth the fretting swell.
No gift can alter the grey Sea's mind,
    But she serves the strong man well.

(As it is when her uttermost deeps are stirred
   So it is where the quicksands show,)
All the waters have but one word –
   'Woe to the weaker – woe!'

The feast is ended, the tales are told,
   The dawn is overdue,
And we meet on the quay in the whistling cold
   Where the galley waits her crew.
Out with the torches, they have flared too long,
   And bid the harpers go.
Wind and warfare have but one song –
   'Woe to the weaker – woe!'

Hail to the great oars gathering way,
   As the beach begins to slide!
Hail to the war-shields' click and play
   As they lift along our side!
Hail to the first wave over the bow –
   Slow for the sea-stroke! Slow! –
All the benches are grunting now: –
   'Woe to the weaker – woe!'

The Changelings

(R.N.V.R.)

('Sea Constables' – *Debits and Credits*)

Or ever the battered liners sank
   With their passengers to the dark,
I was head of a Walworth Bank,
   And you were a grocer's clerk.

I was a dealer in stocks and shares,
   And you in butters and teas;

And we both abandoned our own affairs
    And took to the dreadful seas.

Wet and worry about our ways –
    Panic, onset, and flight –
Had us in charge for a thousand days
    And a thousand-year-long night.

We saw more than the nights could hide –
    More than the waves could keep –
And – certain faces over the side
    Which do not go from our sleep.

We were more tired than words can tell
    While the pied craft fled by,
And the swinging mounds of the Western swell
    Hoisted us Heavens-high . . .

Now there is nothing – not even our rank –
    To witness what we have been;
And I am returned to my Walworth Bank,
    And you to your margarine!

'Late Came the God'

('The Wish House' – *Debits and Credits*)

Late came the God, having sent his forerunners who were not
      regarded –
  Late, but in wrath;
Saying: 'The wrong shall be paid, the contempt be rewarded
  On all that she hath.'
He poisoned the blade and struck home, the full bosom receiving
The wound and the venom in one, past cure or relieving.

He made treaty with Time to stand still that the grief might be fresh –
Daily renewed and nightly pursued through her soul to her flesh –

278

Mornings of memory, noontides of agony, midnights unslaked for her,
Till the stones of the street of her Hells and her Paradise ached for her.

So she lived while her body corrupted upon her.
  And she called on the Night for a sign, and a Sign was allowed,
And she builded an Altar and served by the light of her Vision –
  Alone, without hope of regard or reward, but uncowed,
Resolute, selfless, divine.
  These things she did in Love's honour . . .
What is a God beside Woman? Dust and derision!

Rahere

('The Wish House' – *Debits and Credits*)

Rahere, King Henry's Jester, feared by all the Norman Lords
For his eye that pierced their bosoms, for his tongue that shamed their
    swords;
Feed and flattered by the Churchmen – well they knew how deep he
    stood
In dark Henry's crooked counsels – fell upon an evil mood.

Suddenly, his days before him and behind him seemed to stand
Stripped and barren, fixed and fruitless, as those leagues of naked sand
When St Michael's ebb slinks outward to the bleak horizon-bound,
And the trampling wide-mouthed waters are withdrawn from sight and
    sound.

Then a Horror of Great Darkness sunk his spirit and, anon,
(Who had seen him wince and whiten as he turned to walk alone)
Followed Gilbert the Physician, and muttered in his ear,
'Thou hast it, O my brother?' 'Yea, I have it,' said Rahere.

'So it comes,' said Gilbert smoothly, 'man's most immanent distress.
'Tis a humour of the Spirit which abhorreth all excess;
And, whatever breed the surfeit – Wealth, or Wit, or Power, or Fame
(And thou hast each) the Spirit laboureth to expel the same.

'Hence the dulled eye's deep self-loathing – hence the loaded leaden
    brow;
Hence the burden of Wanhope that aches thy soul and body now.
Ay, the merriest fool must face it, and the wisest Doctor learn;
For it comes – it comes,' said Gilbert, 'as it passes – to return.'

But Rahere was in his torment, and he wandered, dumb and far,
Till he came to reeking Smithfield where the crowded gallows are,
(Followed Gilbert the Physician) and beneath the wry-necked dead,
Sat a leper and his woman, very merry, breaking bread.

He was cloaked from chin to ankle – faceless, fingerless, obscene –
Mere corruption swaddled man-wise, but the woman whole and clean;
And she waited on him crooning, and Rahere beheld the twain,
Each delighting in the other, and he checked and groaned again.

'So it comes, – it comes,' said Gilbert, 'as it came when Life began.
'Tis a motion of the Spirit that revealeth God to man.
In the shape of Love exceeding, which regards not taint or fall,
Since in perfect Love, saith Scripture, can be no excess at all.

'Hence the eye that sees no blemish – hence the hour that holds no
    shame.
Hence the Soul assured the Essence and the Substance are the same.
Nay, the meanest need not miss it, though the mightier pass it by;
For it comes – it comes,' said Gilbert, 'and, thou seest, it does not die!'

The Survival

HORACE, Bk V Ode 22

('The Janeites' – *Debits and Credits*)

Securely, after days
    Unnumbered, I behold
Kings mourn that promised praise
    Their cheating bards foretold.

Of earth-constricting wars,
    Of Princes passed in chains,
Of deeds out-shining stars,
    No word or voice remains.

Yet furthest times receive,
    And to fresh praise restore,
Mere breath of flutes at eve,
    Mere seaweed on the shore.

A smoke of sacrifice;
    A chosen myrtle-wreath;
An harlot's altered eyes;
    A rage 'gainst love or death;

Glazed snow beneath the moon;
    The surge of storm-bowed trees –
The Cæsars perished soon,
    And Rome Herself: But these

Endure while Empires fall
    And Gods for Gods make room . . .
Which greater God than all
    Imposed the amazing doom?

Alnaschar and the Oxen

('The Bull that Thought' – *Debits and Credits*)

There's a pasture in a valley where the hanging woods divide.
    And a Herd lies down and ruminates in peace;
Where the pheasant rules the nooning, and the owl the twilight-tide,
    And the war-cries of our world die out and cease.
Here I cast aside the burden that each weary week-day brings
    And, delivered from the shadows I pursue,
On peaceful, postless Sabbaths I consider Weighty Things –
    Such as Sussex Cattle feeding in the dew!

At the gate beside the river where the trouty shallows brawl,
   I know the pride that Lobengula felt,
When he bade the bars be lowered of the Royal Cattle Kraal,
   And fifteen miles of oxen took the veldt.
From the walls of Bulawayo in unbroken file they came
   To where the Mount of Council cuts the blue . . .
I have only six and twenty, but the principle's the same
   With my Sussex Cattle feeding in the dew!

To a luscious sound of tearing, where the clovered herbage rips,
   Level-backed and level-bellied watch 'em move –
See those shoulders, guess that heart-girth, praise those loins, admire
      those hips,
   And the tail set low for flesh to make above!
Count the broad unblemished muzzles, test the kindly mellow skin,
   And, where yon heifer lifts her head at call,
Mark the bosom's just abundance 'neath the gay and clean-cut chin,
   And those eyes of Juno, overlooking all!

Here is colour, form and substance! I will put it to the proof
   And, next season, in my lodges shall be born
Some very Bull of Mithras, flawless from his agate hoof
   To his even-branching, ivory, dusk-tipped horn.
He shall mate with block-square virgins – kings shall seek his like in
      vain,
   While I multiply his stock a thousandfold,
Till an hungry world extol me, builder of a lofty strain
   That turns one standard ton at two years old!

There's a valley, under oakwood, where a man may dream his dream,
   In the milky breath of cattle laid at ease,
Till the moon o'ertops the alders, and her image chills the stream,
   And the river-mist runs silver round their knees!
Now the footpaths fade and vanish; now the ferny clumps deceive;
   Now the hedgerow-folk possess their fields anew;
Now the Herd is lost in darkness, and I bless them as I leave,
   My Sussex Cattle feeding in the dew!

Gertrude's Prayer

('Dayspring Mishandled' – *Limits and Renewals*)

That which is marred at birth Time shall not mend,
    Nor water out of bitter well make clean;
All evil thing returneth at the end,
    Or elseway walketh in our blood unseen.
Whereby the more is sorrow in certaine –
Dayspring mishandled cometh not againe.

To-bruizèd be that slender, sterting spray
    Out of the oake's rind that should betide
A branch of girt and goodliness, straightway
    Her spring is turnèd on herself, and wried
And knotted like some gall or veiney wen.–
Dayspring mishandled cometh not agen.

Noontide repayeth never morning-bliss –
    Sith noon to morn is incomparable;
And, so it be our dawning goth amiss,
    None other after-hour serveth well.
Ah! Jesu-Moder, pitie my oe paine –
Dayspring mishandled cometh not againe!

Naaman's Song

('Aunt Ellen' – *Limits and Renewals*)

'Go, wash thyself in Jordan – go, wash thee and be clean!'
Nay, not for any Prophet will I plunge a toe therein!
For the banks of curious Jordan are parcelled into sites,
Commanded and embellished and patrolled by Israelites.

There rise her timeless capitals of Empires daily born,
Whose plinths are laid at midnight, and whose streets are packed at
    morn;

THE MOTHER'S SON

And here come hired youths and maids that feign to love or sin
In tones like rusty razor-blades to tunes like smitten tin.

And here be merry murtherings, and steeds with fiery hooves;
And furious hordes with guns and swords, and clamberings over
    rooves;
And horrid tumblings down from Heaven, and flights with wheels and
    wings;
And always one weak virgin who is chased through all these things.

And here is mock of faith and truth, for children to behold;
And every door of ancient dirt reopened to the old;
With every word that taints the speech, and show that weakens
    thought;
And Israel watcheth over each, and – doth not watch for nought . . .

But Pharpar – but Abana – which Hermon launcheth down –
They perish fighting desert-sands beyond Damascus-town.
But yet their pulse is of the snows – their strength is from on high –
And, if they cannot cure my woes, a leper will I die!

The Mother's Son

('Fairy-kist' – *Limits and Renewals*)

I have a dream – a dreadful dream –
    A dream that is never done.
I watch a man go out of his mind,
    And he is My Mother's Son.

They pushed him into a Mental Home,
    And that is like the grave:
For they do not let you sleep upstairs,
    And you aren't allowed to shave.

And it was *not* disease or crime
   Which got him landed there,
But because They laid on My Mother's Son
   More than a man could bear.

What with noise, and fear of death,
   Waking, and wounds and cold,
They filled the Cup for My Mother's Son
   Fuller than it could hold.

They broke his body and his mind
   And yet They made him live,
And They asked more of My Mother's Son
   Than any man could give.

For, just because he had not died,
   Nor been discharged nor sick,
They dragged it out with My Mother's Son
   Longer than he could stick . . .

And no one knows when he'll get well –
   So, there he'll have to be:
And, 'spite of the beard in the looking-glass,
   I know that man is me!

Song of Seventy Horses

('The Miracle of Saint Jubanus' – *Limits and Renewals*)

Once again the Steamer at Calais – the tackles
Easing the car-trays on to the quay. Release her!
Sign – refill, and let me away with my horses.
(Seventy Thundering Horses!)
Slow through the traffic, my horses! It is enough – it is France!

Whether the throat-closing brick-fields by Lille, or her pavés
Endlessly ending in rain between beet and tobacco;
Or that wind we shave by – the brutal North-Easter,
Rasping the newly dunged Somme.
(Into your collars, my horses!) It is enough – it is France!

Whether the dappled Argonne, the cloud-shadows packing
Either horizon with ghosts; or exquisite, carven
Villages hewn from the cliff, the torrents behind them
Feeding their never-quenched lights.
(Look to your footing, my horses!) It is enough – it is France!

Whether that gale where Biscay jammed in the corner
Herds and heads her seas at the Landes, but defeated
Bellowing smokes along Spain, till the uttermost headlands
Make themselves dance in the mist.
(Breathe – breathe deeply, my horses!) It is enough – it is France!

Whether the broken, honey-hued, honey-combed limestone,
Cream under white-hot sun; the rosemary bee-bloom
Sleepily noisy at noon and, somewhere to Southward,
Sleepily noisy, the Sea.
(Yes, it is warm here, my horses!) It is enough – it is France!

Whether the Massif in Spring, the multiplied lacets
Hampered by slips or drifts; the gentians, under
Turbaned snow, pushing up the heavens of Summer
Though the stark moors lie black.
(Neigh through the icicled tunnels: – 'It is enough – it is France!')

Azrael's Count

('Uncovenanted Mercies' – *Limits and Renewals*)

Lo! the Wild Cow of the Desert, her yeanling estrayed from her –
Lost in the wind-plaited sand-dunes – athirst in the maze of them.
Hot-foot she follows those foot-prints – the thrice-tangled ways of them.
Her soul is shut save to one thing – the love-quest consuming her.
Fearless she lows past the camp, our fires affright her not.
Ranges she close to the tethered ones – the mares by the lances held.
Noses she softly apart the veil in the women's tent.
Next – withdrawn under moonlight, a shadow afar off –
Fades. Ere men cry, 'Hold her fast!' darkness recovers her.
She the all-crazed and forlorn, when the dogs threaten her,
Only a side-tossed horn, as though a fly troubled her,
Shows she hath heard, till a lance in the heart of her quivereth.
– Lo, from that carcass aheap – where speeds the soul of it?
Where is the tryst it must keep? Who is her pandar? Death!

Men I dismiss to the Mercy greet me not willingly;
Crying, 'Why seekest Thou *me* first? Are not my kin unslain?'
Shrinking aside from the Sword-edge, blinking the glare of it,
Sinking the chin in the neck-bone. How shall that profit them?
Yet, among men a ten thousand, few meet me otherwise.

Yet, among women a thousand, one comes to me mistress-wise.
Arms open, breasts open, mouth open – hot is her need on her.
Crying, 'Ho, Servant, acquit me, the bound by Love's promises!
Haste Thou! He waits! I would go! Handle me lustily!'
Lo! her eyes stare past my wings, as things unbeheld by her.
Lo! her lips summonsing part. *I* am not whom she calls!
Lo! My sword sinks and returns. At no time she heedeth it
More than the dust of a journey, her garments brushed clear of it.
Lo! Ere the blood-gush has ceased, forward her soul rushes.
She is away to her tryst. Who is her pandar? Death!

The Gods of the Copybook Headings

1919

As I pass through my incarnations in every age and race,
I make my proper prostrations to the Gods of the Market-Place.
Peering through reverent fingers I watch them flourish and fall,
And the Gods of the Copybook Headings, I notice, outlast them all.

We were living in trees when they met us. They showed us each in turn
That Water would certainly wet us, as Fire would certainly burn:
But we found them lacking in Uplift, Vision and Breadth of Mind,
So we left them to teach the Gorillas while we followed the March of
 Mankind.

We moved as the Spirit listed. *They* never altered their pace,
Being neither cloud nor wind-borne like the Gods of the Market-Place;
But they always caught up with our progress, and presently word
 would come
That a tribe had been wiped off its icefield, or the lights had gone out
 in Rome.

With the Hopes that our World is built on they were utterly out of
 touch,
They denied that the Moon was Stilton; they denied she was even
 Dutch.
They denied that Wishes were Horses; they denied that a Pig had
 Wings.
So we worshipped the Gods of the Market Who promised these
 beautiful things.

When the Cambrian measures were forming, They promised perpetual
 peace.
They swore, if we gave them our weapons, that the wars of the tribes
 would cease.
But when we disarmed They sold us and delivered us bound to our
 foe,
And the Gods of the Copybook Headings said: '*Stick to the Devil you
 know.*'

On the first Feminian Sandstones we were promised the Fuller Life
(Which started by loving our neighbour and ended by loving his wife)
Till our women had no more children and the men lost reason and
    faith,
And the Gods of the Copybook Headings said: *'The Wages of Sin is
    Death.'*

In the Carboniferous Epoch we were promised abundance for all,
By robbing selected Peter to pay for collective Paul;
But, though we had plenty of money, there was nothing our money
    could buy,
And the Gods of the Copybook Headings said: *'If you don't work you
    die.'*

Then the Gods of the Market tumbled, and their smooth-tongued
    wizards withdrew,
And the hearts of the meanest were humbled and began to believe it
    was true
That All is not Gold that Glitters, and Two and Two make Four –
And the Gods of the Copybook Headings limped up to explain it once more.

   .   .   .   .   .   .

As it will be in the future, it was at the birth of Man –
There are only four things certain since Social Progress began: –
That the Dog returns to his Vomit and the Sow returns to her Mire,
And the burnt Fool's bandaged finger goes wabbling back to the Fire;

And that after this is accomplished, and the brave new world begins
When all men are paid for existing and no man must pay for his sins,
As surely as Water will wet us, as surely as Fire will burn,
The Gods of the Copybook Headings with terror and slaughter return!

The Storm Cone

1932

This is the midnight – let no star
Delude us – dawn is very far.
This is the tempest long foretold –
Slow to make head but sure to hold.

Stand by! The lull 'twixt blast and blast
Signals the storm is near, not past;
And worse than present jeopardy
May our forlorn to-morrow be.

If we have cleared the expectant reef,
Let no man look for his relief.
Only the darkness hides the shape
Of further peril to escape.

It is decreed that we abide
The weight of gale against the tide
And those huge waves the outer main
Sends in to set us back again.

They fall and whelm. We strain to hear
The pulses of her labouring gear,
Till the deep throb beneath us proves,
After each shudder and check, she moves!

She moves, with all save purpose lost,
To make her offing from the coast;
But, till she fetches open sea,
Let no man deem that he is free!

The Appeal

IF I HAVE GIVEN YOU DELIGHT
  BY AUGHT THAT I HAVE DONE,
LET ME LIE QUIET IN THAT NIGHT
  WHICH SHALL BE YOURS ANON:

AND FOR THE LITTLE, LITTLE, SPAN
  THE DEAD ARE BORNE IN MIND,
SEEK NOT TO QUESTION OTHER THAN
  THE BOOKS I LEAVE BEHIND.

Notes

Verse Heading to 'The "Kingdom" of Bombay'

Prince's Dock, Colaba, Apollo Bunder, Back Bay (ll. 3,4): all sections of
  Bombay's unsavoury coastline.
Swinburne **(adapted)**: see 'The Commonweal'.

In Partibus

title: shortened form of *in partibus infidelium* (in countries of the infidels).
Sandy Hook (l. 27): the entrance to New York harbour.
Barnum's latest joke (l. 40): Phineas T. Barnum, the circus proprietor.
mango-tope (l. 44): mango grove.
'Bus' (l. 83): enough.

Prelude

a sheltered people's mirth (l. 10): that is, the English in England, as opposed
  to those serving in the Empire abroad.

Army Headquarters

super-**Santley tone** (l. 2): Sir Charles Santley (1834–1922) English baritone
  who toured the USA, Australia and South Africa.

The Story of Uriah

Uriah: see II Samuel 11:3 and ff. King David, covetous of Uriah's wife,
  Bathsheba, arranges for Uriah to be killed in battle: 'Set ye Uriah in the
  forefront of the hottest battle, and retire ye from him, that he may be smitten
  and die.'
Now there were two men in one city; the one rich, and the other poor:
  II Samuel 12:1 for Nathan's parable reproaching King David for his conduct
  vis-à-vis Uriah.
Quetta (l. 1): town in what is now West Pakistan, surrounded by mountains,
  but evidently with an unhealthy climate in September.

To the Unknown Goddess

shikar (l. 2): hunting, sport.

thermantidotes (l. 8): mechanical ceiling fans.

as of old on Mars Hill when they raised/To the God that they knew not an altar (ll. 15–16): Areopagus, hill in Athens, west of the Acropolis. See Acts 17:22 and ff.: 'Then Paul stood in the midst of Mars' hill, and said, Ye men of Athens, I perceive that in all things ye are too superstitious. For as I passed by, and beheld your devotions, I found an altar with this inscription, TO THE UNKNOWN GOD. Whom therefore ye ignorantly worship, him declare I unto you.'

La Nuit Blanche

Tara Devi (l. 3): hill at Simla.

Jakko (l. 5): hill at Simla.

M.D. (l. 26): doctor of medicine.

Epigraph to *The Ballad of Fisher's Boarding-House*

the Hughli (l. 5): branch of the Ganges.

Possibilities

Benmore (l. 13): district of Simla, where the public assembly-room was.

Sanjaolie (l. 18): hill near Simla.

'extras' (l. 32): presumably 'encores' which are finally terminated by the National Anthem.

The Betrothed

Suttee (l. 28): the custom by which an Indian widow sacrifices herself on her husband's funeral pyre.

Christmas in India

ghat (l. 12): a place of cremation.

Rama (l. 13): Ramakrishna, Hindu yogi, regarded as saint (1834–86).

Heimweh (German) (l. 21): the road home, the way home, homesickness.

The Grave of the Hundred Head

A Snider (l. 7): rifle.

Eshmitt (l. 27): Indian pronunciation of Smith.

Calthrops (l. 36): an instrument armed with four spikes, so arranged that one always stands upright, used to obstruct an enemy.

Certain Maxims of Hafiz

Hafiz: Persian lyric poet of fourteenth century.

The Moon of Other Days

ferash (Urdu) (l. 5): a menial servant who spreads carpets, pitches tents etc.
babul (Urdu) (l. 24): thorny mimosa.

One Viceroy Resigns

Lord Dufferin: Frederick Hamilton-Temple-Blackwood (1826–1902) under-secretary for India (1864–6); governor-general of India (1884–8).

Lord Lansdowne: Henry Petty-Fitzmaurice (1845–1927) Viceroy of India (1888–93).

Reay (l. 9): an Indian civil servant, untraceable.

Colvin (l. 9): John Russell Colvin: Anglo-Indian administrator, lieutenant-governor of the North-West provinces during Sepoy mutiny.

Lyall (l. 9): either Sir Alfred Comyn Lyall (1835–1911), a British administrator in India; or Sir Charles James Lyall (1845–1920) who served in the Bengal Civil Service. Most likely the former who wrote a biography of Dufferin.

Roberts (l. 9): most likely Roberts of Kandahar, Pretoria and Waterford, nicknamed 'Bobs' (1832–1914) commander-in-chief of India (1885–93).

Buck (l. 9): unidentified.

Westland (l. 14): unidentified.

poor Wilson (l. 15): identity very uncertain, but might be James Wilson (1805–60), the economist who established paper currency in India, or Horace Hayman Wilson (1786–1860), an Oxford Professor of Sanskrit. In point of fact, these identifications are not important since Kipling's point is the blur of recollection.

Hope (l. 16): positive identification impossible. Ditto Aitchinson, Hunter and Marshal.

Sestina of the Tramp-Royal

tucker: (l. 17): food, sustenance, grub.

Song of the Wise Children

the darkened Fifties (l. 1): the upper part of this latitude is more or less level with Bergen, ten degrees below the Arctic Circle.

The Sea-Wife

garth (l. 10): an enclosure, a garden.

the horse of tree (l. 14): ship as a version of the rocking-horse. Compare 'The Long Trail' – 'the bucking beam-sea roll'.

syne (l. 15): then, afterwards.

The Broken Men

Callao (l. 16): Peru's major seaport.

jalousies (l. 40): outside-shutter with slats.

Gethsemane

I prayed my cup might pass (l. 16): compare Christ in the garden of Gethsemane, 'O my Father, if it be possible, let this cup pass from me' (Matthew 26:39; Mark 14:36; Luke 22:17).

The Song of the Banjo

Broadwood (l. 1): brand of piano.

rowel (l. 35): to prick with the wheel of a spur.

the many-shedded levels (l. 54): from 'watershed', the line separating two river basins.

Song of Roland (l. 56): *Chanson de Roland* composed *c*. 1098.

the Stealer (l. 87): Prometheus who stole fire from Zeus and gave it to man.

The Spies' March

the Pale Horse (l. 65): Revelation 6:8 'And I looked, and behold a pale horse: and his name that sat on him was Death.'

The Explorer

dwined (l. 27): *dwine*, to waste away.

recruiting (l. 39): malapropism for recuperating.

Saul he went to look for donkeys, and by God he found a kingdom! (l. 43): see I Samuel 9:3 ff. where Saul, in search of his father's lost asses, seeks directions of Samuel and is appointed by him 'captain over my people Israel'.

The Pro-Consuls

Proconsul: a Roman magistrate with almost consular authority outside the city, originally one whose consulate had expired.

The Runners

Nimrud (l. 5): an Indianized version of Nimrod, for whom see Genesis 10:8, 9: 'And Cush begat Nimrod: he began to be a mighty one in the earth. He was a mighty hunter before the Lord ...' Here Nimrud seems to represent the British Army seen from the Indian point of view, in which rebellious rumour finally gives way to less sanguine fact and hypocritical allegiance.

border-peels (l. 23): a peel is a palisaded enclosure, a fortified post.

The Sea and the Hills

the Line (l. 4): the equator.
berg (l. 17): iceberg.

McAndrew's Hymn

Calvin (originally Jean Chauvin 1509–54) (l. 5): French theologian, author of *Institutes of the Christian Religion* (1536). Creator of the concept of predetermined election, the predestination of the saved and of those condemned to hell-fire.
scoughed . . . jock (l. 36): not in Wright's *English Dialect Dictionary*, nor Mairi Robinson's *Concise Scots Dictionary*, but guessable as 'drenched' and 'joke'.
Forgie's (l. 42): forgive us.
kittlin (l. 44): cuddling, caressing.
Gay Street (l. 46): red-light district.
blind-fou (l. 52): in a blind rage, mad.
meenisters (l. 64): ministers, clergy.
ross . . . (l. 119): rossignol.
Apollyon (l. 130): Greek name of the destroying angel. See Revelation 9:11: 'And they had a king over them, which is the angel of the bottomless pit, whose name in Hebrew tongue is Abadon, but in Greek tongue hath his name Apollyon.'
An' whiles (l. 170): sometimes.
Pelagian (l. 188): heretical Christian sect that challenged St Augustine's conceptions of Grace and Predestination.

The Mary Gloster

the Yards (l. 7): shipyards.
Grub that 'ud bind you (l. 19): make you constipated.
I gave 'em the Scripture text,/'You keep your light so shining a little in front o' the next!' (ll. 57–8): not scriptural, but invented.
best o' the boiling (l. 97): expression derived from 'boiling fowl', a hen too old either to be described any longer as a chicken, or roasted as one.

The Ballad of the Bolivar

Felt her hog (l. 21): to arch, or hump.
Lloyds' (l. 31): the insurance company, primarily concerned with the underwriting of marine insurance.

The Destroyers

twice three thousand horse (l. 65): that is, 6,000 horsepower.

The Long Trail

the Tents of Shem (l. 9): Genesis 9:27: Ham, father of Canaan, saw his father Noah naked when he was drunk. Shem and Japheth, two other sons, entered their father's tent backwards, so as not to see, and covered up their father's nakedness. Noah then said, 'God shall enlarge Japheth and he shall dwell in the tents of Shem; and Canaan shall be his servant.'

the Peter (l. 37): the Blue Peter flag.

the Mouse, the Gull Light (ll. 51, 53): navigational lights.

The Song of the Dead

the warrigal (l. 4): dingo, wild Australian horse, an Australian aboriginal.

kloof (l. 6): a mountain ravine.

The Native-Born

lories (l. 15): a lory is a parrot with a brushlike tongue.

the sluicing stamp-head (l. 71): machine for crushing ore.

The Last of the Light Brigade

See Tennyson's 'The Charge of the Light Brigade'. However, Kipling's account of survivors provoking Tennyson to an angry sequel on the subject of the national neglect of war veterans appears to be a fabrication. There was no such poem.

Bridge-Guard in the Karroo

the Karroo: the semi-arid plateaux of the Western Cape Province of South Africa.

My Boy Jack

Kipling's son John was shot through the head at the battle of Loos, September 1915. He was a subaltern in the Second Irish Guards.

Dirge of Dead Sisters

Maxim (l. 18): the Maxim machine-gun, invented in 1884.

The English Flag

the sea-egg (l. 23): a sea urchin.

the Hoogli (l. 43): a river which is one arm of the Ganges.

'Cleared'

In 1887 *The Times* printed a series of hostile articles called 'Parnellism and Crime', which ended with a facsimile letter signed by Parnell and apologizing for his denunciation of the Phoenix Park murders. The Parnell Commission

(1889) established the letter was a forgery and although some of his activities were censured, Parnell and his associates were exonerated.

to card a woman's hide (l. 21): to comb out into shreds.

the blood-dyed Clan-na-Gael (l. 30): the tribe of Gaels.

you that 'lost' the League acounts (l. 65): in October 1879 the Fenian, Michael Davitt, formed the Land League and persuaded Parnell to become its president. Parnell organized the system of boycotting, but was always wary of extremists among his members. In October 1882 he set up a new organization, the National League.

Gehazi

Gehazi (l. 1): 2 Kings 5 tells how Elisha cures Naaman of his leprosy, refusing Naaman's reward. However, Elisha's servant, Gehazi, follows the departing Naaman and asks, purportedly on Elisha's behalf, 'two talents of silver in two bags, with two changes of garments'. As a punishment, Elisha inflicts the leprosy of Naaman on Gehazi.

In Kipling's poem, Gehazi is Sir Rufus Isaacs, the Lord Chief Justice of England (1913–21) and behind the parable is the financial scandal of the Marconi affair of 1912, when cabinet ministers were thought to have financial interests in the company to which they granted government contracts.

The Ballad of Boh Da Thone

'Kalends of Greece' (l. 41): Kalends (or calends) are days on which settlements of debt are due. Here, humorously meaning 'never', since the Greeks used no Kalends in their reckoning of time.

ghi (l. 94): or *gheé*, sacred butter.

The Feet of the Young Men

ouananiche (l. 7): A French Canadian name for fresh-water salmon of the Labrador peninsula.

A Death-Bed

'Regis suprema voluntas Lex' (l. 9): the wish of the King is supreme law.

The Bell-Buoy

bob-majors (l. 14): a term in bell-ringing for changes rung on eight bells.

bitt (l. 53): post for fastening cables.

trees (l. 53): top of the masts.

colliers (l. 54): ships that carry coal.

The Islanders

the Younger Nations (l. 30): South Africa, New Zealand, Australia, Canada.

Teraphs of sept and party (l. 77): in ancient Jewish religion, images of sect and party.

The White Man's Burden

Kipling's poem was published 4 February 1899. On 6 February the American Senate voted to take over the administration of the Philippines. Only days later a rebellion against American military occupation broke out.

A Song at Cock-Crow

'Ille autem iterum negavit': however, he denied it again.

Tirmonde and Aerschott (l. 25): Tirmonde is probably Tirlmont (*Flemish* Tienen) and Aerschott is another Flemish name once attached to a place.

Recessional

A hymn sung during the retirement of clergy and choir after a service.

Nineveh and Tyre (l. 16): Tyre was destroyed by the Muslims in 1291, Nineveh fell to the Scythians in 612 BC.

Such boastings as the Gentiles use (l. 21): this line makes it clear that Kipling's analogy is with the Jews as the chosen people. Jewish history makes it clear that national fortunes depend on God's will rather than the nation itself. This dependency is what must never be forgotten.

Samuel Pepys

Ostia's mole (l. 6): Ostia was an ancient city of Italy at the mouth of the Tiber. A mole is a massive breakwater.

The beaked Liburnian's triple bank (l. 7): a trireme.

Clio (l. 24): the muse of History.

The Files

Faenza (l. 12): city in north, central Italy.

Père-la-Chaise (l. 19): cemetery in Paris.

Bomba (l. 43): Ferdinand II, King of the Two Sicilies.

Samuel Smiles (l. 66): 1812–1904: author of *Self-Help* (1859), *Character* (1871), *Thrift* (1875), *Duty* (1880), *Life and Labour* (1887).

Conchimarian horns/Of the reboantic Norns (ll. 72–3): conchlike horns of the rebellowing Fates from Scandinavian mythology (either Urd, Verdande or Skuld).

Brocken-spectres (l. 78): an enormously magnified shadow of an observer cast on a bank of cloud in high mountain regions when the sun is low. The shadow is often accompanied by coloured bands and reproduces every gesture in gigantified form.

Quod ubique,/quod ab omnibus means *semper* (ll. 83–4): what is everywhere, what is from everything, means always.

Tomlinson

Empusa's crew (l. 85): hobgoblins sent by Hecate.

The Last Rhyme of True Thomas

flyte (l. 36): to scold, brawl, insult.
row-foot (l. 57): either 'booted' or 'ranked'.
rax (l. 88): wrench.
garred (l. 112): caused.
eyass (l. 124): unfledged hawk.
pye (l. 124): magpie.

The Sons of Martha

Martha, sister of the raised Lazarus. But Kipling refers to Luke 10:38, 39, 40, 41, 42: 'And she had a sister called Mary, which also sat at Jesus' feet, and heard his word. But Martha was cumbered about much serving, and came to him, and said, Lord, dost thou not care that my sister hath left me to serve alone?'

Epitaphs of the War

Native Water-Carrier (M.E.F.) (l. 76): Mediterranean Expeditionary Force.
V.A.D. (Mediterranean) (l. 174): Voluntary Aid Detachment.

Danny Deever

Files-on-Parade (l. 1): ranks are left to right, files are from front to back. Files-on-Parade is the person in the front rank which consisted entirely of old soldiers and non-commissioned officers – that is, experienced, hard-bitten soldiers, whose horror is transferred to the young recruits at the poem's end.

Tommy

Thomas Atkins: the generic name for a private in the British Army.

Gunga Din

our regimental bhisti (l. 12): bhisti is an Indian water-carrier.
a dooli (l. 70): a stretcher between two mules (possibly from French, *douillet*, meaning gentle).

Troopin'

a time-expired man (l. 36): having completed a term of enlistment.

Gentlemen-Rankers

the Curse of Reuben (l. 39): Deuteronomy 27:13 and ff. lists the several crimes for which Reuben's curse is deserved, from incest to bestiality.

'Back to the Army Again'

a ticky ulster (l. 1): a threepenny coat.
slops (l. 41): military fatigues.

That Day

to slope (l. 3): to slink away.
'Ook it (l. 11): to sling your hook, disappear.
sove-ki-poo (l. 11): sauve qui peut.

'Follow Me 'Ome'

swipes (l. 6): poor quality beer.
passin' the love o' women (l. 35): 2 Samuel 1:26 'I am distressed for thee, my brother Jonathan: very pleasant hast thou been unto me: thy love to me was wonderful, passing the love of women.'

The 'Eathen

And now it's 'Get the doolies . . .' (l. 62): stretchers (see note to 'Gunga Din').

The Absent-Minded Beggar

But we and Paul (l. 6): Paul Kruger, leader of the Boers.
sticks and bedding up the spout (l. 30): furniture and bedding pawned.

Lichtenberg

wattle (l. 7): an Australian acacia.
Lichtenberg (l. 7): in South Africa.

Piet

spoored (l. 43): tracked down.

'Wilful-Missing'

Domino! (l. 35): triumphant shout when a player has placed his final domino.

Ubique

Ubique (l. 5): everywhere, anywhere.
De Wet (l. 15): Christiaan De Wet (1854–1922) commander-in-chief of Boer forces after the British captured General Cronjé.
Grootdefeatfontein (l. 21): comic nonceword.

The Return
'Ackneystadt (l. 2): Hackney.

Puck's Song
Trafalgar (l. 4): battle of Trafalgar, 21 October 1805, in which Nelson defeated the French and Spanish fleets.

King Philip's fleet (l. 12): 1588, the defeat of the Spanish Armada.

Flodden Field (l. 15): 1513, English defeated the Scots under James IV.

Poitiers (l. 16): 1356, Edward the Black Prince defeated John II of France.

the day that Harold died (l. 24): battle of Hastings saw Harold killed by an arrow in his eye. William of Normandy (the Conqueror) then succeeded King Harold, in 1066.

When Cæsar sailed from Gaul (l. 36): 55 BC.

Merlin's Isle of Gramarye (l. 47): bard and enchanter of Arthurian romance.

Tarrant Moss
the Reiver (l. 3): border raider, thief.

Whenas (l. 15): when.

Jobson's Amen
neither rule nor calliper (l. 28): ruler nor dividers.

A Song to Mithras
Mithras (l. 1): at first a minor God of Zoroastrian system, but by 5 BC the leading Persian deity. Cult expanded until AD 2 it was more general than Christianity. Found particular favour among the legions, because Mithras was a divine fighter and comrade.

The Winners
Down to Gehenna (l. 5): hell, a valley near Jerusalem where Israelites sacrificed their children to Moloch.

pelf (l. 15): money.

Road-Song of the Bandar-Log
scumfish (l. 26): or 'scomfish', meaning to disgust, but here probably 'scavenge'.

'Our Fathers Also'
By – they are by with mirth (l. 5): they are finished with . . .

mould (l. 16): earth.

the Shewbread (l. 23): the twelve loaves offered weekly in the sanctuary by Jews.

Jubal and Tubal Cain

See Genesis 4:21, 22 sons of Lamech by two different wives, Adah and Zillah.

The Land

Diocletian (l. 2): Gaius Aurelius Valerius Diocletianus, Roman Emperor, abdicated AD 305.
dreenin' (l. 6): draining.
wains (l. 25): carts.
Duke William (l. 31): William of Normandy, William the Conqueror.
sile (l. 39): soil.
spile (l. 40): plug, shore up with piles.
Georgii Quinti Anno Sexto (l. 45): the sixth year of George V.
swapped a hedge (l. 52): cut back a hedge.
evening faggot (l. 55): firewood.
conies (l. 55): rabbits.

The Looking-Glass

Queen Bess (l. 1): Queen Elizabeth I.
Harry (l. 1): King Henry VIII.
King Philip (l. 3): of Spain. Who later sent the Armada.
Queen Mary (l. 15): Mary, Queen of Scots, kept prisoner by Elizabeth I, and finally beheaded for conspiracy.
Lord Leicester (l. 22): Robert Dudley, Queen Elizabeth's favourite, who offended her by his presumptuousness.

The Only Son

steep it in the tyre (l. 13): *tyre*, a name in India for soured milk.

'The Trade'

Zeppelin (l. 5): a dirigible, cigar-shaped airship invented by Count Zeppelin in 1900. An odd target, since 'the Trade' seem to be submarines, which were extensively used by both sides in World War One. But it is possible that submarine attacks were directed at Friedrichshafen, where the Zeppelin Foundation was located, even though this would have involved a breach of Swiss neutrality. Friedrichshafen is on Lake Constanz or the Bodensee.

The King's Task

the years that the lights were darkened (l. 2): the Dark Ages.

St Wilfrid (l. 2): or Wilfrith (634–709) English prelate intent on the overthrow of the Celtic party by the Roman discipline in England.

cottar (l. 5): a peasant whose labour pays for his cottage.

the Witan (l. 9): supreme council of England in Anglo-Saxon times.

loppage (l. 10): timber, trade, loppings from trees.

pannage (l. 10): pasturage for swine.

tun (l. 11): large cask, a measure of liquid.

Hamtun (l. 19): possibly Hampton; hereabouts Kipling's names, apart from Lewes, seem to be variants of Sussex names. For example, Selsea is Selsey and Alresford is Alfriston. It is of no importance, however, once the broad geography is established.

Edward King of the Saxons (l. 43): Edward the Elder, son of Alfred the Great.

Warlocks (l. 47): wizards, magicians.

holden (l. 50): held, obsolete form.

thane (l. 68): noble of lower rank than an earl.

King Henry VII and the Shipwrights

pricking across the down (l. 31): spurring his horse.

The Wet Litany

Libera nos Domine! (l. 8): Free us, Lord.

squattering (l. 15): splashing, fluttering, flickering.

the warning bugle (l. 17): probably a fog-*horn* rather than an actual bugle.

the lettered doorways close (l. 18): accredited harbours.

Thorkild's Song

for Stavanger (l. 2): two possible Stavangers, both in Norway.

'Angutivaun Taina'

title: *Inuit*, 'Angutivaun Taina tau-na-ne taina', Song of the Returning Hunters.

Au jana! Aua! Oha! Haq! (l. 5): directions: Go to the right; stop; whoah.

The Idiot Boy

In fact, the Wordsworth poem parodied is not 'The Idiot Boy', but the lyric 'She Dwelt Among th' Untrodden Ways'.

The Bother

See 'The Bothie of Tober-Na-Vuolich' by Arthur Hugh Clough.

speer (l. 3): to inquire about.

The Roman Centurion's Song

Portus Itius (l. 2): Calais.
Vectis (l. 5): Isle of Wight.
the Wall (l. 5): Hadrian's Wall in Northumberland.
Rhodanus (l. 17): the Rhone.
Nemausus (l. 18): Nîmes.
Arelate's triple gate (l. 19): Arles.
Euroclydon (l. 20): the wind which wrecked St Paul's ship (Acts 27:14).
Aurelian (l. 21): built in the time of Marcus Aurelius Antoninus, Emperor 161–80.
the Tyrrhene Ocean (l. 22): Etruscan ocean, in north-west Italy.

Edgehill Fight

First great battle of the English Civil War, 23 October 1642.

A Departure

Hengist's horde (l. 2): Hengist led with his brother Horsa the Jutish invasion of Britain, founding the kingdom of Kent in the fifth century.

The Changelings

R.N.V.R.: Royal Naval Volunteer Reserve.
Or ever (l. 1): before.
Had us in charge (l. 11): arrested our attention.
pied craft (l. 18): camouflaged shipping.

'Late Came the God'

The God is Eros or Cupid.

Rahere

Compare Tennyson's 'Happy: the Leper's Bride'.
Horror of Great Darkness (l. 9): Genesis 15:12.
Wanhope (l. 18): (*obs.*) despair.

The Survival

Horace has only four books of odes.

Alnaschar and the Oxen

Alnaschar: beggar in *Arabian Nights* who destroys his livelihood by indulging his visions of riches and grandeur.
Lobengula (l. 10): Matabele king (1833–94).
Bulawayo (l. 13): city in south-west Zimbabwe.
Juno (l. 24): Hera, wife of Zeus.

Mithras (l. 27): see note to 'A Song to Mithras'.

Gertrude's Prayer

Ah! Jesu-Moder, pitie my oe paine (l. 17): this appeal to the mother of Christ employs the unusual adjective 'oe'. 'Oe', 'oy' and 'oye' is a Scots noun meaning 'grandchild', so here perhaps Kipling is using it to suggest birth pangs, labour pains. Or 'oe' for 'o' meaning 'one'. Or 'own'.

Naaman's Song

Naaman: see 2 Kings 5:12 and ff. Naaman was a Syrian commander and a leper. The prophet Elisha told him to wash in the Jordan in order to be cured. At first Naaman refused, for patriotic reasons.

Pharpar (l. 17): a river in Syria.

Abana (l. 17): another Syrian river.

Hermon (1. 17): a Syrian mountain.

Song of Seventy Horses

title: that is, 70 horse-power engine.

the multiplied lacets (l. 26): hair-pin bends.

Azrael's Count

Azrael: in the Koran, angel of death. Name is Hebrew, meaning 'help of God'.

yeanling (l. 1): lamb or a kid.

The Gods of the Copybook Headings

title: a copybook is a book where sentences (and maxims, therefore) are laid out for imitation. It is, therefore, very basic.

We moved as the Spirit listed (l. 9): cf. John 3:8 'The wind bloweth where it listeth, and thou hearest the sound thereof, but canst not tell whence it cometh, and whither it goeth: so is every one that is born of the Spirit.'

the Cambrian measures (l. 17): first period of the Paleozoic geological era.

Feminian Sandstones (l. 21): cod category invented to ironize suffragettes.

the Carboniferous Epoch (l. 25): fifth period of the Paleozoic era.

brave new world (l. 37): Shakespeare's *The Tempest* V.v. 183.

Index of Titles

Index of First Lines

READ MORE IN PENGUIN

In every corner of the world, on every subject under the sun, Penguin represents quality and variety – the very best in publishing today.

For complete information about books available from Penguin – including Puffins, Penguin Classics and Arkana – and how to order them, write to us at the appropriate address below. Please note that for copyright reasons the selection of books varies from country to country.

In the United Kingdom: Please write to *Dept. EP, Penguin Books Ltd, Bath Road, Harmondsworth, West Drayton, Middlesex UB7 0DA*

In the United States: Please write to *Consumer Sales, Penguin USA, P.O. Box 999, Dept. 17109, Bergenfield, New Jersey 07621-0120*. VISA and MasterCard holders call 1-800-253-6476 to order Penguin titles

In Canada: Please write to *Penguin Books Canada Ltd, 10 Alcorn Avenue, Suite 300, Toronto, Ontario M4V 3B2*

In Australia: Please write to *Penguin Books Australia Ltd, P.O. Box 257, Ringwood, Victoria 3134*

In New Zealand: Please write to *Penguin Books (NZ) Ltd, Private Bag 102902, North Shore Mail Centre, Auckland 10*

In India: Please write to *Penguin Books India Pvt Ltd, 706 Eros Apartments, 56 Nehru Place, New Delhi 110 019*

In the Netherlands: Please write to *Penguin Books Netherlands bv, Postbus 3507, NL-1001 AH Amsterdam*

In Germany: Please write to *Penguin Books Deutschland GmbH, Metzlerstrasse 26, 60594 Frankfurt am Main*

In Spain: Please write to *Penguin Books S. A., Bravo Murillo 19, 1° B, 28015 Madrid*

In Italy: Please write to *Penguin Italia s.r.l., Via Felice Casati 20, I–20124 Milano*

In France: Please write to *Penguin France S. A., 17 rue Lejeune, F–31000 Toulouse*

In Japan: Please write to *Penguin Books Japan, Ishikiribashi Building, 2–5–4, Suido, Bunkyo-ku, Tokyo 112*

In Greece: Please write to *Penguin Hellas Ltd, Dimocritou 3, GR–106 71 Athens*

In South Africa: Please write to *Longman Penguin Southern Africa (Pty) Ltd, Private Bag X08, Bertsham 2013*

READ MORE IN PENGUIN

A SELECTION OF POETRY

American Verse
British Poetry since 1945
Caribbean Verse in English
A Choice of Comic and Curious Verse
Contemporary American Poetry
Contemporary British Poetry
Contemporary Irish Poetry
English Poetry 1918–60
English Romantic Verse
English Verse
First World War Poetry
German Verse
Greek Verse
Imagist Poetry
Irish Verse
Japanese Verse
Love Poetry
The Metaphysical Poets
Modern African Poetry
New Poetry
Penguin Book of Homosexual Verse
Poetry of the Thirties
Scottish Verse
Spanish Verse
Women Poets

READ MORE IN PENGUIN

POETRY LIBRARY

Arnold	Selected by Kenneth Allott
Blake	Selected by W. H. Stevenson
Browning	Selected by Daniel Karlin
Burns	Selected by Angus Calder and William Donnelly
Byron	Selected by A. S. B. Glover
Clare	Selected by Geoffrey Summerfield
Coleridge	Selected by Richard Holmes
Donne	Selected by John Hayward
Dryden	Selected by Douglas Grant
Hardy	Selected by David Wright
Herbert	Selected by W. H. Auden
Jonson	Selected by George Parfitt
Keats	Selected by John Barnard
Kipling	Selected by James Cochrane
Lawrence	Selected by Keith Sagar
Milton	Selected by Laurence D. Lerner
Pope	Selected by Douglas Grant
Rubáiyát of Omar Khayyám	Translated by Edward FitzGerald
Shelley	Selected by Isabel Quigley
Tennyson	Selected by W. E. Williams
Wordsworth	Selected by Nicholas Roe
Yeats	Selected by Timothy Webb

READ MORE IN PENGUIN

RUDYARD KIPLING

'The most complete man of genius I have ever known' – Henry James

The Light That Failed
A Diversity of Creatures
The Day's Work
Debits and Credits
Wee Willie Winkie
Just So Stories
Traffics and Discoveries
Short Stories
  Volumes I and II
Selected Stories
Kim

The Jungle Books
Life's Handicap
Limits and Renewals
Something of Myself
Plain Tales from the Hills
Puck of Pook's Hill
Rewards and Fairies
Selected Poems
Soldiers Three *and* In Black
  and White

'For my own part I worshipped Kipling at thirteen, loathed him at seventeen, enjoyed him at twenty, despised him at twenty-five, and now again rather admire him. The one thing that was never possible, if one had read him at all, was to forget him' – George Orwell